BIBB
COUNTRY

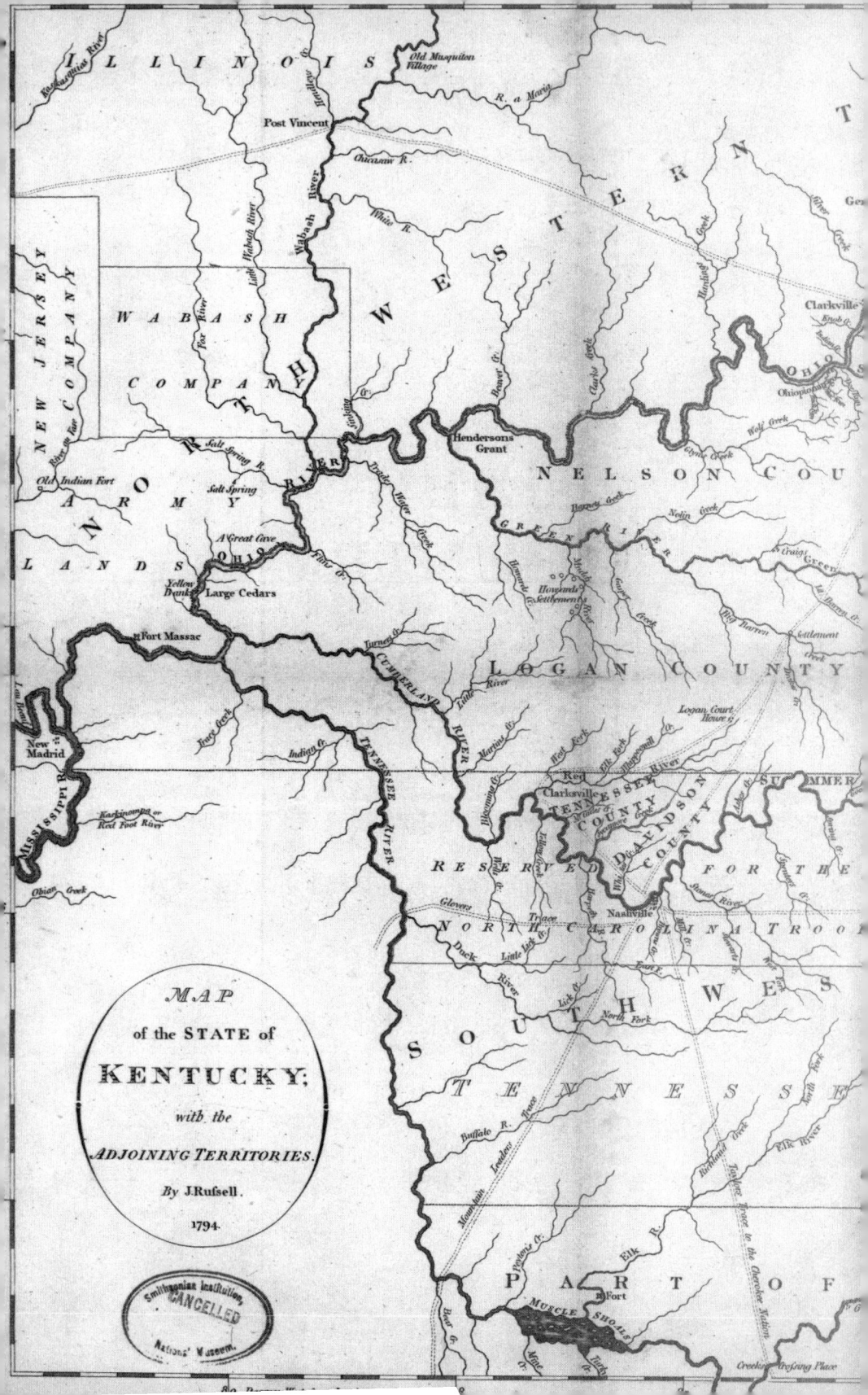

MAP
of the STATE of
KENTUCKY;
with the
ADJOINING TERRITORIES.
By J. Russell.
1794.

UNEARTHING MY FAMILY SECRETS
OF LAND, LEGACY, AND LETTUCE

BIBB COUNTRY

LONNAE O'NEAL

LOS ANGELES   NEW YORK

First Edition, June 2025
10 9 8 7 6 5 4 3 2 1
FAC-004510-25093
Printed in the United States of America

This book is set in Chronicle Text, Adorn, and Knockout
Designed by Amy C. King

Images on pages 61, 82, 91, 291 by Jon Cherry for Andscape
Map of the state of Kentucky with adjoining territories 1797: Library of Congress.
Illustration pages i, iii, 7, 107, and 233 © Shutterstock; pages vii, viii, ix © Adobestock

Library of Congress Control Number: 2024949229
ISBN 978-1-368-08938-8

Reinforced binding

www.AndscapeBooks.com

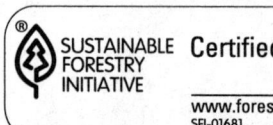

Logo Applies to Text Stock Only

For Momma, may it ever be so

For Thomas, with love

For the descendants of Bibbtown, Northtown,
South Sides, and Black Bottoms everywhere

TABLE OF CONTENTS

PART III: INHERITANCE

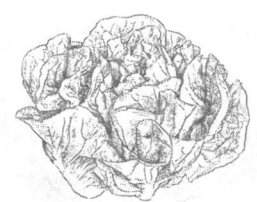

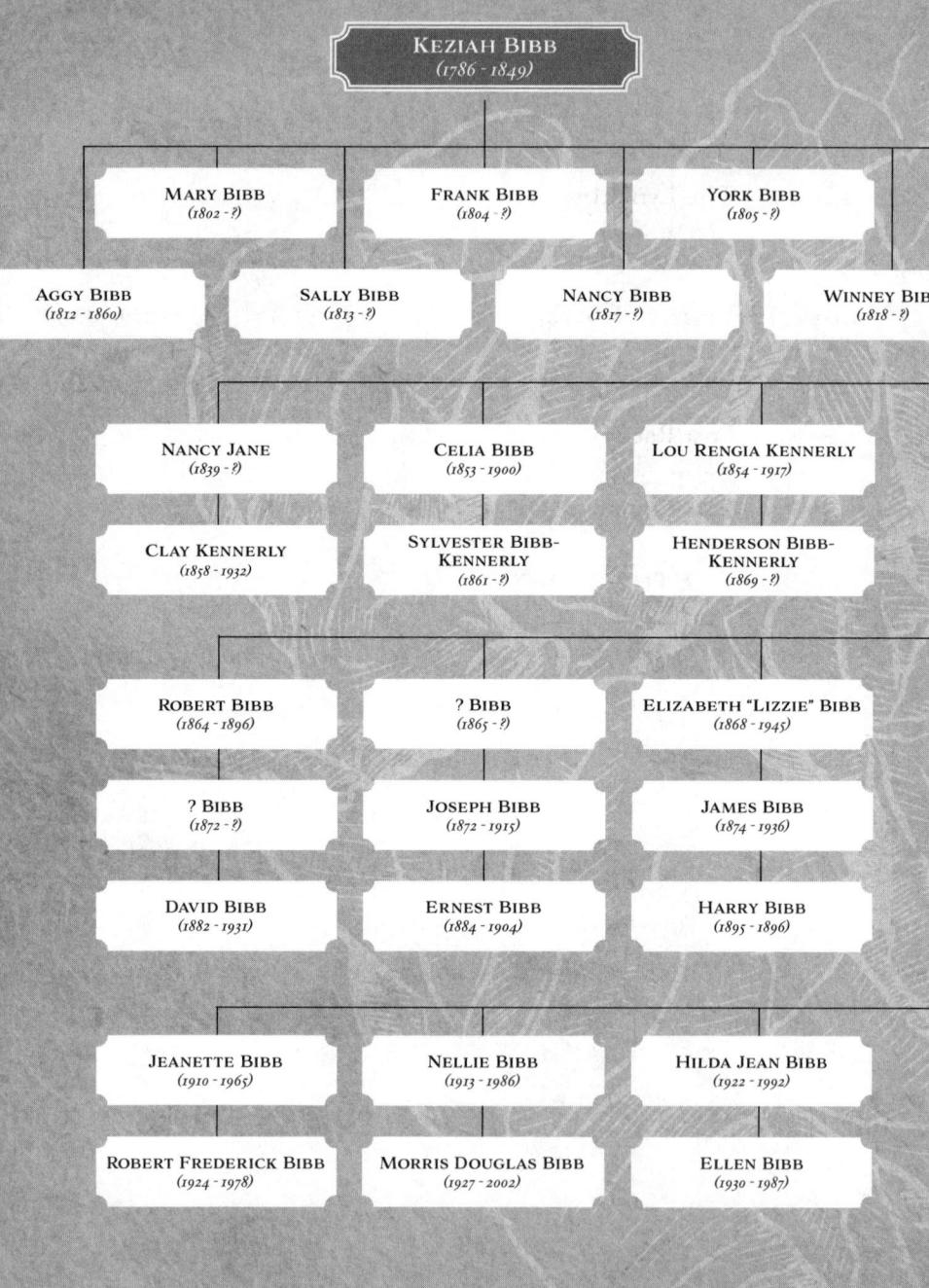

KEZIAH BIBB
(1786 - 1849)

MARY BIBB
(1802 - ?)

FRANK BIBB
(1804 - ?)

YORK BIBB
(1805 - ?)

AGGY BIBB
(1812 - 1860)

SALLY BIBB
(1813 - ?)

NANCY BIBB
(1817 - ?)

WINNEY BIBB
(1818 - ?)

NANCY JANE
(1839 - ?)

CELIA BIBB
(1853 - 1900)

LOU RENGIA KENNERLY
(1854 - 1917)

CLAY KENNERLY
(1858 - 1932)

SYLVESTER BIBB-KENNERLY
(1861 - ?)

HENDERSON BIBB-KENNERLY
(1869 - ?)

ROBERT BIBB
(1864 - 1896)

? BIBB
(1865 - ?)

ELIZABETH "LIZZIE" BIBB
(1868 - 1945)

? BIBB
(1872 - ?)

JOSEPH BIBB
(1872 - 1915)

JAMES BIBB
(1874 - 1936)

DAVID BIBB
(1882 - 1931)

ERNEST BIBB
(1884 - 1904)

HARRY BIBB
(1895 - 1896)

JEANETTE BIBB
(1910 - 1965)

NELLIE BIBB
(1913 - 1986)

HILDA JEAN BIBB
(1922 - 1992)

ROBERT FREDERICK BIBB
(1924 - 1978)

MORRIS DOUGLAS BIBB
(1927 - 2002)

ELLEN BIBB
(1930 - 1987)

BIBB FAMILY TREE

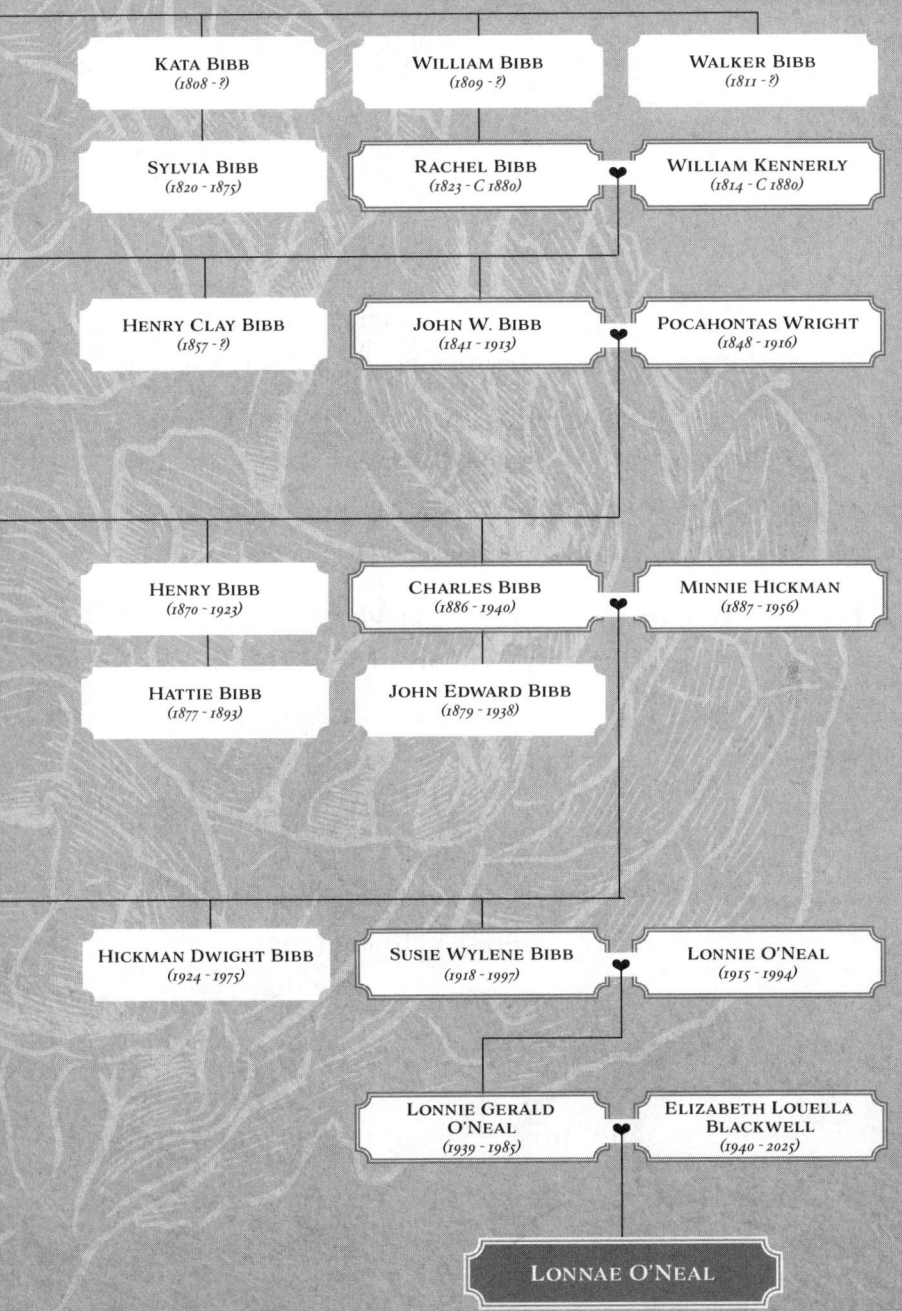

KATA BIBB
(1808 - ?)

WILLIAM BIBB
(1809 - ?)

WALKER BIBB
(1811 - ?)

SYLVIA BIBB
(1820 - 1875)

RACHEL BIBB
(1823 - C 1880)

WILLIAM KENNERLY
(1814 - C 1880)

HENRY CLAY BIBB
(1857 - ?)

JOHN W. BIBB
(1841 - 1913)

POCAHONTAS WRIGHT
(1848 - 1916)

HENRY BIBB
(1870 - 1923)

CHARLES BIBB
(1886 - 1940)

MINNIE HICKMAN
(1887 - 1956)

HATTIE BIBB
(1877 - 1893)

JOHN EDWARD BIBB
(1879 - 1938)

HICKMAN DWIGHT BIBB
(1924 - 1975)

SUSIE WYLENE BIBB
(1918 - 1997)

LONNIE O'NEAL
(1915 - 1994)

LONNIE GERALD
O'NEAL
(1939 - 1985)

ELIZABETH LOUELLA
BLACKWELL
(1940 - 2025)

LONNAE O'NEAL

"To be changed from a chattel to a human being, is no light matter, though the process with myself practically was very simple. And if I could reach the ears of every slave today, throughout the whole continent of America, I would teach the same lesson, I would sound it in the ears of every hereditary bondsman, "break your chains and fly for freedom!"

—Henry Bibb, *Narrative of the Life and Adventures of Henry Bibb, an American Slave, Written by Himself* (1849)

"People say the truth will set you free. But, sometimes, the truth will make you go off . . ."

—Michael Morrow, on the road from Russellville, Kentucky to Centralia, Illinois (2021)

PROLOGUE

This is the story of an American legacy, as seen through a lens of Blackness. A story of enslavement that begins at the Logan County, Kentucky, plantation home of Major Richard Bibb, and ripples through seven generations of Black Bibbs whose freedom dates to twenty-five years before the Civil War.

After the war, they go north. They start businesses, and churches. They become landowners and run for office. They bring suit against the town of Centralia, Illinois, where both my parents were born and raised, forcing it to integrate sixty years before *Brown v. Board of Education*. They fall on hard times during the Great Depression.

When I first heard the story of Major Richard Bibb and Bibbtown, Kentucky, I wondered what my grandmother Susie Wylene Bibb would have said.

Perhaps, if she were taking the long view of history, she would say: *You're entering a conversation that has been unspooling across centuries. Across the whole of the nation, and in the dirt of all its generations. Across the Bibb family in Virginia, Kentucky, Centralia, Chicago, and suburban Washington, DC, specifically.*

If Susie Wylene Bibb O'Neal had been able to go to college like she so desperately wanted to, but could not afford, she might have noted that this conversation is ever pressing at the seams of the nation.

Instead, my grandmother used the issue of her ovens and stove-tops to make dough. Cash dollar bills. To write checks in service of higher education for her descendants. And sometimes to help family, friends, and neighbors make it to Thursday after next, as part of the requirement of Black life on these shores, which is, of course, to put time on the clock, for ourselves and for children unborn. And if that time often came at usurious rates, it was all part of the negotiations required by the deficits of Black citizenship that make Black women such a feature of the underground economies of the nation.

This a story of creativity, culture, community, and resilience. In some ways it is a story of triumph.

Yet it is also a story of trauma. Much of it has been unspoken, *but the body remembers*. It is a story of mental illness, violence, and death. It is a story I'd been reporting for just two days before I learned of four rapes.

It is a story of anger.

Black rage is often seen as disqualifying. Outside the constructive parameters of civic dialogue. *Super scary*. I find it more useful to think of it as human, which is what we have been since we were stolen. Which is what we have been despite all efforts to take us from ourselves.

In any dialogue with Black people, who have not consented to be *y'all's little sin-eaters, or whatever*, there is a point worth remembering. There is no Black equivalent to the spectacle and practice of lynching. To sundown towns, poll taxes, or even the official state song "My Old Kentucky Home."

We must all work out our own salvation with fear and trembling.

As much as anything, this is a ghost story.

I try not to spend a lot of time on it, it's just something to keep in mind. At various points in the reading, writing, and thinking, the emotional and physical labor of pulling these pieces of Americana together, various grace notes or pieces of serendipity would pop up. I took them as a sign that I was on the right track, *so hang in there*, or as an assurance that I was not alone.

They were glimmers of love, perhaps, or maybe a knobby poke in the chest from one of my Black ancestors (which is more on brand) whom I have taken to calling ghosts, just because of the haunting ways they act.

They often gave me these small psychic breadcrumbs. Perhaps they were the type of signs that old Black enslaved people, or even older root people, would have taught their children to read.

John Bigger Bibb, born on my momma's birthday, *okay*. His wife died on my birthday, *fine*. I randomly open a book and land on a page taken from the enslaved narrative of Henry Bibb, *understood*. I'm watching the Ohio State game, I google the name of the Black quarterback and the search pulls up someone named Alonzo Bibb Stroud. *Got it!* (Also, the genealogist, historian, and essential man who brought the Bibb story to light lives on a street that shares the same name as the street I grew up on in Chicago. I take one of my infrequent looks on social media and see the photo of a cousin, from my mother's side, posing with the renowned Cleveland broadcaster Leon Bibb. On a Freedom Monument Sculpture Park wall featuring more than 120,000 surnames adopted by the newly emancipated in the 1870 census, the camera lingers on the Bibb name in an NBC News report.)

I don't make too much of it because there are so many more things I need to make much of. I simply note how I feel, and how it all plays out. I've never seen Bibb lettuce on a menu, but it shows up unexpectedly in Clayton, North Carolina, where Momma lives, and so I learn it's something I have to brace for.

This story is about living in a nation that fools itself into insisting that none of these stories happened, continue to happen, or are relevant to our present day. And it is about the culture that rises up as an affirmation, a release, an off-ramp. Or that sometimes meets white denial with contortions all our own.

The day I first brought home a packet of Bibb lettuce seeds, I happened across a mug shot of my brother, and I began ticking off all the ways I thought those two things were related.

This is a story about my family, and a proxy for what the stories of Black families tell us about America.

Though my grandmother could have passed for white (as long as she remained quiet, because after she started talking, everybody got clear), until a few years ago, I'd never been interested in finding out why. I've come to understand that there are ways that not knowing functions as necessary and protective when it comes to the backstories of Black people.

In some ways, I've arrived late to this telling. People have passed away and taken whatever they knew, wherever they went. But, of course, I had to wait until I could stand to hear the answers to my own questions. Until I could read the ink on the parchment and talk about what this history begat.

I claim a privilege claimed by legions of Black people, to say all the things, as a birthright both as a free Black woman and because it bears repeating. So I will do so.

White fear of American history is simply a projection—an anxiety pulled from their dark imaginings and what they understand themselves to be capable of. It is a photo negative of American history. It should not be honored.

I felt this most acutely on the hardest days of my reporting, when I shed tears with family whose own tears were both old and repetitive. Or far, far worse, utterly inaccessible. I made promises, *promises you understand*, about the secrets I would keep, which at the time felt like the correct exchange for some piece of good—more details, deeper truths. But the more I learned, the more I came to understand the secrets are the truth. At least, they are *the onliest* truth some people can handle.

Yes, yes.

You pull out one pin and the whole thing comes tumbling down, says Michael Morrow, archivist, genealogist and director of the SEEK Museum, who has researched the Bibb family, Black and white alike, for more than three decades.

What you are left with in the Bibb family history are the nested contradictions. But my clearest understanding begins where America begins, with the reprint of a sales notice posted on the wall of the Bibb plantation house turned museum: It reads, "One or two likely Negro boys, about 10-years-old."

It gave me a starting point for our family's adaptations, accommodations, traumas, and violence, and all that flowed from it. And by extension, another set of data points for the American experiment, Susie Bibb tells me.

Sometimes I wonder if we can ever repair. If we can hold ourselves and the nation that birthed us accountable, and with that accountability, change and grow. The answer, when I'm feeling hopeful, or vanishingly optimistic, is *maybe*. But first we must dig up the roots. This won't tell us everything, but it will tell us what was planted.

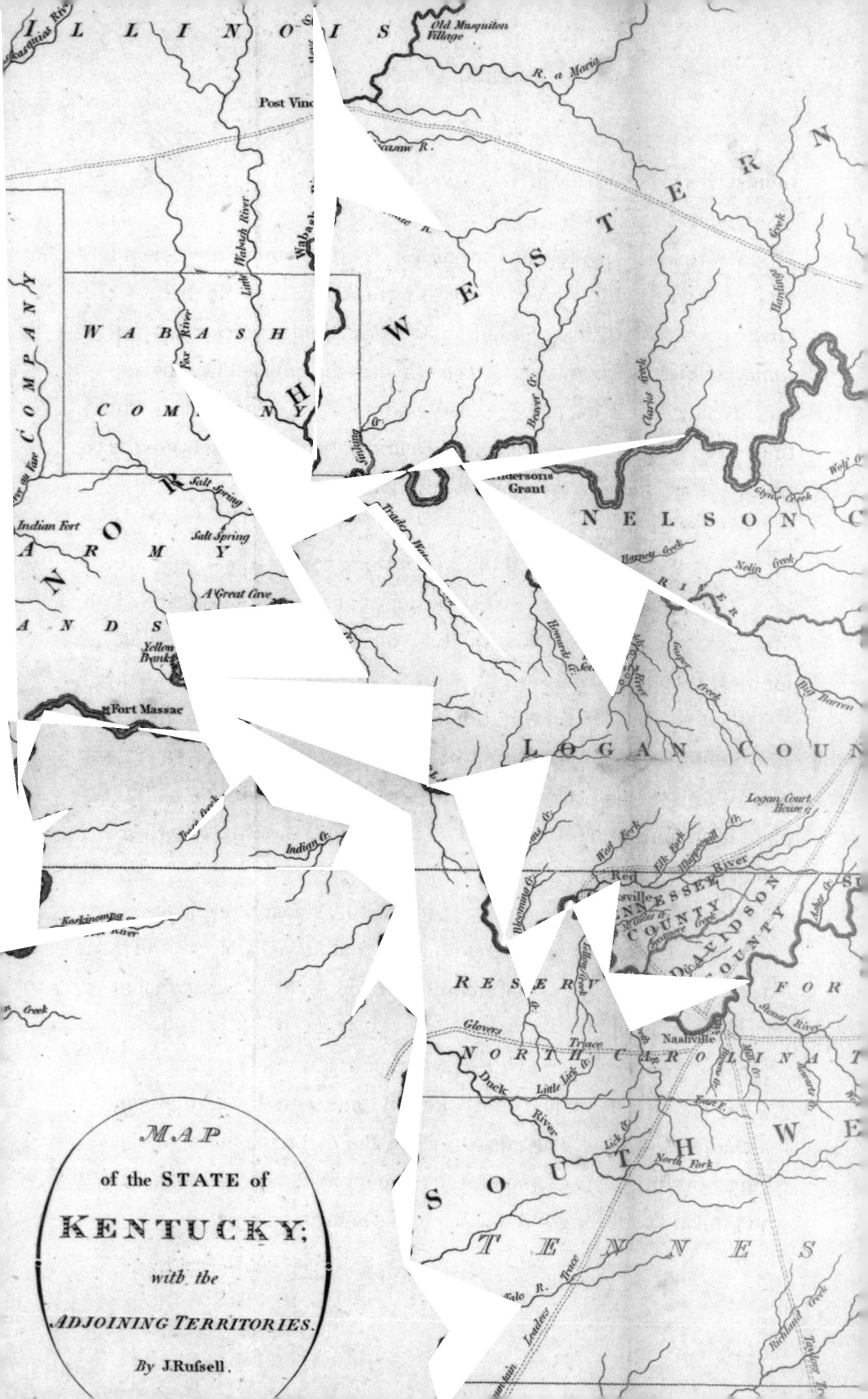

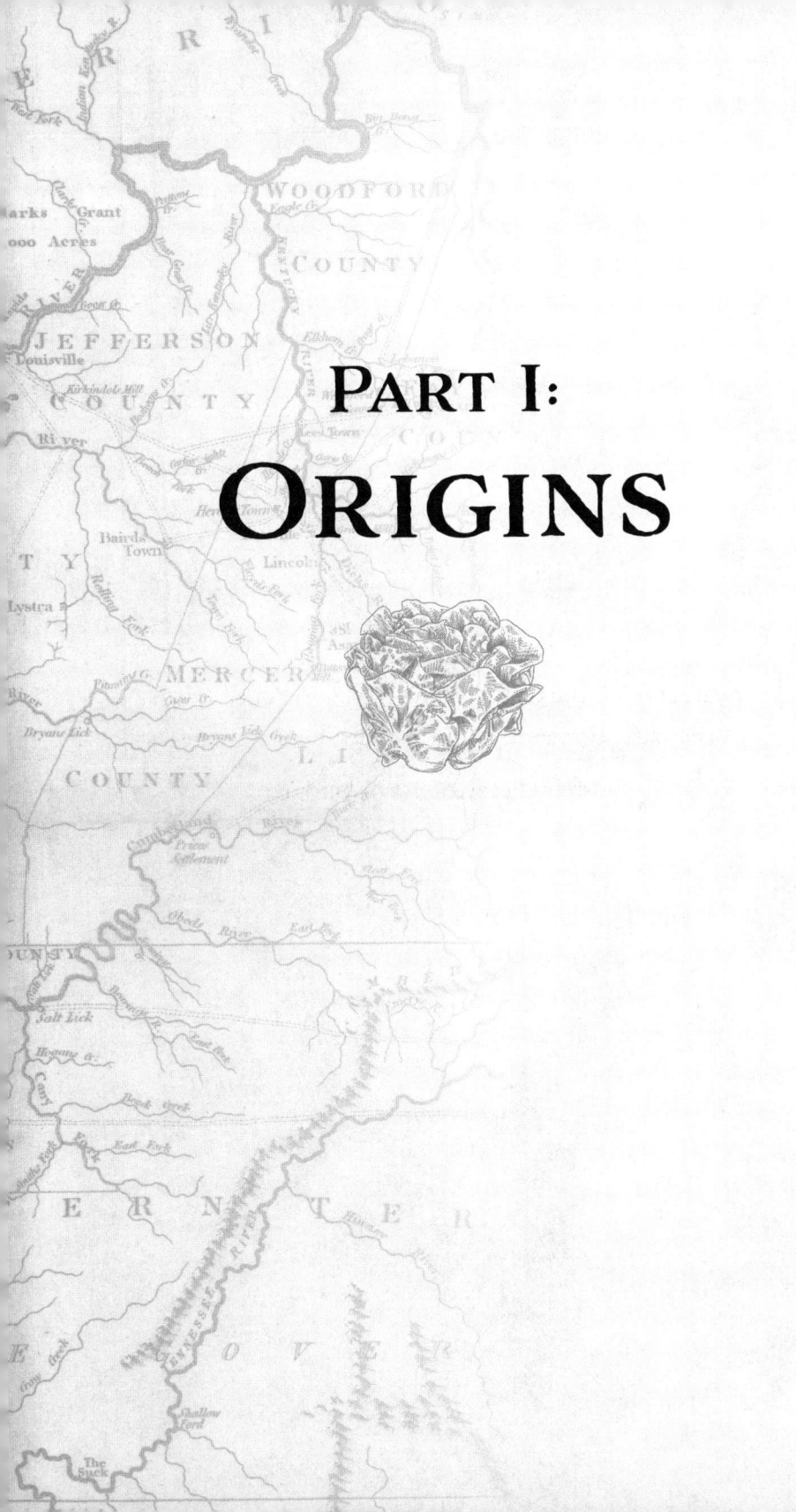

PART I:
ORIGINS

"You'll get lost if you try to look everywhere at once. You have to pay attention somewhere to understand the dance."

—**Imani Perry,** ***South to America***

CHAPTER 1

HARVEST
AND BOND

By mid-April 2020, it was go-time for my garden. It had been a year since I'd moved into my new house in a leafy old neighborhood just outside of Washington, DC. It was my fourth move in less than ten years, and for the first time in a long time, I felt settled.

As a child, I'd helped my mother plant tomatoes and flowers in our backyard on the far South Side of Chicago. My daughter had helped me plant our backyard gardens when she was a young girl, and we'd take turns laying our rows of seed each spring. Gardening, for me, was full of gauzy memories of family and affection. It was about playing in dirt, and a love of growing things. The topography of my life had sometimes felt perilous and uneven, and gardening was about being rooted.

A small, squared-off patch of land extended from my back patio, with three quarters of it carpeted in a lush emerald grass. The final quarter was full of rocks, hard dirt, and overgrown weeds. It was as if the people who'd renovated the house before we bought it ran out of time, money, or the inclination to finish strong when they got to the backyard, and the lawn simply stopped, midway through a roll of sod. I discovered a small pet cemetery (Pet Sematary?) a few yards beyond where the grass ended, with headstones for someone named Gypsy, THE BEST FRIEND WE EVER HAD, and another named Alvin, HE WAS A GOOD BOY. The creepiness of it all helped me keep a wary distance from the overgrown bamboo and poison ivy that separated my yard from that of the neighbor behind me.

All of which made it easy to decide just where my backyard garden would grow.

I moved the rock-scape and broke the dirt on the closest grassless patch to my house, far from the pet cemetery and poison ivy, as I day-dreamed of fresh herbs. But for all my optimism and nostalgia, I had some real growing pains to contend with. I'd really only ever been a dilettante as a planter. I was more in love with the idea of my garden than the work of it, and I never acquired any depth of knowledge or literacy. I'd watched seeds turn into leaves and stems that withered back into the dirt without even doing anything so earthy as a Google search to determine what to pick, from where on the plant, and when to do so.

Why, for example, had my cilantro turned into flowers, and where did the actual garlic cloves grow? This explains how I found myself overstimulated in the seed aisle of Home Depot, rushing to get in and out, in a time of covid.

I reached, first, for what I knew. I grabbed packets of green onions, parsley, peppers, and tomatoes. I bypassed the cucumbers, vowing never again to be spooked by their scary, invasive vines. I was scanning the leafy greens, looking for mustard or collards, which I remembered Momma growing on the South Side, when I spotted a name that caught me unawares, although looking back, it should not have. Either way, it stilled my motion and changed my mood. Maybe changed everything.

I cursed softly, under my breath. I picked up a packet of Bibb lettuce seeds and stared at the photo of leafy rosettes open to the sun. Then I turned it over to read. The packet detailed features of color, texture, and signs of maturation. It offered best practices on sowing, spacing, and optimal sun. It said everything necessary about germination and water. But there was no word on the man credited with originating Bibb lettuce.

There was nothing about the hundreds of people he and his family had enslaved or how they might have factored in the development of the delicate, eponymous heirloom vegetable.

No mention of how the Bibb family wealth and influence were seeded into America, and how they spread across the nation.

I had no intention of planting the lettuce, but I threw the packet in my cart to bring home for further rumination. It's not as if I thought it held some important clue to my past, I reasoned, or why America never was America to me. But then again, perhaps it did.

This part of my identity was less than a year known to me, and I hadn't even remotely come to terms with whether I wanted any part of it. Whether I could ever reckon with the tortured, blues-song ways my family history fit into the sweep of American history, and how angry and destabilized both those histories made me feel.

I was struggling with the bitter harvest of Major Richard Bibb. And where to begin?

Perhaps I should begin on a late summer morning in 2019, when I arrived in the city of Russellville, in Logan County, in western Kentucky, and took my measure of the place. It was a day before the inaugural Bibb House reunion, where the descendants of Revolutionary War veteran Major Richard Bibb and the descendants of those he enslaved, and emancipated, would meet. Some participants had long known this family history. Some, like me and mine, had heard it for the first time that summer and had not gotten past the laceration of it.

I was not yet reconciled to the idea of a "reunion." More than that, I was still mad at having been invited. Mad that enslavement had occasioned such a reunion. Mad that America had sanctioned Black bondage, and that it had touched every generation thence. Mad that I was going to have to talk about this with white strangers. Mad, in advance, about all the emotional labor I was going to have to do just to be polite. Looking back on it, I shouldn't have been so mad about that one, as I don't think I was especially polite. I've settled on being mad that I ever felt like I needed to be. Mad that enslavement was still tasking us, taking from Black people labor we would not have chosen to give.

I toured the Bibb plantation-house-turned-museum and explored the nearby work cabins, lingering near the fireplace stove to imagine the Black hands that had labored between the fire and brick. I walked the perimeter of the antebellum structures, and I paid attention to my footfalls, noting the soft spots and the ways ground shifted beneath me. Or maybe it was just my understanding of how I walked in the world that I felt moving all around.

By early afternoon, I'd settled in the community room with musem director and reunion organizer Michael Morrow, a tall, deeply brown brother, a native of Logan County who looked and sounded like the kind of Black people I'd known my whole life. He grew up on stories of Major Richard Bibb, and in the enclave of those Black people Bibb had enslaved and emancipated, bequeathing them money, tools, and the land, just outside Russellville, that became known as Bibbtown.

The *onliest* thing Morrow wanted was for this history to be told, he said. He was plainspoken, folksy, watchful. We'd fallen into an easy rapport by the time some of the white families arrived for a tour. I heard their voices in distant parts of the house, and I was startled by the sound of them, as I later wrote in a 2019 article about the reunion. I sat up straight, and I felt an almost feral sense of danger rise in my throat. My reaction was dark, sudden, impolitic, impolite. I'd thought I wouldn't have to see white descendants for another day. I was not yet ready to meet these people. They had done nothing to me, but it felt as if they had.

Do not come in here, I warned silently.

Their voices got closer, and I became more rattled, though no one would have known by looking at me, except maybe for Morrow. He knew, like we all did. We wear the mask. But it felt like mine was about to slip.

Weeks earlier, my cousins and I, the Black Bibbs, the only Bibbs I'd ever heard of, joked that we needed to come up with a code word or signal in case this "reunion" started going "south," and we had to "get out" fast (my vote: the crow caw from the Parliament song "Aqua Boogie"). We were being lured into a trap, we joked, not without an edge of mania. But at that moment in Russellville, the trap felt real. It was the plantation house, the work cabins, the white voices moving ever closer. I had stepped into a house of mirrors. I wanted to escape.

A couple of white could-be relations reached out to shake my hand, and I extended mine to them as well.

Why had they come? I wondered.

Lord, why had I?

❊ ❊ ❊ ❊

The invitation to come to Russellville had kicked around Facebook for several months before I saw it. The event would bring together the descendants of the Revolutionary War veteran Major Richard Bibb and the descendants of those he enslaved during his life and emancipated in his 1839 will.

Three generations later, my grandmother Susie Wylene Bibb was born in southern Illinois, where my Black Bibb ancestors migrated after the Civil War. We called her Momma Susie.

My family and I, the children and grandchildren of Momma Susie or one of her seven siblings, were told that we were potentially descendants of both. Of the white enslaver and the Black enslaved.

Miss me on those plantation happenings, I told my cousins. I had not searched out this history, or ever even wondered about it. That way lies pain, and I had enough to deal with in the here and now without tripping over ancestral traumas. There was no consensus, or pressure, about whether to attend the reunion among family, and I was, initially, a no. Hard pass. Deuces. I was clear about my decision not to go. Or at least, I thought I was. But something kept nagging at me, and I couldn't name it or give it voice. As near as I could figure, it was the weight of all these new unknowns from the past that felt beyond my capacity to make sense of. This was the first time I'd ever heard tell of any such thing as white Bibbs. The first time I'd heard anything about where my grandmother's people came from. A couple of the white descendants were working on a documentary and would be filming at the reunion, we were told. I considered my options. None of them felt safe.

I had constructed a life as a reporter and writer with the resources and standing that allowed me to encounter white people largely on my own terms. Or so I imagined. To decide for myself when and where I entered.

But this so-called reunion would be a departure from that. It represented something aching and unresolved that put me and mine on the *fear and trembling* side of a racial power dynamic. And of American history. Something sinister and frightening. The thought of it made me feel vulnerable and afraid in ways that I could not reason myself past.

Joe Gran Clark, president of preservation group Historic Russellville Inc., had once argued to the Kentucky Supreme Court for the Bibb House to be a public charitable trust. He wanted it to be "a realistic memorial to the Old South." But deciding what that meant was a whole different fight. And not merely with white people.

It was not a fight I wanted. I didn't know if I had it in me.

As I seesawed back and forth about whether to attend, I reached out to Clark. He'd helped found the SEEK Museum (Struggles for Emancipation and Equality in Kentucky), which, in addition to SEEK at the Bibb House, includes six other historic structures located in Russellville's historic Black Bottom, an area settled by three free Black families *prior* to the Civil War. Clark had emailed me a picture of an elderly, light-skinned Black woman who'd been the matriarch of Bibbtown. Oral history passed down for generations held that she was the daughter of Major Richard Bibb, Clark said. She reminded me of Momma Susie.

This light-skinned woman stared out at me, unsmiling, from the photo, and I felt implicated in her gaze. Dead Black people are always judging. Having put their own burdens down, they're always asking the rest of us what we're fittin' to do.

I met her eyes, but I had no answers.

My cousin Marvin had driven to Russellville from Texas with his mother, Sharon . Our grandparents had been siblings, and he made the twelve-hour drive to get some answers of his own. On the morning of the reunion, Marvin and I sat in his truck, watching people go in and out of the Bibb House, trying to piece the fragments we knew of our family history into whole cloth. Or at least a shred that halfway hung together.

He told me something his grandfather, my uncle Morris, had told him over and over growing up. Something my grandmother had never even whispered my way. A story that compelled Marvin to take a DNA test, which is precisely how Morrow had found our family:

"Granddaddy always said that his granddaddy was the son of a white slave owner in Kentucky."

This was why my cousin came to Russellville. This was what he wanted to know: If the white Bibbs were so wealthy, why did we end up with such shit portions? We could be a part of the family that they don't even talk about.

I had called my sister that morning for a consult on what I should wear to the reunion. I decided on a green wrap-style dress to remind me, and all the Bibbs who knew the score, of the green armchair where Momma Susie planted herself for much of our childhoods. It was as if she just sat in her chair in her pajamas one morning and simply decided there was nowhere more important for her to be.

That green armchair was where she had the most power and influence. It was where she received a steady flow of Black Centralians— those from that southern Illinois town of Centralia—looking to borrow a little cash when there was too much month at the end of their money. I lingered in the hotel parking lot and prayed to Momma Susie that I might speak for her at the gathering.

I had decided the only way I could attend the reunion was to write about it. To show up under my own agency, with enough power to balance out whatever it was that white folks, or the Commonwealth of Kentucky, or the kind of baleful spirits that hover over old plantation houses, might be bringing to the gathering.

The afternoon of the reunion, the Bibb House front lawn was crowded with chairs and tables. Dozens of strangers, clusters of Black and white from far-flung places, were milling about, with more arriving. I walked up in my green dress, with my reporter's notebook. Even as I reminded myself I was there to do a job, I was tremulous. The sky darkened, and rain began to fall in sheets, displacing plastic tablecloths, sending everyone fleeing inside the Bibb House, where we'd be forced to talk to one another. I thought it likely the work of spirits, asserting their will, though I couldn't decide if the spirits were Black or white or where they were coming from. Who had more to lose, and who had what to gain? My thoughts felt piecemeal, like fragments of things I used to understand but now had forgotten. I couldn't make sense of them. I couldn't figure out the stakes.

I clutched my notebook, but I couldn't find my pen, and I had a hard time making my mouth agree to conversation. I took deep breaths and forced myself to focus on small details, to take the edge off of feeling haunted, or hunted, or whatever it is that Black people are made to feel in the Southern plantation houses that carry their grandmomma's last name. I shivered.

The wide center hallway of the white Palladian-style house museum featured two pairs of iron shackles under glass that had been found in the dirt on the grounds. They looked rusted, old, evil. I tried to imagine the heaviness of them around my wrists. I imagined trying to slide my wrists out of them, but being unable to, and trying harder and harder, until my knuckles popped and the iron shackles started tearing my skin. It was a panicky thought heading down a spiral staircase. So, I tried to step away from it.

A copy of an enlarged notice hung center wall in an adjacent room, announcing: FOR SALE, ONE OR TWO NEGRO BOYS, ABOUT TEN YEARS OLD.

I white-knuckled my notebook, gripping it with both hands, and forced my feet, which were not acting like feet, which were in open rebellion, to make for a nearby white woman to interview. I learned she was a descendant of one of Major Richard Bibb's daughters, which she'd found out from a cousin who'd taken a DNA test. She'd traveled from California; she told me she was there with her son and daughter-in-law, who were both from Illinois.

Attendees of the 2019 Bibb House Reunion, which includes Maj. Richard Bibb's 1798 sales notice for "likely Negro boys about 10-years-old."

She was open and smiling and pleasant. She had shortish blond hair, as I recall. She spoke generally about embracing our shared history and trying to make sense of it, all of which was fine, none of which was offensive. But I felt like I was about to hyperventilate. I had to will myself not to bolt.

O-aw, O-aw

Aqua boogie, baby.

My Lord, I was coming undone.

I excused myself and fled to a nearby Black family, who acted as a reset. Who had an instant, calming effect on my nervous system. I regained my composure as I introduced myself and started asking questions.

Before getting word of the reunion, the wife had never known of any white Bibbs either, she said. The husband said he was full of feelings he didn't want to feel. I nodded. I knew just what he meant.

I followed them around, taking notes, until I felt me come back into myself. Until I felt marginally less frightened.

At some point I went looking for my cousins Amber and Traci. Their late father and my late father had been brothers. Traci had spent time by herself in the attic, where the enslaved had slept, where the risen heat acted as another overseer: an oppressive supernatural force pushing at Black people, crowding the room. Traci had been asked to be the reunion speaker and she was taking a few moments to gather herself. She was, she said, trying not to come unglued.

Soon after, the sky cleared, everyone went back outside, and the formal program began. Morrow talked about discovering Major Richard Bibb's will and how he'd made finding the Bibb descendants his life's work.

"The Bibb family and these Bibb slaves went all over America and done all kinds of things," he said. The Bibb story "is a story about race. It's a story about family. It's a story about slavery. It's a story about wealth. It's a story about abuse. It's a story about neglect."

Traci stepped to the lectern on the Bibb House lawn and told the hushed crowd, "When I pulled up, voices started in my head. Normally, I don't hear voices." She talked about sitting alone in that windowless, 110-degree attic, holding a quilt made by one of the enslaved. She was, she said quietly, enraged.

My cousin asked the descendants of the enslaved: What would you want to say to the slave owners? And much later, when the moment was long gone, I thought up plenty of words. They went like this:

We are not like you.

We will not do to you what your people did to us.

We are not going to burn your teenagers alive or put your

grandmothers to work scrubbing our floors. We won't break every bond of fellowship or citizenship to gain advantage, then lie to ourselves and others about how, precisely, we've hoarded privilege in every institution of American society. We won't call the police every time we feel uncomfortable or are made to share space. You are so afraid of us, of our anger and emotion, only because you know what you would do. It is everything you've already done. This is why you're always marveling at our power to forgive, because you, yourselves, do not.

That's what I came up with later, but in that moment on the Bibb House lawn, I had just two bitter words. I said them out loud. Clearly. And I meant every bit of them.

My cousin Sharon whipped her head around and tried to shush me, but I just faced forward, gazing steadily at my cousin and at the plantation house behind her. I didn't apologize. I said what I said. I felt calmer than I had since I'd arrived in Kentucky. For the first time, everything I was looking at made sense.

I do believe it was the spirit of my grandmother Susie O'Neal (née Bibb) answering my prayer.

The idea of Major Richard Bibb as an emancipator had been a source of local and family legend, and pride. It was the animating feature of the Bibb House reunion. But from where I sat, which was on the front lawn of a

Portrait of Richard Bibb.

21

Kentucky plantation house, it was simply a reminder that a complex 250-year system of violent plunder and human trafficking could only be sustained by intersecting policies of pressure and release.

To me it just meant Richard Bibb was, arguably, better than some. Not necessarily good.

The next day, eight carloads of Black Bibbs and some of the white descendants toured parts of Bibbtown. Nearly fifteen hundred acres, land as far as you could see, said those who used to know.

Arnold's Chapel AME Zion Church was founded by that light-skinned woman in the picture, the matriarch of Bibbtown, who'd been known as Granny Kate. Some of us might still own property in Bibbtown, Michael Morrow told us. It was going to be difficult to sort out, to disentangle from the white hands that were laying claim to it, and he wanted our help.

It all felt like a very old story. And having come to the end of the reunion, I thought to keep it at a far remove, shunted away somewhere distant and manageable, where the known world was more legible and my feelings all used their indoor voices. I was eager to get home, beyond the reach of Bibb history, family history, Kentucky history, American history. Beyond the violence of the past.

Even at a distance, some of us feel it always, Faulkner said, and I know it to be true. I've felt it my whole life. The South he called a vanished society, full of "garrulous outraged baffled ghosts." I have not, to my knowledge, been visited by white spirits, so it's not something I can speak to. But I know Black ghosts. They come at you in the midnight hour. They wake you up with their bitter, unreconciled strivings. They shake their chains, or wag their fingers, or play their records until you just don't want to hear them anymore. Black ghosts put your soul on ice.

I wanted to get back to a place where the ground felt steady beneath my feet, and the ghosts were less restive, or at a minimum better behaved. I wanted to replant myself, in my own Black place and time, in my own Black yard, which is exactly what I was trying to do when I seized up in the seed aisle of Home Depot. Because that's not how history, or ghosts, for that matter, work. They do not adhere to boundaries of place and time. Once they decide about you, they follow you home. They write their stories in blood, and then they read behind each other. They leave blood on the leaves and on the roots.

I decided to start there.

CHAPTER 2

THE BIBB
BEGOTTEN

The white Bibb family, most likely Huguenots, French Protestants who migrated to Wales to escape religious persecution, arrived in Virginia nearly a century before the American Revolution.

There is a James Bibb listed in records (the Bibb name alternately appears in records as Bibbey, Van Bibber, Bebe, and Bibbs) who appears to have at least visited the colony in 1629. Another early name, Charles Bibb, shows up as a witness to a land lease in 1635. But Benjamin Bibb, also known in the genealogical literature as "the Colonist," was considered the first permanent Bibb in America. He migrated with his wife and four sons to Hanover County, Central Virginia (which became part of the greater Richmond area), sometime prior to 1685.

Three of Benjamin Bibb's four sons formed separate branches and geographies of white Bibbs in America. The Colonist's second son, William Bibb (1665–1744), fathered the most storied branch of the white Bibbs—this includes a US senator from Georgia who became the first governor of Alabama, and the namesake for Bibb Counties in both states; his brother, who succeeded him as Alabama's second governor; and the Bibbs of Logan County, in western Kentucky, who enslaved my ancestors. William Bibb begat John Bibb (1703–1769). And John Bibb's youngest child, Major Richard Bibb (1752–1839), moved with his family to Kentucky around 1798.

Major Richard Bibb, one of the wealthiest men in western Kentucky, is the starting point for where I first learned of the white Bibbs, and where me and mine enter this story.

According to lore, i.e., stories kept in family bibles recounted on genealogical sites, an enslaved person prompted Major Bibb's change of soul regarding the peculiar institution. The Episcopalian—a land speculator and tobacco farmer who owned a whiskey still and dabbled in the burgeoning Kentucky concern of thoroughbred horses—became a lay Methodist minister (called by God to preach, is how I've heard it said) who gradually turned against enslavement. Most significantly when he was dead.

Major Richard Bibb begat three sons and three daughters, including: John Bigger Bibb, the executor of his father's will and an amateur horticulturist credited with developing Bibb lettuce.

When Major Richard Bibb died, his son John had a detailed will to follow through. But his brother George Mortimer, renowned Kentucky legal mind, would spend many years advising his brother how to circumvent and delay the full execution of their father's wishes.

The Black Bibbs

My Black Bibb ancestors descended from an enslaved woman named Keziah who was born around 1786.

It is believed that Keziah came from Virginia with Major Richard Bibb. She became known as Old Keziah to distinguish her from a granddaughter called Young Keziah.

Keziah had twelve children between 1802 and 1822, and she was one of those emancipated in Major Richard Bibb's will.

(There is no father listed for any of Keziah's children. They were only property. Where they came from was of no consequence to white record keepers.)

Keziah's youngest child, Rachel Bibb, was roughly seventeen years old when Major Bibb's will emancipated her. The emancipation rolls for Logan County describe her as being about five feet tall, "well made," and the "ordinary color of negroes."

Census records list Rachel as Black.

But Rachel had a one-year-old son named John Wesley Bibb around the time of her emancipation. He is not listed in Richard Bibb's will, or on the rolls of the Logan County emancipations, but he shows up by name in 1850. He is listed as Black in the 1860 census records. But in 1870, in Centralia, he is listed as white.

Thereafter, he is most often called "mulatto" in census records. A man who would be listed as Black, *white*, and mulatto? He is the product of a nation that was unsure how to categorize what it was doing, but still felt compelled to do it. The paper trail follows John Wesley as he grows up, takes a bride, starts a family, registers to fight for the Union in the Civil War, and when the war ends, moves to southern Illinois, where he works as a farmer and fathers more children, a total of thirteen in all.

John Wesley Bibb was my great-great-grandfather.

John Wesley's father, my great-great-great-grandfather, was almost certainly a white man. For me, the question of who he was and what that meant hung over the 2019 reunion. It was the one question that would answer so many others, I thought. That would give me the kind of purchase an enslaver, if that's who he was, would never have intended. I wanted to find the roll, the letter, the document that would tell me. I wanted blood, or I wanted, at least, the proof of life it represented. But there was nothing official, just breadcrumbs for me to follow, if that's what I wanted to do. So very many times, I did not know if it was.

John Wesley and his wife, Pocahontas, known as Pokey, had one child in Bibbtown, and twelve others in Centralia, a railroad town in southern Illinois where so many of the Black Bibbs, and other Logan County residents, migrated after the Civil War.

John Wesley Bibb begat Charles Smith Bibb, his tenth child.

Charles Smith Bibb and his wife, Minnie Bibb, begat eight children who lived to adulthood. His third oldest was Susie Wylene O'Neal (née Bibb).

Momma Susie and her husband, Lonnie O'Neal Sr., begat Jacqueline Rivers (née O'Neal), Ronald Dwight O'Neal, and my Lonnie Gerald O'Neal.

Lonnie Gerald, as everyone called him, and his wife, Elizabeth Louella, who everyone called Betty Lou, begat

Momma Susie as a young woman.

Lisa Allen (née O'Neal); *me,* Lonnae O'Neal; and adopted my brother
Charles O'Neal at six months old. He was six weeks younger than me.

I was named after my father. He wanted a boy. His spirit hung over
that first Bibb House reunion in 2019 for me. Over it, around it, all the
way through it. And like many thousands of Black people gone and
unaccounted for, his spirit and shadow loom over the Bibb history and
descendants, known and unknown.

Uncle Roy, Uncle Morris, Uncle Hickey, and Uncle Bobby, World War II portrait.

CHAPTER 3

BIBB LETTUCE

I must have heard of the mildly sweet, smooth-textured lettuce before that first Bibb reunion, although when or where, I cannot say. It was a food reference slightly beyond the tables where I usually sat. Though I don't ever remember eating Bibb lettuce, the name sounded instantly familiar.

I have often wondered why, having surely, at some point, heard the name Bibb lettuce, I never even remotely associated it with Momma Susie, or our extended Bibb family. It could be that I never got close to connecting Bibb lettuce with my grandmother's table because there was zero similarity or cultural vernacular between the two. I don't know if Momma Susie was familiar with the heirloom garden vegetable that bore her maiden name, even though she and my grandfather ran a restaurant and tavern in the small southern Illinois town of

Centralia, where I spent every summer of my childhood in the 1970s and '80s. Perhaps it was because on Momma Susie's table, as on most tables in America and every table where I ate growing up, lettuce only ever meant iceberg, like the phone company meant Illinois Bell. And iceberg lettuce was only ever meant to be drowned in French dressing. Or perhaps Catalina, if you were putting on airs.

I have long been a salad (bar) lover. I eat it almost daily, such that often young relatives who lived with me would reliably lose weight after a month or two of shared meals at my table. This prompted the better cooks among my family and friends to fret over my propensity to serve my "great big ole husband [one current, one former] leaves," which they saw as a form of spousal neglect. Or at the very least, a cultural betrayal. To the extent I'd ever thought about it, I'd always considered lettuce to be a fairly anodyne vegetable. It's not like garlic or cilantro or onion. The aroma of freshly cut lettuce never wafts through a kitchen or brings water to your eyes.

And although it's green and leafy, I'd never seen anyone fry it up in the bacon grease that always sat, congealing, in an old Crisco can between the back burners on the kitchen stoves of my childhood. Or even simmered with smoked turkey.

It was several years after that first Bibb reunion that I finally sat down to a plate of Bibb lettuce salad. But it took some doing to get to that point. I'd started off determined to fix my own Bibb salad at home. Over time, my salad tastes had grown marginally more sophisticated—I'd graduated from iceberg to spring mix, garlic kale, raw mustard greens, and even arugula (which I'd learned to pronounce after hearing President Obama once complain about the high price). I'd bought a cruet and mixed up my own olive oil, balsamic vinegar, and Italian herb dressing, which, admittedly, was easy enough since it all came in the same box, with clear instructions. Still, I felt confident that I'd be able to handle this new lettuce challenge, no matter how high-end its reputation.

I was going to buy a head of Bibb, I was going to dress it perfectly, and I wasn't going to allow any bottles of French (or Catalina, Thousand Island, etc.) anywhere close. I was determined to see why people thought this vegetable was so special and what all the fuss was about.

I tried to find it at a nearby farmers market first. I met a young farmer who said he and his brother used to sell Bibb lettuce for three dollars a head, but they'd stopped a few years earlier because there wasn't enough demand. Next, I searched the produce aisles of a few local grocery stores, but none of them carried anything in the Bibb lettuce family. Finally, I found two kinds of butter lettuce, of which Bibb is a type, at Whole Foods, and decided that would have to do.

Having secured the greens, I shifted gears. I willed myself to evolve into a better and higher version of my salad-fixing ways. I remembered what I'd read about the softness of Bibb lettuce leaves and vowed to dress it lightly. As I walked the grocery aisle, everything I was tempted to buy prompted me to think deeply about complementary pairings and ideal ways to awaken lettuce flavor.

I bought a lime because it seemed like the right thing to do. Then I bought a lemon, because a lime might not be right. I rejected a classic ranch or chunky blue cheese, or an organic creamy Caesar dressing, as too heavy for the tender Bibb constitution, and I looked instead for something that telegraphed sophisticated and fresh. Something new in my experience, with a considerable number of vowels in the name, like lemon herb tahini. And I searched high and low for an appropriate vinaigrette (because how many Bibb salad recipes had I read that championed vinaigrette?). I saw a lemon basil dressing—which wasn't a vinaigrette, but I picked it up anyway. A lemon vinaigrette would have been perfect, but that I could not find. There was, however, a champagne vinaigrette that married well with my need to combine two French names in my salad that were not French dressing, which I was starting to wonder if Whole Foods carried. That one was even spelled with an *a* in the vinaigrette, which felt fancy until I looked it up and found out that's how vinaigrette is spelled. So that was less of a win than I thought.

In the end, my choices came down to Italian Romano cheese vinaigrette, with notes of citrus (I felt good about the *notes* part), or herbes de Provence vinaigrette, which was "fragrant, savory, robust, and herbaceous." As I read the labels in the refrigerated section of the produce aisle, I shook my butt a bit because I liked the way that last word sounded. Maybe I myself was feeling herbaceous. Or robust. Anyway, I'd lost the thread. I just went ahead and bought the champagne vinaigrette. And the lemon basil. Also the lemon herb tahini, because I decided whatever this Bibb salad was going to be, it was going to work. Except then I felt pressured. After returning home and spreading out three containers and one plastic bag of butter and baby butter lettuce and nearly thirty dollars' worth of salad dressings, I opted for a new plan. I would find a restaurant that served a true Bibb lettuce salad and I would order from there. In that way, I wouldn't have to wonder if I had the right stuff in terms of both the lettuce and my aptitude for dressing it correctly.

As it turned out, finding a local restaurant that served a Bibb salad also took a considerable amount of intention and effort. It was on the menu at one Italian restaurant for Washington's bian-nual restaurant week, but by the time I called, they'd switched their lunch menu to serve a kale salad instead. I found other restaurants with Bibb lettuce menu mentions that were outdated or limited to an important but supporting role on lobster rolls or burgers. I'd nearly resigned myself to having to become a food tourist, to wander the mid-Atlantic or perhaps travel all the way back to central Kentucky, before I would finally score. But then I found a strawberry Bibb salad with candied walnuts, goat cheese, and a Dijon vinaigrette at McCormick & Schmick's seafood restaurant in downtown Washington. I ordered it to go so I could eat in private and descend into the experience.

I took three bites, just the lettuce first so I could take in the unvar-nished taste and texture. Then I added a few blue cheese crumbles and I allowed myself to spear a few pieces of strawberry. I dipped the leaves in tiny drops of vinaigrette. In very short order, I understood why I'd heard of Bibb lettuce, and why it was considered a gourmet favorite. It was late afternoon and I hadn't eaten anything, so I was at the point in my program where anything I'd eat would taste like the best I'd ever had, but these leaves were the real thing: whole, soft, and absolutely buttery in my mouth. They felt, very nearly, creamy. And, yes, sophisti-cated. It was the best lettuce in the best salad I'd ever tasted, and even that descriptor was foreign to me since lettuce was not something I'd ever considered in terms of superlatives.

On the theory that everybody is a critic, I permitted myself just the slightest quibble. The leaves were supposed to be mild, I knew, but I wondered if I'd actually enjoyed the vegetable's full nuance and taste potential. Or had this Bibb lettuce been grown hydroponically, for efficiency's sake, shipped over great distance, perhaps, and had that affected my ability to experience some of the more flavorful "notes"? I wouldn't have known the difference, but that had been the debate among some gardening and food experts. But now I'm getting ahead of the story.

Bibb lettuce grows in small, round heads of loose, tender leaves that open in layers, like a rose in bloom. It is a type of butter lettuce, so named for its smooth, velvety texture, but it also goes by limestone lettuce, for the sedimentary deposits in the soil in Inner Bluegrass, Kentucky, where it was first cultivated. It is the limestone alkaline that is said to give a mild sweetness to the thin, satiny leaves that can be served whole, particularly if they are lightly dressed. That is, unless they become the perfect wrap (in place of tortillas!) for shrimp, or chicken breast in a slightly warmed peanut butter sauce.

The niche popularity of Bibb lettuce is part of the contemporary evolution of farming and eating that prioritizes variety. That places a premium on fresh, organic greens—preferably locally grown—and all the good feelings therein.

But Bibb lettuce has made disparate, high-profile appearances in and around food and gardening cultures for nearly a century—since it first became commercially available, and Kentucky newspapers began to crow: "The world comes to Kentucky for lettuce."

Former First Lady Michelle Obama grew Bibb lettuce in her White House kitchen garden, part of her "Let's Move!" initiative to encourage healthy eating. It was an ingredient in the White House garden salad recipe, with snap peas and radishes. It marries well with apple and blue cheese, with persimmons or horseradish, or a bourbon vinaigrette. The small inner leaves are also especially well suited for cups with pork, turkey, chicken, chopped seafood, or tofu, all tasty options for a protein filling.

In 2016, Bibb lettuce was added to the *Ark of Taste* global catalog of historically important and flavorful foods that require intentional preservation. They called it the "sine qua non," the most essential part, of any restaurant salad. That is, if it is a good restaurant.

A 2021 *New Yorker* appreciation piece about the late essayist and food writer Laurie Colwin used it as an analog for refinement: "She had a taste for delicacies, recommending Bibb lettuce with chunks of pate de foie gras and lobster meat, but was never delicate about them. . . ."

And in 2022, it played a key role in the conservation effort to keep a manatee named Corleone, and others of his species, from starving to death along Florida's Atlantic coast. Biologists charged with their care and feeding "took the unprecedented step of setting out fresh heads of romaine and Bibb lettuce daily for hungry manatees gathering in the warmer outflow waters of a power plant near Cape Canaveral," according to an account in the *Washington Post*. Officials thought all their efforts had come to naught, until one day when "some three dozen sea cows were observed munching on the lettuce. Wildlife officials said the animals ate 450 pounds of produce in a day."

But for all its wide travels, Bibb lettuce, which was not commercially produced until the 1920s, is, most essentially, a staple of Kentucky identity. Steeped in the Bluegrass State terroir. A product of the dirt where it was first grown.

After the classic old-fashioned (a Kentucky-bourbon-and-bitters mix with fruit and a touch of sugar served in a lowball glass), it serves as a proprietary refinement of the Bourbon, Horses, and History region of central Kentucky and acts as a cultured offset to less savory parts of Kentucky history. It makes an annual appearance during the commonwealth's most celebrated victory lap, the Kentucky Derby, a horse race where Bibb lettuce is always in good taste.

"My earliest memory of lettuce with actual flavor was biting into a leaf of Bibb, sprinkled with salt," remembered Frankfort native Donna Hecker, a food writer and former associate chef in the Kentucky Governor's Mansion. "Not flakes of hand-raked fleur de sel or fine grains of Himalayan pink or even kosher crystals, but ordinary iodized table salt from the blue canister so ubiquitous in my 1960s childhood." Hecker was visiting friends in northern Kentucky who'd grown the lettuce in their garden. Having previously been relegated to "the soulless crunch of iceberg left to languish at the local A&P, Bibb was a revelation—tender yet tasting of sunlight and the color green."

Hecker specialized in salads at the Governor's Mansion from the mid-1990s to the early aughts. While Kentucky Governor Paul E. Patton and his wife, Judi, were partial to hearty salads with obscenely buttery, garlicky croutons and rich blue cheese dressing for themselves, Hecker served a Bibb salad with strawberries and pecans for guests. Once, for a visiting Japanese business group, she made a Bibb salad with peeled green grapes and balls of honeydew and cucumber with a light tarragon cream dressing (just lemon juice, fresh tarragon, heavy cream, and salt and white pepper). There "may" have also been a few chives involved.

A highlight of her tenure was the "all-Kentucky" dinner for Princess Anne where they served Bibb lettuce with a light vinaigrette and a chiffonade of thin-sliced country ham. The menu for the late April dinner had to be approved by Buckingham Palace by February; the Bibb lettuce was specially grown by a local family who'd been farming organically since 1975 in Casey County, Kentucky, an hour and a half south of Frankfort. The timing worked out to allow the dinner to feature one of the first harvests of the season.

It wasn't the first time the lettuce had been served to British nobility (or royalty, in the case of Princess Anne). Bibb salad first appeared on the Kentucky Derby menu at Churchill Downs in 1930, a decade after its public introduction, to help give Lord Edward Montagu Cavendish Stanley, son of the Earl of Derby, an authentic Kentucky welcome.

That authentic Kentucky welcome remains an important ingredient of the culture and foodways of the Bluegrass region. The Holly Hill Inn, just outside Lexington, riffs on the history of locally famous Bibb salads with their Woodford salad, which is served with a bourbon sorghum vinegar dressing. In 2024, the Holly Hill garden grew seventy-four heads of Bibb to supply their eight family-owned central Kentucky restaurants on the theory that Bibb lettuce must be blessed by dirt, or at least be in conversation with it, to reach peak flavor, or to have much (if any) flavor at all. Hecker, who writes about food and culture for *Holly Hill and Co.*, called the lettuce a ghost of itself when grown hydroponically—although that technology, which swaps water for soil to eliminate pests and chemicals, and increases yields year-round, has allowed a new iteration of John Bigger Bibb's lettuce to travel the world.

Lettuce was first cultivated by the ancient Egyptians for its seed oil. It soon became an important food crop grown for its thick stem and upright leaves. This also made it a phallic symbol. As a sacred plant of Min, a god of fertility, it was thought to increase sexual endurance, appetite, and vitality, and was depicted on temple walls as part of the deity's harvest festival.

It spread to the Greeks and Romans, who cultivated different strains and began using a romaine antecedent as a salad before meals. Of the five types of lettuce, three—leaf, head, and romaine (which is also called cos for the Greek island where it was cultivated)—each with numerous varieties, spread throughout Europe. By the early sixteenth century, lettuce had arrived in the Americas and has been grown in the US since colonial times.

As a young man, John Bigger Bibb joined the Fourth Kentucky Volunteer Brigade during the War of 1812. He was promoted from private to major after the Battle of the Thames, in which the Shawnee leader Tecumseh, who had united Native peoples' fight against white settlers, was killed. John Bigger Bibb returned to Russellville, became a lawyer, and served in the Kentucky House of Representatives, and then as a state senator.

By the 1850 census, John Bigger Bibb, sixty, is listed as having no occupation and is, perhaps, retired. He and his wife, Sarah P. Horsley, have no children. By 1856, the couple had moved to the state capital of Frankfort, where they lived in the neighborhood that came to be known as the "corner in celebrities" historic district for its concentration of notables. These included Supreme Court Justice John Marshall Harlan, high-ranking state and federal officeholders, military officers, and John Bigger Bibb's brother, George Mortimer Bibb, who'd been chief justice of the Kentucky Court of Appeals and a US senator and treasury secretary.

In 1860, census records list John Bigger Bibb as a lawyer in Frankfort, though he hadn't practiced law since before he entered public office in Russellville. In this season of his life, he is written of as kindly, gentle, loath to harm another living creature, and referred to as Major Jack. In a family of "aggressive and successful" men, Major Jack Bibb, who dropped the Major upon leaving military service, was regarded as "shy and retiring."

"In a day when violence was rife and bloodshed was common, even in high places, this gentleman would not even go hunting. While his contemporaries were fighting duels and contributing another page to Kentucky's bloody history, Mr. Jack Bibb busied himself with gardens and flowers," according to one newspaper account. The Gothic Revival home he built in 1856, known as Gray Gables, situated on the old Petticoat Lane and fashioned after an English country home, is known today as the Bibb-Burnley house. The corner property, which stretches from Frankfort's historic Wapping Street to the Kentucky River, features a wrought iron entryway, expansive gardens, and an inside wall of Tudor bookcases with ceiling-high arches. But it was at the rear of the property, in the gardens and under the hothouse glass, where John Bigger Bibb devoted himself to his horticultural passions.

He used a strain of lettuce his family had brought from Virginia (and possibly England before that) to develop his "Kentucky limestone" lettuce. A key difference between the Virginia and Kentucky cultivars was the alkaline in the sedimentary limestone deposits in the Inner Bluegrass, Kentucky, soil. This is credited with giving Bibb lettuce its signature satiny texture and sweetish leaves.

In the late 1860s, Bibb began giving samples of the lettuce to his wealthy, influential friends and family in and around the state capital, people who celebrated his ingenuity and refinement, and grew his legend.

"The influential and the wealthy considered it a great honor to receive the lettuce or the seed as gifts from the 'Major.' It had no name, so people simply called it Bibb lettuce because 'Major Bibb' had given it to them," a 1961 *Louisville Courier-Journal* article noted.

"My lettuce has been unusually good," John Bigger Bibb boasted in an 1878 letter to his nephew Samuel Sterling, of Hopkinsville. "Two or three families have been getting some. At least one or two are beginning to save seeds and help me in giving it to others."

John Bigger Bibb died in 1884, at age ninety-four, and took the secrets of his Bibb lettuce cultivar with him to the grave. None were able to replicate the precise combination of strains, along with soil, fertilizer, and production, to grow the lettuce from scratch, and in Russellville and Spring Station (now part of Louisville), the lettuce died out. But members of the Frankfort upper class were determined to keep it growing. They allowed a portion of their Bibb lettuce heads to bolt—to flower and reproduce seeds—which they then replanted, season after season, for decades. It was only a chance dinner in Louisville in 1919 that broke that cycle and saved Bibb lettuce from eternal hyperlocality, or even extinction, and launched it on a brief, star-making national run.

There are differing accounts of how Bibb lettuce found its way out of the high-class homes of Frankfort, but the broad strokes are fairly consistent. The story goes that, one night, a young Louisville woman named Viola Genenwein had dinner with a friend who served salad featuring a small, delicate lettuce of a type Viola had never had. The friend told of a wealthy employer (alternately the friend's father) who grew the lettuce on his estate, touted its rarity, and was very particular about who he gave it to. Viola came home and raved about this new lettuce to her father, William Genenwein, a modest truck farmer with a hundred-dollar greenhouse measuring thirty by ninety feet he'd bought from the city of Louisville and expanded. Genenwein was intrigued by this new lettuce and set about trying to score some of that green for himself.

Genenwein asked his daughter's friend to ask this wealthy employer if he would part with some of his lettuce seed. "In all probability, he [had] obtained the seed from someone in Frankfort, or from some descendant of a friend of old Mr. Jack Bibb," according to a 1939 *Louisville Courier-Journal* article. And he guarded it jealously. The friend (alternately reported as a young woman or a young man) was doubtful. The gardener on the wealthy employer's estate may have been enlisted to help, a premium bottle of whiskey may have figured in the negotiations, and whether the employer reluctantly agreed, or was unaware, a half teaspoon of seeds, or "just enough to keep one family in lettuce for a season," was passed to Viola. That was plenty for William John Genenwein, who wasn't interested in dinner; he was interested in dynasty. He began letting the lettuce plants go to seed. In short order, he'd become the only grocer supplying enough of the lettuce to satisfy a growing local hunger that he himself helped create.

By the mid-1920s, Genenwein owned a thirty-two-acre vegetable garden in western Louisville, a third of it irrigated, where he grew cucumbers, carrots, sweet corn, and potatoes. But Bibb lettuce was his moneymaker. He grew the cool-season vegetable year-round in an acre-and-a-half stretch of greenhouses, under nearly thirty-five-thousand feet of glass.

"Mr. Genenwein took a truckload of lettuce to market every weekday—50 to 100 bushels a day. This lettuce was sold at a premium, usually," a 1925 article in the *Louisville Courier-Journal* noted.

Genenwein's near decade-long commercial monopoly ended when he seeded his lettuce outdoors instead of inside his greenhouses, and persons unknown, who had presumably been itching for their chance, slipped the fence and nabbed enough lettuce to put the world in business. Bibb lettuce seeds spread to other regional commercial producers, and eventually around the country. By the mid-twentieth century, the Kentucky original was a national brand.

It was served in the "higher heeled haciendas of Hollywood." New York's 21 Club and Nino's made a production of it in their Caesar salad, as did the famed Little Club where opening act Doris Day was said to have wolfed hers down one night while talking to a reporter at dinner. In Chicago, the Pump Room served a Bibb salad before its flaming-sword-swallowing act "with Saladier George Sotos abaft the bowls."

Frankfort native John Glover South, the former US ambassador to Portugal, took Bibb lettuce with him to Lisbon. The climate and soil of the peninsula allowed it to thrive and gain an enduring place in the Portuguese national diet.

By 1969, Kentucky newspapers trumpeted Bibb lettuce as the "finest in the world" and the "orchid of the salad world." It was "among the world's famous foods," earning a "magnifique" from French gourmets—especially the ones who'd moved to Kentucky.

But a few years later, the salad days for Bibb lettuce began drawing to a close. The restaurant salad bar was spreading across the country, but Bibb lettuce was constitutionally unable to make the trip. It just didn't travel well. Its delicate leaves bruised easily, making it unsuited both to the buffeting of salad bars and to the practice of chain grocery stores selling prewashed lettuce in plastic bags.

"It returned to being a signature regional lettuce, jealously protected and employed famously in food celebrations surround[ing] the Kentucky Derby," according to the Slow Food Foundation for Biodiversity, and "has not been in mass field cultivation since [the] 1970s." It has been mostly grown by home gardeners, in heirloom gardens, in greenhouses, and increasingly through the water-for-soil substitution method known as hydroponics. For the epicurean, though, nothing replaces Bibb lettuce grown in Kentucky limestone soil. Kentucky food aficionados, regional cooks, and garden bloggers have been the true believers who've carried the Bibb lettuce mystique into the twenty-first century in ways that feel delightfully ambrosial.

Albeit a bit incomplete. Because there is another side to this story.

I remember the first time I heard Black Bibb descendants talk about Bibb lettuce.

The two women, mother and daughter, were sitting in the Bibb House front room, surrounded by old photos, drawings, pastoral images of Logan County, and maps demonstrating its centrality to western Kentucky. Quotes with portraits from Civil War–era politicians hung on the wall behind them. The older woman, LaVaughn Duncan, breathed through an oxygen tube that wrapped her ears and snaked down the front of her sleeveless blouse. Her face was unlined, her hair more pepper than salt. She is too young to need oxygen, I thought.

"We used to say that Bibb lettuce belonged to us," Duncan said. "And that we were going to be rich!" She giggled lightly at the thought. For a moment, her daughter, Loretia Seals, dropped her head to shut her eyes, like she might need to pray on the matter. Then she looked up and joined the giggle, laughing right along with her momma. She is in on the joke, you understand. We all are. Seals's eyes crinkled lightly at the corners.

The brief scene is from *Invented Before We Were Born*, a documentary on the legacy of Major Richard Bibb, by filmmakers Jonathan and Rachel Knight, white Bibb descendants who had been heavily involved in organizing the inaugural Bibb reunion.

But that exchange felt palpably Black.

I immediately understood what I was looking at as I watched Duncan and Seals. Their laughter was protective. Their smiles were resistance. Their ruefulness was, most precisely, a reflexive Black defense mechanism against the consumptive flames of our own, American, Babylon.

Or, put another way, it was just part of that old Black knowing.

I thought we were going to be rich!

Hahahaha.

Whatcha goin' to do?

In the vast majority of history and backstories I've come across detailing the origins of Bibb lettuce, Major John Bigger Bibb's role as an enslaver was never mentioned. The contribution that enslaved people might have made to kindly Jack Bibb's horticultural triumph was never entertained or raised as a line of inquiry. Camille Glenn, famed author of *The Heritage of Southern Cooking*, who called Bibb lettuce one of the "aristocrats of the genre," did take note, however, of "the gardener and helper in [John Bigger Bibb's] small greenhouse, knowing his secretive ways, [who] wisely slipped a few plants" out of the door.

I, of course, have questions about that "gardener and helper."

I wonder if he or she was akin to those Black helpers mentioned, as culinary historian Michael W. Twitty puts it, in "the canon of cookbooks written by white women whose worlds were populated by black cooks and servants, whose presence can be read across the pages in recipes in dialect, recipes with only first names, or recipes with descriptions of plantation life." Twitty specifically cites *The Kentucky Housewife* cookbook with its thirteen hundred recipes, which also includes helpful information on "established rules for domestics and slaves" in the introduction, just so there's no confusion. Apparently a Kentucky housewife was wise to avoid confusion.

I wonder if John Bigger Bibb's "gardener and helper" syncs up with the persistent, although unproven, supposition that it was a Black woman who originated the recipe for Kentucky Fried Chicken. Enslaved cooks had married the Scottish tradition of deep-frying chicken with their own creative seasonings, popularizing fried chicken in Southern cuisine and turning it into an enduring staple of communal Black meals. But it was a white former insurance salesman, filling-station operator, and motel owner, Kentucky Colonel Harland Sanders, who shrouded his "top secret, original recipe" chicken, with eleven herbs and spices, in mystery, and made it a central part of the KFC identity and appeal. Colonel Sanders (colonel not being a military rank but rather an honorific bestowed by the Kentucky governor) operated a motel/restaurant precursor to his Kentucky Fried Chicken franchise in Corbin, Kentucky, where, by the way, a white mob drove its entire Black population out of town in 1919. Largely never to return.

Sanders once became right proprietary about the Bibb lettuce name at a Kentucky Tourist and Travel Council meeting. Apparently "some Yankee up in Chicago" was selling Kentucky Bibb lettuce and "not just making barrels of money at it," Sanders bristled, but stripping *Kentucky* from the name and simply calling it limestone lettuce. If you can imagine.

I wonder if John Bigger Bibb's "gardener and helper" was a similar figure to the enslaved Tennessee man Nathan "Nearest" Green, "Uncle Nearest," who taught a young Jasper "Jack" Daniel how to distill whiskey. Daniel used that knowledge to become one of the most famous whiskey makers in the world. A corrective to the long-ignored history of Nearest Green, the brand's first master distiller, was added to the Jack Daniel's website in 2017.

There is one story about John Bigger Bibb that recounts how he used to take a "Negro boy" fishing with him to bait the hook and cast his line out into the water. The story goes that one day, the boy called Bibb's attention to the surface of the pond. The frog he'd used for bait was swimming with all its might, away from the fishing line he'd just been attached to. Bibb instructed the boy to allow the frog-bait to escape, to let it swim to safety instead of meeting its death at the business end of a fishing pole. The point of the story, in this telling, was to illustrate John Bigger Bibb's tender heart. To bolster his legend as an animal philosopher, a lover of flora and fauna, and a man possessed only of the most kindly inclinations toward even the lowliest of creatures. My takeaway was he was an enslaver. He trafficked in human beings and profited from a violent system of labor exploitation at a time when other white people, men and women of their times, made different choices, and the millions of enslaved were not consulted as to their choices at all.

We do not know if the story of John Bigger Bibb and that "Negro boy" took place during enslavement. But even if the young boy was not enslaved, he was not free. The circumscribed state of Black lives includes a question, among many, as to whether he would have chosen to help an old white man go fishing if the choice had been put to him or his parents.

My takeaway is that every glowing descriptor that amplifies John Bigger Bibb's name, that lionizes him as a Kentucky original and a man of the gentlest persuasions, elides that simple fact. It is that inability to make room for complexity in the American story, for many things to be true at once, that feels pathological to the descendants of enslavement. That bent toward the most reductive history and blinkered understanding reeks of innocence. It is white people wondering publicly how we got here, as they fervently tell each other this is not who we are, while some are passing memory laws, and banning books, to make it ever so. They don't contextualize John Bigger Bibb as an enslaver, because they don't want to see the centrality of that role in his triumph, or in the American culture, character, and belief system that rose up from what he, and by extension the slaveholding nation, begat.

"Kentucky producers are often asked from whence [Bibb lettuce] came, or in true Kentucky style, who was its grandpappy. The answer to that probably passed on with Maj. John Bibb," a 1942 *Louisville Courier-Journal* article contends. "We are told it bears a resemblance to some of the fine old cottage lettuces of England. . . . But it is unnecessary to grope with the past."

As a descendant of enslavement, I disagree.

Who are the ones, we Black Bibbs wonder, who walk away with the spoils of colonialism and bondage and deem the process that gave rise to a white narrative primacy, and most assuredly generational wealth, as pre-political? As naturally occurring, rather than an amalgamation of brutal choices, policies, and legal maneuvers that created that very same narrative primacy and wealth. Who closed off that process to review, and deemed the foundational joists of American inheritance off-limits? Who gets to declare that legacy beyond reconsideration, un-subject to adjudication, remuneration, or the reapportionment of cultural and reputational shine?

Who is the white Simon who ever stops the music when he's holding all the chairs? And when did Bibb lettuce shake the shackles off its leaves to enter the public domain fresh, innocent, and free of blight to become an heirloom treasure, menu delicacy, and source of Kentucky pride? What is that process called? Who do we see about that?

It is against this fuller history, and not separate from it, that I engage questions of Bibb lettuce cultivation, provenance, and cultural rise. That I assess its creditworthiness. That I think about kindly old Major Jack, boasting about the prized lettuce he's giving away to his estimable friends into his eighties.

Lettuce is typically a cool-season crop.

It gets seeded in late March, just after the chance of heavy frost has given way to early spring, at about a dozen seeds per square foot (sometimes many times that, which will require thinning out). Planting every week or two, March through May, yields a continuous supply from April through June, or until the weather gets hot. That's when the lettuce starts bolting, or going to flower, and the leaves turn bitter.

Lettuce seedlings that germinate indoors are transplanted outside in small, inch-and-a-half plugs, spaced eight to twelve inches apart. Outdoor seedlings also have to be transplanted, plant by plant, eight to twelve inches apart. This way, the roots don't compete for nutrients, and the leaves don't fight for sun.

As lettuce goes, Bibb doesn't have a big head. Even fully grown, the leaves are small and compact. They extend from the core and can lie relatively flat once you pull them off the outside edge to harvest. Alternately, you might cut the top off the plant an inch or so above ground level. Cut off all the harvest leaves at once, and the plant will continue to yield two or possibly three more heads.

Lettuce is not a princess vegetable, like those preening tomatoes, which need constant attention. But all planting and gardening is labor intensive, and that was especially true before twentieth-century advances in agricultural mechanization. When John Bigger Bibb grew his lettuce outdoors in Russellville, before he moved into his Gray Gables home in Frankfort, the soil would have had to be tilled and spread with manure to fertilize it. Or perhaps in lieu of fertilizer, he might have grown other crops to provide nutrients for his lettuce. The work of managing weeds and pests, of deterring rabbits, which, by the way, love lettuce, would have been constant.

It is unclear whether the "greenhouse" behind Gray Gables was simply a hothouse tunnel—a glass-covered structure with seeds planted directly into the soil beneath—or if it was a covered and enclosed greenhouse, which would have changed the nature of Bibb's gardening, giving him better control over weeds and insects. But he would have needed to ready his pots, or whatever container he used to hold his lettuce. He would have had to customize his growing medium—a mixture of soil, manure, and nutrient additives—all of which he then would have had to move inside the greenhouse.

He had to plant enough lettuce to harvest for his own dinner table—enough to give away to his rich friends, and enough to bolt and provide seeds in sufficient numbers to meet his growing ambitions for the next planting season.

John Bigger Bibb was in his mid-sixties when he moved to Frankfort. He was in his mid-seventies when he began giving his lettuce away shortly after the end of the Civil War, an annual practice he continued until his 1884 death, at age ninety-four.

I have found no records detailing the role enslaved labor may have had in the development of the lettuce cultivar that bears my grandmother's maiden name. There are only clues to puzzle out against the racial contours of the times, the physical demands of the task, and the scientific movement that animated English planters in the New World.

The development and management of Bibb lettuce would have been labor intensive. It would have required daily monitoring, repetitive bending, stooping, and hands-on dirt work. It is work that John Bigger Bibb may not have done alone, particularly since he reportedly long suffered from rheumatism, and was the type of fellow who was apt to bring a Negro boy along fishing with him simply to bait his line. John Bigger Bibb developed his lettuce as an aging man, in chronic pain, at precisely the time that he enslaved dozens of Black laborers. It is no stretch to say they would have played a role in the development of Bibb lettuce: Given the labor arrangements that marked the institution of slavery. Given the fact that he did not start giving his lettuce away, to "keep it going" in his words, until enslavement had ended. (Which, in his case, meant during the Civil War, when some of his enslaved men left to fight in the Union army and he swore fidelity to the Union—even though his nephews, and much of his extended family, were Confederates—so he could collect the reparations for their loss.)

And enslaved labor was never simply physical. It was always conjoined with the creative, intellectual, deductive thought work that often gets discounted or ignored.

In the development of limestone Bibb lettuce, as it was first called, enslaved labor would not have come only at the end of the process. And it would have transcended moving dirt. The development of a new cultivar requires generations of genetic monitoring. It requires season-by-season, strain-by-strain decisions about the most favorable outcomes: the properties, traits, and characteristics that align with a grower's preferences—good taste, high yield, a promising crop to market and sell. In the case of Bibb lettuce, as it came to be called after John Bigger Bibb's death, maybe the end goal was something less evanescent and earthy, and more everlasting and rewarding. Something stemming, perhaps, from that Enlightenment spirit of his forefathers that was often based on collaboration.

The intellectual and cultural movement that swept through western Europe in the seventeenth and eighteenth centuries centralized reason and science in a philosophical reconsideration of society. The seventeenth-century idea of English improvement was that anything could be made better through science and natural philosophy, and through tools of experimentation. It corresponded with the belief that the highest job of the Englishman was to master the land and the earth. In this movement, powerful enough to spur advancements in agricultural practices that had been unchanged for centuries, the master/servant relationship was crucial.

According to Andrew Agha, a scholar who specializes in the origins of colonial agriculture: "The owner-slave relationship began in the laboratories in England—with the master-servant relationship where the man in control is the scientist. He's the White man whose name you read in books." He is the master who writes what Toni Morrison famously called "the Master Narrative," which, she explained, is simply "whatever ideological script that is being imposed by the people in authority on everybody else."

The seventeenth-century Puritan minister Cotton Mather was credited with introducing disease inoculation in colonial New England and advocating its use to prevent smallpox. But it was the West African man enslaved by Mather, Onesimus, who first acquainted him with what he said was a widespread West African practice.

The renowned twentieth-century surgeon Alfred Blalock was known for pioneering the corrective procedure for the congenital heart defect known as "blue baby" syndrome. But it was a Black man, Vivien Theodore Thomas, initially hired as a Vanderbilt University janitor, who partnered with Blalock on the breakthrough. (A portrait of Thomas hangs on the wall of the Alfred Blalock Clinical Sciences Building at the Johns Hopkins Hospital in Baltimore.)

It was the servants, unnamed, uncredited, often historically silent, doing the lab work: collecting information, maintaining version control, bringing the data to the scientist who bounced his (always "his") ideas off of these servants, thinking aloud, perhaps soliciting feedback and reading body language. And it was this template, an antecedent to the enslaver/enslaved relationship, that English planters brought with them across the ocean. That spirit of scientific innovation and servant labor would have been the agricultural ethos John Bigger Bibb was born into. That was passed down from his grandfather, the Virginia tobacco farmer John Bibb, who was the grandson of the colonist, Benjamin Bibb, who immigrated to Virginia from seventeenth-century Enlightenment England. This ethos would have shaped the Virginia planter class. It would have been part of John Bigger Bibb's cultural and intellectual inheritance, helping to govern how he moved through his gardens and his days. It is the canvas the story of Bibb lettuce is written on. And part of the story of the Black Bibbs.

The commercial potential of his prized lettuce does not seem to have motivated John Bigger Bibb, whose land speculation, inheritance from his wife, and compensation for the enslaved who fought for the Union during the Civil War, along with various pensions, allowed him to die a wealthy man. That doesn't mean it didn't occur to others in short order. "Properly handled, it can be a reliable money crop," noted the *Lexington Herald-Leader* a century after Bibb lettuce was developed, and there are numerous ways growers, especially the ones who got in on the ground floor, have profited.

The Kentucky Derby serves as its own distinctive proof-of-concept category in that regard.

Meriwether Lewis Clark Jr. (grandson of the Lewis and Clark expedition's William Clark) began the Kentucky Derby after returning home to Louisville following an 1872 European visit that included taking in the near-century-old Epsom Derby in England.

Billed as "the most exciting two minutes in sports," the Kentucky Derby is the culmination of a series of events infilled with 150 years of Southern-customized, English-derivative ritual and tradition—ornate hats inspired by British royalty, peacock costuming along the racetrack rails with dress codes getting dressier as you climb toward millionaires row. In his seminal 1970 article "The Kentucky Derby Is Decadent and Depraved," Hunter S. Thompson, a Kentucky native (whose *Rolling Stone* publisher and childhood friend was a man named Porter Bibb) wrote about the performative excesses of the "whiskey gentry," as Thompson called Derby goers, with their rheumy, dissolute strivings.

It's Kentucky bourbon in every mint julep! Kentucky Bibb salad on every Derby menu! And at every turn, there is racism, riding a dark horse.

Enslaved horse trainers and caretakers built American horse racing, and Black jockeys dominated the race early on, winning fifteen of the first twenty-eight Kentucky Derbies before being violently and systematically forced out of the sport after 1921. Black jockeys didn't run for the roses again until 2000, with just four Black jockeys racing from 2000 to 2024.

Dozens of enslaved people ran the distilling operations of a Fayette County Baptist preacher named Elijah Craig. He became known as the "Father of Bourbon" in the rolling horse country of central Kentucky.

And shortly before post time, there's the spectacle of Derby goers, overcome with sentiment, wrapped in false witness, crying thug tears (for sheer cultural brutality) as they sing along, en masse, to "My Old Kentucky Home." The longtime Derby anthem is a rejiggered minstrel song—one of those disordered fantasies of Black pathos that helped form a distinctively American popular culture—that white Kentuckians saw fit to make their official state song in 1928.

The Stephen Foster tune, inspired by the Harriet Beecher Stowe novel *Uncle Tom's Cabin*, was originally entitled "Poor Uncle Tom,

Goodnight." It tells of a weepy, old enslaved man, sold downriver, and longing to return to the Kentucky plantation he loved, and it is a whole-ass mood. Emily Bingham, a daughter of one of Kentucky's oldest and most prominent families, clarified the ground "My Old Kentucky Home" covered on the way to its state-sanctioned officialdom, writing post–Civil War: "It smoothed the path to a cross-sectional American reunion defined exclusively to meet white needs, feelings, and desires, a unity that self-consciously discriminated against its Black citizens. . . . Amid mass immigration, industrial strife, women's suffrage, world war, and racial unrest, the classic tune, a white tonic spoken through a supposedly Black tongue, evoked rural safety, gentility, and a lost world where Black people knew their place."

That place, of course, became less likely to be Kentucky. Black people, including my Bibb ancestors, fled or were driven from the state, as it descended into a sustained period of racial bloodletting, post–Civil War and beyond.

All of this is the broad backdrop against which Bibb lettuce was first cultivated in the gardens and hothouse of John Bigger Bibb, during a period in which he enslaved Black people by the dozens and, after the Civil War, employed some as servants.

This is the state of the commonwealth in which Bibb lettuce first rose to prominence.

As with any commercial offering, there are layers and interconnections to the stages of Bibb lettuce production. Farmers cultivate the seeds for different brands, who then sell them to whoever's buying—in the case of my ill-fated backyard garden, it was the Burpee-bred heirloom seeds at Home Depot.

Though William Genenwein (or John Bigger Bibb, for that matter) never patented the seeds and did not know the secrets of Bibb lettuce hybridization, Genenwein's ten-to-fifteen-year near monopoly over the vegetable paid off handsomely. He initially sold exclusively to one local Louisville grocer, eager to supply his clientele—a group of doctors who swore Bibb lettuce had medicinal properties and recommended wealthy patients add it to their diets.

Genenwein expanded his production and began selling to other "fashionable groceries." He continued growing his lettuce supply, and, along with his sons, opened a stall at the old Haymarket in downtown Louisville, advertising it in the newspaper one Saturday for "25 cents a pound—'all you can carry!'"

That "cut rate" price prompted a weekend run on the vegetable, and market goers from near and far flocked to the Genenwein stall until their fifteen-hundred-pound supply sold out. (Another account of the same event, by the same writer, put the supply at twenty-five hundred pounds three decades later, when Bibb lettuce was at the height of its popularity and its origin story was becoming something of a fish story.) Each head was carefully cut above the root so no other grower could propagate it for seed. The exclusivity and mystique of the lettuce continued, as did the Genenwein family's lucrative monopoly. Genenwein bought more land and invested in irrigation pipes. By the time he began growing an additional crop outdoors—outside the privacy of his greenhouse, which allowed others to nab it and get in on the business—Bibb lettuce was selling for 50 percent more than any other lettuce on the market. The Genenweins bought land in the Rio Grande Valley in Texas, devoting much of their expanded acreage to Bibb lettuce, though it was deemed less tasty, didn't ship well, and lacked the same regional demand.

Meanwhile, by the early 1940s, hundreds of dealers were selling Bibb lettuce seeds in Kentucky and neighboring states. California eventually became a mainstay for the seeds. Profit margins varied depending on quality, capacity, and the individual grower's ability to expand the market and forge relationships with stores and restaurants. By the 1950s, Bibb lettuce sold at peak winter wholesale prices of fifty cents a pound and twenty to twenty-five cents per pound during spring and summer. "Now do you begin to understand why some people refer to currency as lettuce?" a *Courier-Journal* article asked.

But by 1969, regional differences in taste and quality had emerged, along with packing and shipping problems that caused the leaves to bruise easily. A premium was put on "Kentucky grown." In central Kentucky, a winter crop, grown under glass for "the highest quality Bibb," retailed for a summer price of forty-five cents per pound and seventy-five cents in the winter. In that same period, Bill Genenwein Jr., who took over his father's greenhouse, packed his "Kentucky Limestone Bibb" in five- to seven-pound baskets and shipped eighty to ninety thousand baskets to Chicago yearly. Soon after, national ambitions for Bibb lettuce were thwarted, though epicureans everywhere continued its story.

In the past two decades, advances in shipping, refrigeration, and, particularly, lighting and hydroponic growing technologies have again widened the aperture for Bibb lettuce and given it a national profile. New names and varieties, Butterhead, Buttercrunch, Boston Bibb, Speckled Bibb, Mini-Bibb, have sprouted up, with Kroger, Whole Foods, and Trader Joe's among the stores that carry the vegetable, often singly packaged, roots and all. Though it always remains an heirloom garden darling.

The original Bibb lettuce cultivar remains secret. "It is called a mystery lettuce because no one has figured out which roots Kentuckian Jack Bibb used to hybridize his lettuce in 1865," Camille Glenn once wrote.

For my ancestors, the Black Bibbs, it is just one secret among many.

I don't know if John Bigger Bibb ever imagined how far his eponymous lettuce would travel. But if given a chance, perhaps my great-great-grandfather, Momma Susie's grandfather John Wesley Bibb, could have come up with some ideas. Right after the Civil War, when he was about twenty-four years old, John Wesley Bibb moved with his extended family nearly 230 miles northwest to the young railroad town of Centralia, Illinois. I imagine that secret lettuce cultivar that John Bigger Bibb was beginning to give away to his high society friends in Frankfort, Kentucky, would have been most welcomed by John Wesley Bibb. It could have potentially changed his family's generational fortunes, as it did for the Genenwein family in Louisville. Or at least, it might have bought them time to grow fortunes of their own. Especially since, like William John Genenwein, my great-great-grandfather John Wesley Bibb was a truck farmer.

Both the passage of time and the layers of production and technology (not to mention American jurisprudence) make it hard to wrap Bibb lettuce around questions of credit or remuneration to the descendants of the enslaved. But that information is knowable. Per capita, lettuce consumption ranks second only to potatoes nationally, which has got to be worth something. And that order is reversed in my house.

When those who write the American story writ large are so often one kind of person, with one kind of skin color, economic background, and origin in the world, "then it's more than just the victors with the stories that become our history . . . in America, there is a unique kind of victor that writes our master narrative," said Andrew Agha.

And often that is not the descendants of enslavement. For our part, we are looking to round out, correct, or even replace the record with a larger, more encompassing truth.

Blood on the leaves and at the roots.

Or we are simply refuting falsehoods, like the one about how "Bibb lettuce is a symbol of peaceful life," and "Jack Bibb's final tribute is the happy sigh of the gourmet still unborn." We're looking to engage in what author and scholar Jabari Asim calls "narrative combat," because, you see, the fight is all in the telling.

In the master/servant relationship, servants had to innovate to make things work. In colonial Virginia, and frontier Kentucky, mutuality often equaled survival. For white planters, it meant not having to return to England. And for the enslaved, it meant not being starved or sold away. This often meant rallying around the highest—most profitable, most emotionally rewarding—outcome to the master. Or, in the immediate short term, it at least meant buying yourself and your family time, although whether the nature of those mutual arrangements and that "rally" esprit de corps worked for the enslaved, not to mention Native Americans, can be argued to a fare-thee-well. But Black ingenuity in Kentucky alone—horse racing, Southern cuisine, bourbon—tells its own stories.

It's a spirit of creation that lived on the front lines of American work—from people who were forced to try new things constantly to keep white people at bay. From people who saw crop failures happen and then tried to correct them to appease the person controlling their lives, and the lives of their children. And also because deep in the human spirit is a desire to make things work, says Agha, regardless of our status and position in life. "When it comes to what we're doing today on planet earth, you know, we need to keep innovating, and we need to know the origins of our innovation, our scientific work on the planet. We need to know where did that come from and who was involved."

I am moved by the expansive vision, not simply of what we think to be Enlightenment ideals, but of human innovation, which all societies have had their own version of. And I wonder if that vision, to some degree, may have been part of the story of Bibb lettuce, which shares the name of my grandmother, who herself shared in nothing of its cultural and economic triumphs.

There is a historic and methodological process by which we identify, name, and reverse engineer human achievement and advancement to better understand its origins. To enable us to replicate or build upon the science, whether it involves global breakthroughs, or hyperlocal delights, like a new garden cultivar. But this can't be done without a set of agreements. And in America, by white agreement, the process often obscures, changes, or omits facts in ways that arrest certain questions and lines of inquiry so that they atrophy or become verboten. The precise fact pattern, such as it may have existed, is necessarily lost in order that full understanding and credit is also buried, or maybe never germinates, or dies on the vine.

So that the only place you're going to even begin the inquiry is: How did Bibb lettuce become a staple of the Kentucky Derby? And: What are the best recipes? Not: I wonder what role the enslaved played in the development of Bibb lettuce, which took place during slavery, at the hands of an enslaver. So that you're going to look for the influentials in the time line, but never look at the beginning, in the hothouses, to grow your understanding from underneath the dirt, making the yield more legible, and the fruit more equitable, because it's rooted in truth.

I find the philosophical underpinnings of innovation—those expansive ideals of mutuality, the nature of scientific advancement, and human creativity—inspiring. Every bit of that spirit moves me and feels intuitively right about leaps in knowledge and discovery throughout history. It's good stuff.

But, now, it does leave unanswered the central question posed by the descendants of the formerly enslaved who lived in Bibbtown. People like LaVaughn Duncan and her daughter, Loretia Seals, and my late grandmother Susie Bibb O'Neal and her siblings, among others. And it is for those Black people, and all their generations, for whom I stand as proxy, that I still must ask, must require an accounting for, perhaps the main question that remains unanswered:

Who, precisely, is going to run me my coin?

Lonnae's daughters read a descriptor of Major Richard Bibb at the Bibb House Museum, with a portrait of the man credited with developing Bibb Lettuce, John Bigger Bibb, in the background.

CHAPTER 4

CHANCELLOR BIBB AND THE WHITE MAN'S BURDEN

I first heard of Major Richard Bibb's oldest son, George Mortimer Bibb, at that inaugural Bibb House reunion in 2019.

We were in Upper Bibbtown, actually, which was quite fitting since the old farming community, about ten miles northwest of Russellville, was on one of the two main land parcels bequeathed to the sixty-five people Major Bibb had emancipated in his 1839 will. He also left them livestock, tools, and the sum of five thousand dollars.

John "Bigger" Bibb, developer of the gourmet lettuce which bears his name, was executor of his father's estate. His brother, George

Mortimer Bibb, was the ardent pro-slavery politician and chancellor of the Louisville Chancery Court who John Bigger Bibb wrote to for help on how to execute his father's wishes.

Help to get his head around all that slave-freeing.

Enslaved people as beneficiaries and inheritors?

Instead of aiding his brother, who was also a lawyer, in executing the estate, in a legally famous letter—"a rare example of legal opinion-letter writing in the antebellum era"—George Mortimer Bibb advised John Bigger Bibb on how to get around fulfilling their father's wishes. All the while, passionately denying he would ever do such a thing.

Major Richard Bibb's conversion to an emancipation stance included his membership in the Kentucky Colonization Society, under the auspices of which he sent thirty of his enslaved people (and one enslaved by his son-in-law Dr. Boanerges Roberts) to the newly American-established colony of Liberia, Africa, in 1832.

The various state colonization societies, and Liberia itself, were constituted as a way to gradually end enslavement by freeing Black people, specifically to ship them away, and compensating enslavers for their loss.

> In the name of God, I, Richard Bibb, Senr. of Russellville, County of Logan and state of Kentucky do … hereby emancipate all my slaves from and after the first day of January next after my death, and desire that all of them, who have not wives or husbands in bondage, be sent to Liberia.
>
> I give to my slaves hereby emancipated five

thousand dollars to be divided out among them and paid out to them from time to time according to the discretion of my executors, and all my stock of horses, cattle, sheep and hogs, farming tools, wagons and carts and crops made the year of my decease, or that may be on hand, and each slave hired out the hire due for the year in which I shall decease.

I also give to said slaves all my lands which are unsold or undisposed of . . . in the county of Grayson of this state, this land in the county of Logan to be divided to them at the discretion of my executors, . . . hereby authorized to sell and convey any of the land or other property hereby given to my emancipated slaves and divide or lay out the money for their benefit.

Major Richard Bibb had been one of the wealthiest enslavers in western Kentucky, and his 1839 will reflected the final iteration of his decades-long emancipationist conversion.

Neither George Mortimer Bibb nor any of Major Richard Bibb's other five children who enslaved people converted with him.

George Mortimer Bibb was born in Prince Edward County, Virginia, and attended nearby Hampden-Sydney College and the College of New Jersey at Princeton (later renamed Princeton University).

He was a Kentucky state legislator, a two-time chief justice of the Kentucky Court of Appeals, and served two nonconsecutive terms as a US senator, the first of which he spent as part of the Senate "War

Hawks" pushing for the territorial expansion, among other things, that led to the War of 1812 against Great Britain.

He was appointed secretary of the treasury under President John Tyler in 1844, after which he remained in Washington as a prominent part of the Supreme Court bar, practicing law until his death in 1859.

Chancellor Bibb (as George Mortimer Bibb was known in the winter of his

George Mortimer Bibb.

life), a states' rights, pro-Unionist judge, was a steadfast supporter of enslavement in the border territories and states. He was part of a brain trust of Kentuckians (including the "Great Compromiser," Henry Clay; Senator John J. Crittenden; and Vice President and Confederate General John C. Breckinridge) who had a significant hand in shaping the political character of antebellum America.

George Mortimer Bibb was philosophically opposed to his father's emancipationist conversion. Perhaps even offended by it.

"Discussion of freedom between master and slave was an implicit criticism of bondage," wrote historian Marion B. Lucas. It was an indictment of enslavement as wrong, and an embrace of freedom as an inherently, intuitively higher, more ethical order of society.

Yet it was George Mortimer Bibb who was called upon to render judgment about how the Black Bibbs would get their bequest, their land, their money, and answers to questions about their newly unshackled proportions. His writing offers a chance to read between the lines of American jurisprudence, which just so happens to contain a lot of white space.

When you put aside the deep legal reasoning, the takeaways are unvarnished and simple: Major Bibb died in 1839. The enslaved were freed, per his will, in 1840. The fifteen hundred acres of Bibbtown land were not formally deeded to the formerly enslaved Black Bibbs until 1872.

At that 2019 Bibb reunion, two dozen or so descendants gathered near the decaying old AME church, Arnold's Chapel, founded by Granny Kate.

Along with another land tract around nine miles northeast of Russellville, the fifteen hundred acres was known collectively as Bibbtown, Upper and Lower. "Heirs' property" is a form of land ownership that passes through families without protective legal formalities, common to Black folks. And the Bibb heirs' property, descendants said, spread out in every direction, as far as the eyes could see.

On land that the Black Bibb ancestors of Muhammad Ali had known, it was an American legacy built on a singular kind of rope-a-dope. A will to plant your feet, hold strong, and outlast the hits of those who would deny Black people their title.

When John Bigger Bibb finally deeded Bibbtown to the Black Bibbs in 1872, Catherine, who had been emancipated as a toddler, and who was by then grown and married, and her aunt—my great-great-great-grandmother—Rachel immediately donated a combined two acres for the Arnold's Chapel Church and a Bibbtown school.

The deed to the church land was signed in 1876 by John Bigger Bibb. It included a note that the women had donated the land four years earlier, as soon as they'd gotten their titles to it, that he was carrying out their wishes, and that the church had, in fact, already been built. Because the Black church was vital to how the formerly enslaved understood themselves, essential to their collective work, and a haven from the whites who would beset them. And because the Black Bibbs had no time to waste.

The Black Bibbs had been living and dying on land they were entitled to but not legally given for more that thirty years, and by 1872, only fifty-four people, children and grandchildren of the formerly enslaved, were finally deeded their land. Of that number, only four were part of the original sixty-five Black Bibb legatees, Michael Morrow explained as we stood in a half-moon before him, with more than a century's worth of questions.

Was the land held in trust for them? Why did it take more than thirty years?

※ ※ ※ ※

Chancellor Bibb settled in Georgetown, and he and his wife, Martha Tabb Scott Bibb, also owned land and enslaved people in Montgomery County, Maryland, just north of Washington. He was regarded in local circles as a throwback to a more formal time. "In Washington, the old man was a reminder of a bygone era. The Chancellor continued to wear the old-style knee breeches and ... his frame, like his mind, was compact and well knit together. His whole demeanor and appearance proclaimed that he was a gentleman." A gentleman who, on the eve of the Civil War, still dressed like a Founding Father.

His letter to his brother regarding their father's estate begins with the Chancellor's disappointment in the Methodist Church's encouragement of emancipation, and his own financial difficulties, along with colorful claims of high ethical concerns:

> What effect the experiment our father has made in sending negroes to Liberia and in setting out some to work for themselves near him might have had in changing his mind upon the subject of emancipation I did not know. The will which he has left shows that his mind was unaltered. It is done. Poor as I am, struggling at my time of life, by the most intense application to the duties which does not afford any surplus at the year's end above the expenses of my family, yet I would not, for the property bequeathed by the will, for all the negroes, nor the value ten times told, insult the memory of our father by and attempt to set aside the writing he has published as his last will and testament.
>
> Whoever suggested an intention on my part to oppose the will, or to endeavor to break it, did but little understand my thoughts or temper, spoke at random, without colour [sic] of

authority from me and did me great injustice. . . .

Wealth has no such charms for me as to induce the purchase at the price of dishonour [*sic*] by abusing our fathers' memory and litigation with my nearest kindred.

Having gotten that out of the way, Chancellor Bibb set about rendering his analysis of the will and his prescriptives in accordance with the laws of the Kentucky Commonwealth. It was a tricky business as state legislators were quite protective about the rules of enslavement.

At the time, Kentuckians, as citizens of a border state, which acted as middle ground between North and South, with cultural and economic ties to each, were wary of both increases in slavery and of free Black people. And, most especially, of any possibility free Blacks might become a burden to the white people around them.

The legal result of this provision was that "oral testimony of a promise to a slave of future freedom was forbidden," wrote legal historian Kurt X. Metzmeier. There are numerous examples in Kentucky case law where people were promised emancipation and it did not happen. Better to err on the side of harshness, to make clear the law, was the prevailing sentiment.

It reminds me of the judge who remanded Margaret Garner back to slavery after she and her family had escaped to Ohio from Boone County, Kentucky, in 1856. Garner had slit her baby daughter's throat rather than see her returned to bondage. Her story was the inspiration behind the Pulitzer Prize–winning Toni Morrison novel *Beloved*. In his ruling, federal commissioner John L. Pendery made it plain: "The question is not one of humanity that I am called upon to decide. The laws of

Kentucky and of the United States make it a question of property."

Kentucky bondsmen would recall masters who made a habit of pledging freedom, "both idly and seriously," without taking any action to emancipate, wrote scholar Marion B. Lucas.

One enslaved man recounted the masters who "frequently made vague promises of 'freedom in a few years,' which were promptly forgotten before their words got 'cold' . . . and many men who expected to be freed at their master's death found that they had, instead, become the property of his heirs or were to be sold as part of the estate."

Enslavers would guarantee funds to provide for those they wished to emancipate that would never materialize, or the formerly enslaved would post bonds that they'd inevitably forfeit if they couldn't support themselves. White heirs would challenge emancipations in court, forcing bondsmen to prove their right and ability to be free, and prolonging their enslavement until they could do so. "Obviously, emancipating slaves was not something to be entered into lightly by either party, and masters resorted to it infrequently."

All formerly enslaved people, including the Black Bibbs, had to have a certificate of freedom, on parchment, with an official seal, which they would have to carry with them until they died—or the institution of slavery ended. In the Logan County emancipation records, Frank, who would have been my three-time great-uncle, was listed as "about 25, ordinary color of Negroes, about 5' 8", stout, well made." Another Bibbtown resident, Ben Winn, who was "about 60, about 5' 11", straight, well made, yellowish complexion," got the added description of "pleasant countenance, quick spoken."

Successive Kentucky "slave codes" included curfews, expanded usage of the death penalty, and the establishment of county "slave patrols" made up of white men who would ride out at night to enforce laws governing the enslaved.

All of this was the legal and cultural context against which George Mortimer Bibb rendered his analysis.

"Emancipation was the general object of the will," he wrote. Every division had to be "just and proper," though not necessarily equal or timely. The land and money fell under the "absolute and unconfined discretion" of the executors to keep the formerly enslaved from "becoming a charge to the county." To contend otherwise would be "a manifest perversion of the beneficent intentions of the testator," wrote Bibb. Ask your wife, "a woman of vigorous intellect," he urged his brother. After all, he'd often asked his own wife and been heartened by how frequently her judgments coincided with his own.

It would almost seem progressive (at a time when white women could neither vote nor own property, except enslaved people). But that's belied by the overarching thrust of the letter, which always inures to the enslaver's own interests at the expense of the enslaved. Or it simply shows that many self-serving and superficial nods to equality, couched in bracing and self-serious language, can be true at once. It is in those intersections, as a descendant of Bibbtown, that I found clarity. That I came to understand the foundational disconnect in the systems of language, law, habit, and customs white men invented, and the moralities they feigned. They used their "beneficent intentions" and "vigorous intellect" to separate their waking minds from what their plundering hands were doing.

It became an argument to effectively withhold the entirety of the bequest for such a sustained period of time that, in many ways, it largely contravened the intent of it.

Chancellor Bibb predicted John Bigger Bibb and Richard Bibb Jr., who'd been named coexecutor but fell ill and died the same year as his father, would have difficulty executing the trust.

They'd have to protect the emancipated from "interested knavery" that "will stimulate the negroes," he warned.

George Mortimer also advised his brothers to gather their own receipts and "not to rely on receipts from the negroes alone."

The whole of his advice added up to this: The discretion to pay out "from time to time" and "according to circumstances" necessarily meant the power to subvert the rights of individual legatees to preserve the bequest, supposedly for the benefit of the group. Except, in Chancellor Bibb's estimation, the group would always be potentially problematic. If they weren't careful, he wrote, "The emancipation of a large number of negroes, male and female, helpless and infirm, old and young, would prove a nuisance to society, as well as an injury to the negroes. . . ." In his thinking, individual legatees could always be deemed unsuitable in some way to receive their inheritance, in full or otherwise. Perhaps at some point the formerly enslaved Bibbs would come of age and rise to the level of productive citizenship.

But not for decades.

I remember the day I first stood in Bibbtown, where the lands of my ancestors stretched out in every direction. And I've come away with my own conclusions. Each generation of would-be oppressors necessarily suspends their powers of discernment, investing a little more of themselves into the con, until at some point, much sooner than they would have imagined, they no longer realize that's what it was at all. Or at least they cannot admit it. So they wrap the con in layers to insulate it from cold, hard, American truths.

At the end of George Mortimer Bibb's letter, having dispensed with the legal strategizing, the chancellor pivots to family matters—how his son-in-law, Albert T. Burnley, has turned a handsome profit from the slave trade in Texas, which was not yet part of the United States. It was "a stunning example of the antebellum tendency to compartmentalize the institution of slavery," wrote Metzmeier.

The Bibb letter, with its high-level legal reasoning and interpretation about the granularity of emancipation in antebellum America, is rare, Metzmeier said.

The white Bibbs could have simply ignored or suppressed their father's will and taken possession of the enslaved people and the property. The fact that they did not is another standout data point in Bibb history.

Although what is also true is that the emancipated Bibbs weren't able to leverage their bequest to do all the things that people do to build wealth and better their situation, when they have a clear title to their own land and legal systems that allow them to advantage themselves of that fact.

The Black Bibbs "weren't getting much of a benefit out of their purported ownership of the property, because of the way it was held in trust," said Metzmeier.

Most of the Black Bibbs that Major Richard Bibb emancipated were not able to sell the land and leave, borrow against it, or use it for whatever industry or purpose they could have imagined or built for themselves—for thirty-two years after the will was executed, and seven years after the end of the Civil War. And these consequences of Chancellor George Mortimer Bibb's advice on the lives of the Black Bibbs rarely attach to his storied legacy.

CHAPTER 5

MY OLD
KENTUCKY HOME

I sometimes think about that most American of journeys that carried my fourth great-grandmother, Keziah Bibb, as an enslaved child from the Piedmont region of Virginia, west of Richmond, to Logan County, Kentucky, at the close of the eighteenth century.

Keziah would have been roughly twelve years old in 1798, when she and dozens of others enslaved by Major Richard Bibb and his family set out on the perilous, monthslong trek through the Appalachian Mountains to the Kentucky frontier. It was a migration fueled by settler dreams of land, wealth, and all the expansive possibilities of the young American nation. But for the enslaved, such as Keziah, the forced migration geographically widened their exploitation, and deepened their precarity in ways scarcely imaginable, even for a child growing up in hereditary bondage.

The white Bibbs were part of Virginia's planter class, landed gentry who invested heavily in tobacco farming, livestock, and enslavement.

Major Bibb, who was studying to enter the Episcopal ministry, became a Goochland County militia commander in the Revolutionary War, and afterward served as a delegate in the Virginia House of Representatives. He inherited nearly eight hundred acres of plantation land along with at least a dozen "Negro and mulatto slaves and their future increases" from his father, John Bibb, in 1769, when Virginia was still a British colony.

And, like many Revolutionary War veterans, he was awarded bounty—land warrants for his military service. These land grants amounted to little more than certificates for distant acres marked by vague coordinates and rough geological descriptors: *the clearing at the foot of the mossy hill beside the great fallen pine*. It was paper land, unless you could survey it and claim it. Major Bibb added to his fortune as a land speculator, buying up land grants awarded to his fellow soldiers, who wrote letters to Congress attesting to the fact that they'd served under Major Bibb to give what was essentially a land grab the new US government stamp of officiality.

Channeling the spirit of his European ancestors, no doubt, Major Bibb and others in the extended Bibb clan who had journeyed ahead left the colonies of their fathers to lay claim to the fertile Bluegrass region of central Kentucky, or farther west to the Pennyrile region with its limestone soil (which proved to be quite useful for cultivating a new variety of lettuce), and on toward the river lands that later included the Jackson Purchase region. They followed in the wake of tens of thousands of settlers from Pennsylvania and North Carolina, but mostly from Virginia, where the descendants of those early colonists sought room to spread out into new territories they could stamp with their own cultural and political sovereignty.

In the mid-eighteenth century, early Kentucky explorers, hunters, trappers, and surveyors had found a land of beauty and abundance: miles of savannas with herds of bison, rolling hills, and woodland animals.

But Major Bibb set out for Kentucky after decades of settlement had taken up so much land so quickly the Kentucky frontier was closing. He would have been anxious to stake his claims before they were lost. And there were other complex reasons that would have compelled the Bibb migration as well. The American Revolution had changed the social and political order of the young nation. It challenged the primacy of the elite planter class, with its European-based class structures and hidebound traditions. Instead, it was the self-made "common man" who was ascendant. Who began to capture public imagination, seeding broad new possibilities of identity, less bound by old-world customs and traditions.

If you were a white man.

With land to be tamed and wealth to be built, every white man could win(!) if he simply headed West, carried along by tales of rugged individualism. It's an ethos that's been applied to other places and times, but it was well baked in Kentucky. And like his European ancestors, this new, self-made everyman, this rugged individual, could only triumph, at scale, over the burial grounds and on the backs of Indigenous and enslaved people, who, as it turns out, had their own Kentucky frontier stories.

The early records are silent about who, if any, of Keziah's people traveled to Kentucky with her. I don't know if she was torn from a mother and father who reached for her as she was carried away, or if the love of family was even known to her. But based on kinship records and enslaved family structures, she almost certainly had brothers and sisters owned by the Bibb family, who were either part of the Kentucky migration, or who remained behind in Virginia for her to long for.

I wonder if my fourth great-grandmother was cold, or lonely, or frightened about the future. Or maybe terrified, too, because she'd heard tales of fierce mountain lions passed from the tongues of the enslaved and worried, as my twelve-year-old self would have worried, that mountain lions might eat young Black girls.

Or perhaps, as an enslaved child, she had no time to fantasize or imagine after attending the immediate needs of those who commanded her bondage in service of their own longings and anxieties. After working from can't-see-in-the-morning to can't-see-at-night, perhaps sleep was Keziah's only dream—the only time when she felt free. To consider the interiority of twelve-year-old Keziah Bibb is to add Black childhoods to the tally of all that was stolen in the push for "elbow room, elbow room," as my Saturday morning *Schoolhouse Rock!* jingle put it. And I happily sang along.

The trail west had other perils. A British colonial law, the Proclamation of 1763, had forbidden settlement on Native lands west of the Appalachian Mountains, likely in fear that the expansion of white settlement would incite violence and would overwhelm the British capacity for governance and tax collection. But colonial settlers had simply ignored that prohibition and moved west anyway.

By the mid-eighteenth century, only remnants of the Native

nations—the Iroquois (the Five and later Six Nations), the Chickasaw, the Shawnee, the Cherokee—that inhabited the region prior to European settlement remained. But Native people continued their bloody battles with white settlers over the fertile lands and hunting grounds of their forefathers. The lore and gore of these brutal conflicts, decades of regional fighting over nationhood and territorial control, seeped deep into the dirt of Kentucky. And deeper still into Kentucky's sense of itself.

In 1773, during legendary frontiersman Daniel Boone's first attempt to settle Kentucky, he and future Revolutionary War general and Russellville founder, William Russell, both lost their eldest sons along the Wilderness Road. James Boone, Henry Russell, and several others were returning from a supply run when a party of Delaware, Shawnee, and Cherokee launched a sunrise attack that saw Boone and Russell, both teenagers, brutally killed along with several others, including an enslaved man named Charles. Another enslaved man, Adam, was able to escape and carried word of the massacre to Daniel Boone.

Whites and Blacks had entered Kentucky together in the mid-eighteenth century, giving rise to rousing narratives of mutuality, interdependence, and esprit de corps. White enslavers and their trusted Black enslaved bound together, braving the isolation and the perils of the Western frontier with its many and varied ways to die. And frontier stories of resourceful and heroic enslaved people abound.

At a homestead near Lexington, an enslaved man called Black Sam rescued his master's young daughter from a Native raiding party that had killed the master's wife and two sons. When one of the attackers took the child and laid her aside while he reentered the homestead,

Black Sam scooped her up and fled into the surrounding woods. After wandering for days, he left the little girl at a settler's station and rushed back to his ruined homestead. There, he found his master despondent, before Black Sam cried out with the news that his little girl was alive.

Black people chopped, cleared, and cultivated Kentucky. They provided the massive physical and intellectual lift necessary to turn wilderness into farmland. But that spirit of frontier freedom, and the courage and loyalties of the enslaved, did not occasion a wholesale reconsideration of their chains. Instead, it solidified slavery's centrality to the future prospects and, increasingly, the self-conception of white Kentuckians, regardless of whether they themselves enslaved people.

The 1790 census puts the population of Kentucky, on the brink of statehood, at 73,077, with the 11,830 enslaved and 114 free Blacks, making Black people 16 percent of the total population. By 1830, Black people, including almost 5,000 who were free, constituted nearly 25 percent of a total population that had grown to almost 700,000. The enslaved lived primarily in households with fewer than five other enslaved people, as only in Virginia and Georgia was enslavement spread among more owners. In some central Bluegrass counties, which included the cities of Lexington, Louisville, and Frankfort, and rural southwestern counties along the border with Tennessee, the antebellum Black population was 30–40 percent of the total inhabitants.

The Commonwealth of Kentucky, part of the "Upper South," became the first US state west of the Appalachian Mountains seven years before Keziah's forced migration from Virginia. The enslavement laws of Virginia were enshrined into the state constitution in 1792. In 1798, the Kentucky legislature customized its own "slave codes" restricting movement, prescribing punishments, and codifying restrictions on emancipating enslaved people—witnesses, seals, attestation on parchment paper, and monetary guarantees ensuring support for the formerly enslaved would never fall on white people—to make the practice rare.

Though a vocal contingent of religious leaders opposed the expansion of enslavement, the tens of thousands of white Virginians crossing the Appalachians were too determinative, and the "free land" demands for unfree labor too compelling, for any antislavery religious fervor to carry the state.

By the time Keziah Bibb arrived, Kentucky—with its varying topography and bound by rivers on three sides—had become a confederation of contrasting geographic, economic, political, and cultural loyalties. Unlike the Deep South, it was not suited to the vast cotton, rice, and sugarcane plantations. The work of the enslaved was more wide-ranging, and sometimes included work for pay.

The mountainous eastern and southeastern regions enslaved fewer people than the rest of the state, and these were skilled craftsmen, domestic workers, or service workers catering to the incoming migrants. The enslaved in the northern counties along the Ohio River, which was also an escape route to the free states of Ohio and Indiana, were skilled carpenters, brickmasons, riverboat workers, cooks, seamstresses, and midwives.

Enslavement was primarily concentrated in the central Bluegrass and western regions of the state that were conducive to tobacco and hemp plantations, along with corn, wheat, and barley crops. Enslaved laborers and skilled tradesmen were sometimes leased out to other farmers. The enslaved tended livestock, and they trained the thoroughbred horses that grazed on the abundant pastureland of the Bluegrass. It was this region, which included the large urban areas of the state, whose cultural, political, and economic order most approximated that of colonial Virginia.

Major Richard Bibb would have fit in here. He and his first wife, Lucy Booker Bibb, stepdaughter of his brother William, along with the youngest of their six children, likely arrived in Kentucky via the Ohio River, a potentially easier route than the overland route likely taken by Keziah and the other Bibb enslaved. Major Bibb moved first to Bullitt County, in north central Kentucky, where he bought a salt mine, had a whiskey still, and grew tobacco. He then moved to Lexington, where he was involved in the burgeoning concern of racing and breeding thoroughbred horses. His ongoing land speculation, including in the Illinois and Arkansas territories, made him increasingly wealthy, and yet restless. He moved to Logan County, where he struggled to figure out what he thought God wanted from him.

In 1813, the first governor of the commonwealth granted Richard Bibb two hundred acres of land in Logan County, western Kentucky, "at the headwaters of the Muddy River." He had settled in the county with his family a few years earlier, growing tobacco and raising livestock. After Lucy Booker Bibb died, he married Mary Ann Jackson and built her the Bibb House in Russellville. Decades of Kentucky census records show a white Bibb family surrounded by enslaved workers, from early in the morning until they closed their eyes at night, encountering few other white people on a daily basis. There were six white Bibbs and fifty-five enslaved Black people at Richard Bibb Sr.'s Logan County plantation outside Russellville in 1810. (That same year, Richard Bibb Jr. was the sole white person in a household with nine enslaved people.) Three white Bibbs and a dozen enslaved Black Bibbs lived at the Bibb House in Russellville in 1820, while a decade later, there were two white Bibbs and thirty-two Black Bibbs enslaved by Major Richard Bibb in Russellville.

The lives of the Black Bibb enslaved revolved around the routines of bondage. They rose with the sun to begin their work—emptying chamber pots first, then lighting fires, cooking, and attending to every request, demand, or sudden whim of their white Bibb masters. They remained attuned to the mood of their enslavers, ever watchful for anger, for mental or financial instability, for changes in the master's or mistress's health that could cause a crisis that might hurt or tear asunder their own Black families. They would have kept a keen eye out for visitors, white Bibb relatives passing through who might make demands, including sex. They stayed ever alert for shifts in household loyalties, politics, or prevailing winds that might occasion an opening to negotiate with their God and their white Bibb masters

Shackles are seen on display at The Bibb House SEEK Museum.

and nudge them for better terms. It made for a fluid, soft-tissue intimacy, a daily connectedness in conversation and thought. It was a construct of these interactions that saw Major Richard Bibb spend the majority of his days with the Black people he was increasingly uncomfortable holding in bondage. It was there, in Logan County, where he began his slow-to-come-to-it emancipationist conversion.

He chose a tough part of the state to do that work.

Logan County is situated in the middle of a farm belt that stretches nearly one hundred miles along western Kentucky's border with Tennessee. It was known as a "Rogue's Harbor," attracting folks looking for a fresh start—or running from the law. These included killers, and charismatic ministers preaching their personal witness of the Spirit. At least in one instance—that of Dr. Beverly Anthony Allen, a Methodist minister who shot and killed a Georgia lawman and fled to western Kentucky, where he became Logan County's first physician—those were the same person. "Murderers, horse thieves, highway robbers and counterfeiters fled here until they combined, and actually formed a majority," wrote one late-eighteenth-century observer.

Western Kentucky land was among the most amenable to plantation agriculture in the state and the most socially associated with the South, to which it was culturally and commercially connected by waterways, including the Mississippi River. Along with central Kentucky, western Kentucky had the highest concentration of enslavers and the most enslaved people. As in some central Bluegrass counties, by 1860, Blacks made up between 30 and 40 percent of the residents in parts of western Kentucky, including Logan County.

Major Bibb's second wife disdained the isolation of country living.

So sometime between 1815 and 1820, he built the Bibb urban plantation town house in Russellville, the seat of Logan County, about fifty miles north of Nashville and a few miles from his rural plantation, where the enslaved grew tobacco and raised livestock. The Russellville property included a kitchen and laundry outbuilding where the enslaved—including, perhaps, Keziah—spent their days cooking for, cleaning after, and in service to the white Bibbs and their frequent visitors. Every night, they slumbered in the attic or stared out of its one tiny window and dreamed, surely, of somewhere else.

Legend has it that, at some point, one of those enslaved by Major Richard Bibb prompted a change of heart in him about enslavement (or perhaps it was fear over the biblical skepticism about whether a rich man could get into heaven). By the early nineteenth century, when he settled in Logan County, the former Episcopalian devotee was a Methodist circuit rider: a lay minister for the newly chartered Christian denomination rapidly adding souls to its frontier churches. At the 1814 Red River district campground conference and revival, white preachers and at least two enslaved Black preachers ministered to the ecstatic with "robust shouting," calling on the Lord, and inveighing against sin in the deep wilderness of north Logan County.

The night before the revival, Bishop Francis Asbury spent the night "in the comfortable home" of the "wealthy and cultivated" Richard Bibb. Asbury was the lone British minister—sent by the founder of Methodism, John Wesley—to remain in America post-Revolution, and I wonder if Keziah met him. That is, if she was serving or cleaning or cooking, and caught a glimpse of this devout white apostle of God. Perhaps she heard the piety and empathy for the poor in his voice and felt lifted? Or maybe betrayed?

Bibb established his own—sparsely attended—Bibb's Chapel six miles east of Russellville, and tried to come to conceptual and practical terms with the idea of Black freedom. (John Wesley opposed enslavement, and the Methodist Church split in half, along geographical lines, over the issue in 1844.) Bibb joined the Russellville chapter of the Kentucky Colonization Society, an affiliate of the umbrella American Colonization Society. The organization of plantation owners and abolitionists, founded in 1816, promoted gradual emancipation, compensating enslavers for their loss, and establishing the African colony of Liberia, where they could ship the enslaved. The organization was predicated on local control, and Major Richard Bibb and his youngest son, John Bigger Bibb, were officers of the Russellville chapter.

The elite membership of the national ACS included Daniel Webster, Francis Scott Key, and Bushrod Washington, a nephew of George Washington, among others. Kentucky's famed "Great Compromiser," Henry Clay, a founder and charter member of the organization, was a friend of Major Richard Bibb and visited him in Russellville for the Fourth of July in 1807. He was, at various times, Speaker of the House, secretary of state under John Quincy Adams, and a US senator (succeeded in his seat by Major Bibb's son George Mortimer Bibb). Clay remained publicly sad about the evils of slavery throughout his life, though he once sought to imprison an enslaved woman who sued the then secretary of state for her freedom in 1829 and lost. She is listed as property on his tax records in 1837. Clay sought compromise on the institution of slavery, without compromising the ways the enslaved added to his wealth, until his death in 1852, when he emancipated some of the 122 enslaved on his six-hundred-acre estate near Lexington.

My fourth great-grandmother Keziah would have been maybe sixteen years old in 1802 when she had the first of her twelve children. The 1815 Logan County tax records list Keziah as over sixteen and worth three hundred dollars (her son York, who is under sixteen, is worth two hundred dollars, while her daughters Aggy and Sally, little ones, presumably, are only valued at sixty dollars each). In 1821, she is still valued at three hundred dollars, and more of her children have been added to the ages-sixteen-and-under property records of Major Richard Bibb, which show him owning more than eleven thousand dollars' worth of human beings, and nearly five hundred dollars' worth of horses. By the late 1830s, Major Bibb owns 418 acres of land in Logan County, and the records list my fourth great-grandmother as "Old Keziah" to distinguish her from her son Frank's baby girl, her granddaughter Young Keziah.

But those were the records kept by enslavers, with naming conventions that worked for trafficking. As I have never encountered a Black woman of advanced age (or middle age, in Keziah's case) whose Black family called her Old *Anything*, and as I called my grandmother—Keziah's great-great-granddaughter—Momma Susie, I've taken to thinking of my fourth great-grandmother as Momma Keziah. And as I spoke the words *Momma Keziah* and reclaimed her for myself, I began to cry.

For the first time since 2019, this family history didn't feel so reductive. For the first time since I'd heard tell of white Bibbs, I hadn't lost my ancestors to slavery; I had gained a Big Momma—a Black woman who I could name, and who, two centuries ago, held generations unborn in her mind's eye and called us free with every mile she walked along the Wilderness Road. And I could see the Bibb history

An 1815 listing of the age range and "value" of the Bibb enslaved, including the author's fourth-great-grandmother, Keziah, along with the names and value of Bibb Horses. (Filson Society)

more clearly, when I filtered it through Momma Keziah's eyes. It gave me a sight line that extended throughout the whole of Kentucky and beyond.

In 1832, Major Richard Bibb emancipated thirty people and, along with one enslaved person belonging to his son-in-law, Dr. Boanerges Roberts, shipped them by way of mercantile vessel, the brig *Ajax*, to Liberia. It was part of the Kentucky Colonization Society–championed process to gradually end slavery by sending Black people "back" to Africa (where most had never been). Colloquially, it became known as "voluntary emancipation."

This was, of course, an enslavers' representation. A sleight of mind to soothe white psyches riddled with anxieties about whether they were good people, while leaving the operant conditions of those enslaved people "volunteering" for the voyage utterly unconsidered. I wonder if many didn't, in fact, volunteer, especially if their choices were framed as eternal bondage or *this new place where we're sending Black people.* When I consider "voluntary emancipation," I think of a half million Black people who escaped to Union encampments during the Civil War, prompting President Lincoln to issue the Emancipation Proclamation in 1863. I think of the 198,000 Black men who volunteered to fight for the Union, for their people, for freedom during the Civil War.

An 1897 *Louisville Courier-Journal* retrospective on Major Bibb and the establishment of Bibbtown called the Liberia migration the initial part of Bibb's "long cherished plan." The article, by Russellville native and longtime newspaperman Marmaduke Beckwith Morton, is written in racist, infantilizing terms. In Morton's rendering, Major Richard Bibb is a saintly, Christlike figure offering salvation to the bondsmen who are portrayed as either troublesome, or grateful and childlike. In fact, more than two dozen of those Major Bibb shipped to Liberia were children, most under ten. The last name of six of those emancipated by Bibb and sent on the *Ajax* also happened to be Morton, as they'd once been owned by the newspaperman's family.

"Major Bibb had cared for the enslaved since his youth, and many of them, or their parents, had been owned by his father in Virginia," Morton wrote. "He believed slavery was wrong" and he was putting that belief into action. He'd sent that first group of enslaved people he deemed "shiftless and hard to manage" (Morton's words) to Liberia so they would not be a bad influence on those he planned to emancipate and provide with land, tools, and money upon his death.

"He read a chapter in the Bible and had given out a hymn, and when his prayer was finished, many a black face was bathed in tears, and the slaves gathered about and shook Old Master's hand for the last time and heard the accent of his kindly voice." Morton had purportedly based his account on the recollections of Andrew Bibb, who was a young child at the time. (Not to be confused with the builder and carpenter by the same name, who'd been emancipated by Major Bibb as a teenager and moved to Louisville at the dawn of the Civil War, where he became a business owner, landlord, and elder in the Colored Methodist Episcopal Church.) And perhaps that was the account the Andrew Bibb who had grown up with this story, and some other formerly enslaved Bibb, told the former enslaver/newspaperman on the eve of the twentieth century, during a sustained period of reactionary white violence and backlash in Kentucky. But I believe the Black Bibbs were very careful with their words. Even today, we understand that Black folks often will not speak their piece in front of white people. In front of company. Especially when company has made a habit and practice of bigotry, might turn savage under cover of darkness, or law, and has a penchant for breaking things when they get news that they don't like, or are not willing to accept. And much of what gets broken are the lives of Black people.

I suspect Momma Keziah would have remembered events differently, if her truth be told. Two of her daughters, Catherine, twenty-five, and Mary, thirty-one; one son, William, twenty-four; and eight of her grandchildren were sent on that ill-fated voyage to Liberia on which most of them perished. They died of whooping cough or worms, "brain disease" or a painful lung condition called pleurisy. They died in the outbreak of cholera that claimed nearly all the *Ajax* children on the first leg of the passage to Louisiana, before they even left US soil.

The *Courier-Journal* article notes only that most of the emancipated died. "The remainder lapsed into original barbarity," it contends, allegedly based on the report of a Black missionary sent to Liberia to check on the Kentucky contingent.

When Richard Bibb's 1839 will emancipated his remaining enslaved people, it stipulated that the childless and unmarried enslaved "voluntarily emancipate" themselves to Liberia, but that never happened. In 1950, Leonara Foulks, one of the few remaining residents of Bibbtown, told an interviewer that the granddaughter of Granny Kate and the preacher she married named Armstead Arnold had received a letter from the State Department telling them someone in Liberia had died and left the family some land. But Foulks was told the family did not look into the matter any further.

Kentucky enslavement—with its smaller plantations, varied crops, and types of labor performed by the enslaved, who also sometimes earned wages hiring themselves out—differed from the vast plantation enslavement of the Deep South. That dissimilarity gave rise to the

A bedroom sits on display in the attic of the Bibb House SEEK Museum. The unventilated attic area served as enslaved quarters before emancipation.

deeply held, self-serving belief that Kentucky engaged in a "milder," more benign form of the practice.

The enslaved begged to differ.

"I once knew a Methodist in the state of Kentucky by the name of Young," Henry Bibb—whom I now claim, at the very least, as fictive kin—wrote in his 1849 memoir, *Narrative of the Life and Adventures of Henry Bibb, an American Slave, Written by Himself.* Bibb, an enslaved mulatto man whose father was James Bibb—"doubtless one of the present Bibb family of Kentucky"—used Young's story to address critics who claimed he'd failed to show the "best side" of enslavement.

According to Bibb, Mr. Young was a religious man, whose enslaved people were always well fed and clothed. He'd allowed them a small house and garden and never overworked or beat them. Mr. Young worshipped alongside the bondsmen, at the same church. But when

Mr. Young fell into debt, his property, who were also his church brethren, were put up for sale. Mr. Young vouched to the slave traders and speculators for the fidelity and "good Christian character" of one old, gray-haired enslaved man named Richard, who stood on the auction block with his wife, begging that they not be parted.

"But the marriage relation was soon dissolved by the sale, and they were separated, never to meet again.... After the men were all sold they then sold the women and children. They ordered the first woman to lay down her child and mount the auction block; she refused to give up her little one and clung to it as long as she could, while the cruel lash was applied to her back for disobedience. She pleaded for mercy in the name of God. But the child was torn from the arms of its mother amid the most heart-rending shrieks from the mother and child on the one hand, and bitter oaths and cruel lashes from the tyrants on the other. Finally, the poor little child was torn from the mother while she was sacrificed to the highest bidder. In this way the sale was carried on from beginning to end.

"Having thus tried to show the best side of slavery that I can conceive of," wrote Henry Bibb, "the reader can exercise his own judgment" about the "mild" enslavement practiced by Kentucky Christians.

In *Narratives of the Sufferings of Lewis and Milton Clarke*, Lewis Clarke, who worked as one of four "house slaves" in Madison, Kentucky, as a child, wrote that those enslaved in the home of the master were "constantly exposed to the whims and passions" of every white person in the house, from the greatest to the least. But all the calamities of bondage, wrote Clarke, "were as nothing to the sufferings experienced by being separated from my mother, brothers and sisters.... My thoughts continually by day, and my dreams by night were of mother and home, and the horror experienced in the morning, when I awoke and beheld it was a dream, is beyond the power of language to describe."

Momma Keziah would have known that anguish at every stage of her life. Torn and split families were what white wealth was made of in America. It was what white Bibb wealth was made of, from Momma Keziah's Virginia girlhood until the last day someone called out for "Old Keziah" in Kentucky. And beginning in the early nineteenth century, that forcible separation became more pronounced as Kentucky became known as a "breeder state."

As demands for Southern plantation labor, especially cotton cultivation, increased, enslaved people in excessive numbers deemed necessary for tobacco and hemp plantations, domestic service, and raising livestock were loaded onto steamships bound for Alabama, Mississippi, Georgia, and Louisiana. The phrase "sold downriver"—as a lamentation, a dirge, an expression of dread, fate, and grievous betrayal—is said to have originated in the "slave pens" of Louisville, from where, by some estimates, 22 percent of young Black adult males were shipped to the Deep South. As one enslaved man explained, "Going to New Orleans was called Nigger Hell, few ever returned...."

The practice was often considered an even more craven form of profiteering than other ways of selling off the enslaved. It could also be a punishment, or a more desperate form of white debt relief to send Black people downriver. White men would threaten Black people they were considering shipping away. *I'm about to fold you up and put you in my pocket.*

Breeding seems to have been a job white Kentucky men put their backs into. Neither of the two "Slave Schedules" published by the US Census in 1850 and 1860 saw fit to record the names of the enslaved, or any of their family ties, but along with their age and gender, their race—recorded as either Black or "mulatto"—was something white men were keenly interested in, as the original people to make everything about race. By 1850, the "breeder state" of Kentucky, along with Arkansas, Missouri, and Texas, was home to the largest population of enslaved "mulattoes" in the nation. Young, light-skinned women, known as "fancy girls," were trafficked for sexual exploitation and could command four to five times as much as enslaved women sold as cooks, or fieldworkers, who were also sexually exploited.

In 1850, Major Richard Bibb's son John Bigger Bibb (the creator of Bibb lettuce) enslaved five people in Russellville, three of them mulatto, and of the three, two were under ten years old. By the 1860 census, taken after he'd relocated to the state capital of Frankfort, John Bigger Bibb was enslaving forty-eight people, twenty-seven of them mulatto, eight of those people under the age of ten. Like Major Richard Bibb, his son Richard Bibb Jr. also died in 1839.

In Logan County, before the Civil War, the number of enslaved people increased from 5,382 in 1850 to 6,364 by 1860. Of that increase, 272 were Black, while the numbers of enslaved mulattos nearly doubled from 791 to 1,501. During that same period, the number of free Blacks in Logan County decreased from 301 to 265, while the number of free mulattoes increased from 64 in 1850 to 105 by 1860.

By 1860, Bibbtown had been an enclave of free Blacks and mulattos for decades.

In 1840, the sixty-five people from five enslaved families emancipated by Major Richard Bibb's will the year before were finally freed and able to settle on two land tracts totaling roughly fifteen hundred acres. Twelve hundred acres of the most arable land, with ample water, good timber, and good soil for growing, roughly ten miles northwest from the Bibb House, was known as Upper Bibbtown. It went to three families. Two other families inherited three hundred acres known as Lower Bibbtown, nine miles northeast of the Bibb House. It featured a changeable elevation, the majority of which was steep and mountainous with no potential for income. About 10 percent was flat land with a thin layer of poor soil over the rock base just beneath the surface, and it was barely serviceable and of minimal value. It sufficed for growing food for personal use, but not for producing large volumes of commodities for sale.

Upper Bibbtown is thought to be where the descendants of the Bibb enslavers, the daughters and sons of the Bibb masters, were settled. These were the light-skinned formerly enslaved. This is where Momma Susie's people came from. Lower Bibbtown is where the formerly enslaved who were not understood to be blood relatives of the white Bibbs were thought to have settled, though there was a great deal of intermarriage between the two.

The first crop in Lower Bibbtown failed.

The first crop in Upper Bibbtown turned a profit.

Of all the money and all the lands left to the enslaved people who Major Bibb freed when he died at eighty-six, Catherine, a light-yellow child who was three years old at the time, was given the most and the best, the soonest: 250 acres of the choicest land in Upper Bibbtown, which she, her grandmother Momma Keziah, and Momma Keziah's children Frank and Winnie were all settled on two years before Major Richard Bibb died. (There is no record of what happened to the infant

Catherine's mother, Keziah's daughter Nancy.) The oral history, passed down for generations, was clear on the reason why the child was singled out: Catherine was Major Richard Bibb's daughter.

Catherine established a school and the AME Zion Church, Arnold's Chapel, which stands today. It was Granny Kate's eyes that stared out at me from that turn-of-the-century photograph before the 2019 reunion. It was her face that reminded me of Momma Susie.

By 1840, Momma Keziah had lived to be a free woman and head of a twelve-person household. By 1850, she had fallen out of the census records. I felt her loss. I will be looking for her the rest of my life. I believe that before she died—even with the national mood darkening and the question of enslavement unsettled, and despite all she had been through—my fourth great-grandmother saw reasons to be hopeful about the future of her family in Bibbtown.

Momma Keziah's youngest child, Rachel, who was seventeen or eighteen when she was emancipated, quickly acclimated herself to her newly freed status. She set about ordering provisions against her $64.47 share of the $5,000 Bibb inheritance. Over two years, she bought a new pot and skillet, fabric for new dresses, leather for shoes, and, notably, the first bed she'd ever owned. She bought cotton, cups, knives, and forks. She went in half for a plow horse and shared in the cost for a plow harness. She bought salt and nearly 450 pounds of pork, at three cents a pound.

Momma Keziah didn't live to see her daughter Rachel and granddaughter Catherine donate two acres from their own lands for the Arnold's Chapel AME Zion Church in 1872. Or to see Rachel's son—her grandson, my great-great-grandfather—John Wesley Bibb (named, perhaps, for the founder of Methodism) register to fight for the Union in the Civil War. He had never personally known bondage, but Bibbtown Blacks all had family enslaved by the children and grandchildren of Major Bibb. Other residents of Bibbtown were deceived and re-enslaved by Logan County Confederates who coerced some of the freedmen, telling them if they didn't voluntarily return to enslavement they'd be sold downriver.

John Wesley Bibb was one of three free Bibbtown men who signed up to fight for the emancipation of others.

In the 1860 presidential election, white Kentuckians voted overwhelmingly for John Bell, the pro-Union candidate in a four-way race that included Kentucky native son and the then vice president, John Breckinridge. (Breckinridge, who served under President James Buchanan and, at thirty-six, remains the youngest ever US vice president, became a Confederate general and secretary of war.) Abraham Lincoln, who opposed the spread of enslavement into US territories, was elected, and six weeks later, South Carolina seceded from the Union.

The governor declared Kentucky neutral the next year, at the start of the Civil War, and when forced to choose a side, Kentucky remained pro-Union. Though, crucially, pro-Union did not necessarily mean they were pro-emancipation. It's another historical paradox of the state.

With the nation on the brink of war, the fault lines over enslavement in Kentucky became source material for competing visions of the state. They were portentous and seemingly full of providence.

President Abraham Lincoln, savior of the Union, was born in

central Kentucky. A year later and just over a hundred miles away in western Kentucky, Confederate President Jefferson Davis was born in Todd County, the immediate western neighbor of Logan County.

Kentucky was the setting for Harriet Beecher Stowe's 1852 abolitionist novel, *Uncle Tom's Cabin*, which became a national sensation. It so effectively and efficiently salves white sensibilities with portrayals of simple *"Negro inferiority"* that its main character, Uncle Tom, becomes a safe, pitiable, emotive agent for white identity trying to come to terms with enslavement, and the idea of Black emancipation.

Kentucky was built by enslavement, and the moral, political, philosophical, and economic issues central to the institution that split the country in two broke Kentucky into shards. Many of them small, hard, and ridiculous. Western Kentucky, with its Southern borders and mindsets, was especially vulnerable.

In a letter to the newly elected president, Abraham Lincoln, Sue Burbridge, whose husband was a Russellville farmer, enslaver, and staunch Unionist, and whose brother-in-law was the reviled Union general known as the "Butcher of Kentucky," gave voice to the ways enslavement had turned fear, rage, and fetid entitlement into a grotesquerie.

Logan County, Kentucky

Jan 20nd 1861

Dear Sir

The negros have taken up the notion, or rather it has been taught them by beggars and Gipsies [*sic*], that as soon as you were elected they would all be free. They have commenced their work of poisoning and Incendiarism. Now all

I want to know is, if you do not intend such a thing, make them know it, so that they may go to work and wait until the next presidential Election to cut out again. I wish you would ask your Estimable Lady how she would like, just as she gets a good cook, for some straggling beggar, peddler or fortune teller to come along and persuade her that someone would give her higher wages on the other side of town. For God's sake, Dear Sir, give us women some assurance that you will protect us, for we are the greatest Slaves in the South.

Respectfully,

Sue H. Burbridge

Later that same year, Kentucky Confederates held a convention in Russellville and designated Bowling Green as capital of their shadow government, which never replaced the elected representatives in Frankfort and, as the war progressed, existed mostly on paper and in hearts and minds. For white Kentuckians, even those far from the front lines, the Civil War divided brothers, fathers and sons, and extended families.

Major Richard Bibb's grandson—Titus Pomponius Atticus Bibb (son of George Mortimer Bibb), an attorney (who John Bigger Bibb described as an alcoholic in letters to family!)—took two of his sons when he left Logan County for Alabama to fight for the Confederacy. After some of his enslaved men ran off to fight for the Union, John Bigger Bibb (Bibb lettuce) filed paperwork swearing Union allegiance so he could be compensated for their service, which was the practice in all the enslaver states—including Delaware, Missouri, and Maryland—that did not secede.

Between the Emancipation Proclamation in 1863 and 1865, twenty-three Black Kentucky regiments were formed, making up 13 percent of all Black Union soldiers, second only to Louisiana.

Having been assured of their centrality to the Union—"I hope to have God on my side, but I must have Kentucky," President Abraham Lincoln was reported to have said—perhaps white Kentuckians thought their decision not to secede would enable them to keep their enslaved, or their wealth, if not their understanding of themselves, which was, of course, indexed to Black people. In fact, they weren't able to keep any of it. And tens of thousands of them died trying.

The vast majority of Black and white Kentuckians fought for the Union (not the Confederacy). But after the war the state's factionalized identity—from white Confederates to white Unionists, some for emancipation and some against, to Black Republicans, eager to build upon their Union service and extend their claims to full citizenship—went up for grabs.

White Kentuckians, both Unionists and Confederates, reacted to postwar destabilization, to their profound grief, and, especially, to the upending of the racial order they had coiled their identities around, like ivy on a chain-link fence, "with unheard of violence, even by Kentucky standards." The formerly enslaved were whipped by their former masters. Some of the enslaved, who were not freed by the Emancipation Proclamation, which applied only to states that had seceded, were held in bondage until the Thirteenth Amendment abolishing enslavement was ratified by Congress in late 1865. Returning Black Union soldiers were targeted by roaming bands of white men, who attacked them, especially as they met at the newly formed Union Leagues. The end of the war found Kentuckians "in a mood to hate, retaliate, and destroy," and reactionary white violence grew, without restraint.

In petitioning for a Freedmen's Bureau in Kentucky, a state that had not seceded from the Union, the assistant commissioner of the Tennessee bureau cited the "brutal treatment of returned colored soldiers and their families." One field agent cited sixty cases of "outrage," which he called "unparalleled in their atrocity and fiendishness; cruelties for which in no instance . . . is there the least shadow of excuse of palliation."

Logan County, in particular, gained a national reputation for white violence. White people flew Confederate flags at public gatherings, and a large number of Confederate soldiers returned home to Russellville, where they were openly hostile to returning Black soldiers. The secret "I Am Committee"—one of those hyperlocal, violent white Confederate affiliate groups that sprang up across the South post–Civil War—distributed a handbill establishing rules for Blacks and whites alike regarding interaction between the races, and the limitations of this new Black freedom. The bill threatened "one hundred lashes" for perceived first offenses and "looking up a sapling," a euphemism for lynching, for a second offense. For "Negroes found stealing . . . death is the first penalty." The bill warned, "Anyone that may not like these rules can try their luck, and see whether or not I will be found doing my duty." I do not know if they confronted some of the Black Bibbs, who might have met their hostility armed with weapons, or simply a belief in the justness of their own freedom.

Leave the state, the Confederates in Russellville warned returning Black soldiers. And Momma Keziah's grandson John W. Bibb—my great-great-grandfather—along with his wife, Pocahontas, and their young son, members of the extended Black Bibb family, and other Blacks from Bibbtown and all over Kentucky did just that.

From 1860 to 1870, the Black population of Kentucky went from 20.4 percent to 16.8 percent. By 1900, the Kentucky Black population was just 13.3 percent, and after a brief rise to just under 20 percent a decade later, the numbers plummeted to the single digits, where they've remained for over one hundred years.

Emancipationist Unionist Republicans, both Black and white, continued to fight for a multiracial, democratic Kentucky after the Civil War. Other Kentuckians, whatever their Civil War loyalties, bonded over a covenant organized by race. Whiteness began to re-form its lines, and the former frontier state of Kentucky, once central to the political life of the nation and the outsize possibilities of its people, began a decades-long march backward into the Confederacy. Or, perhaps, in some ways, it simply lapsed into its native barbarity.

I sometimes wonder about how the post–Civil War realignment would have felt to the Black Bibbs who had been free for twenty-five years. It was, after all, a singular kind of starting over. I believe the grandchildren of Momma Keziah would have welcomed their new future, even as emancipation would have wiped out aspects of their head start as free Black people in a state that now had hundreds of thousands of them, surrounded by white people who refused to come to terms with that fact. Even as they were likely forced from Russellville by white Confederates, my great-great-grandfather John Wesley and his extended family would have been feeling some sense of their new proportions. Would have perceived the longer reach of their arms, outside of Kentucky, the new possibilities in a free state, in a reconstructing nation, where their gifts could take root and their children could flower. Or so they must have prayed, even as they whispered their doubts on the wind to Momma Keziah.

Besides, their head start wasn't totally wiped out, they would have thought to themselves. They were still light-skinned Black people, and that meant something, they surely thought. Generations later, we still heard it. We hear it today. It was a "privilege" they carried with them, that spoke for them. That opened doors. To a point, of course. After all, they were still Black people wherever they went. But being light-skinned was central to how they understood their prospects for the future, and who they were in the world. *We're not like the rest of*

Lonnae and family in front of the Bibb House.

these Negros. It was a fact they were proud of, protective of, and clannish about. It was 1865, and they were free Black people and experienced landowners, able to read and write from childhood, heading for a place that was full of work for people looking to begin again. Even if they were uncertain or angry because they'd been forced to leave Logan County and relocate to Illinois, they'd find themselves in good company.

And as it turns out, the white Bibbs had already seeded much of the ground.

MAP

of the STATE of

KENTUCKY;

with the

ADJOINING TERRITORIES.

By J.Russell.

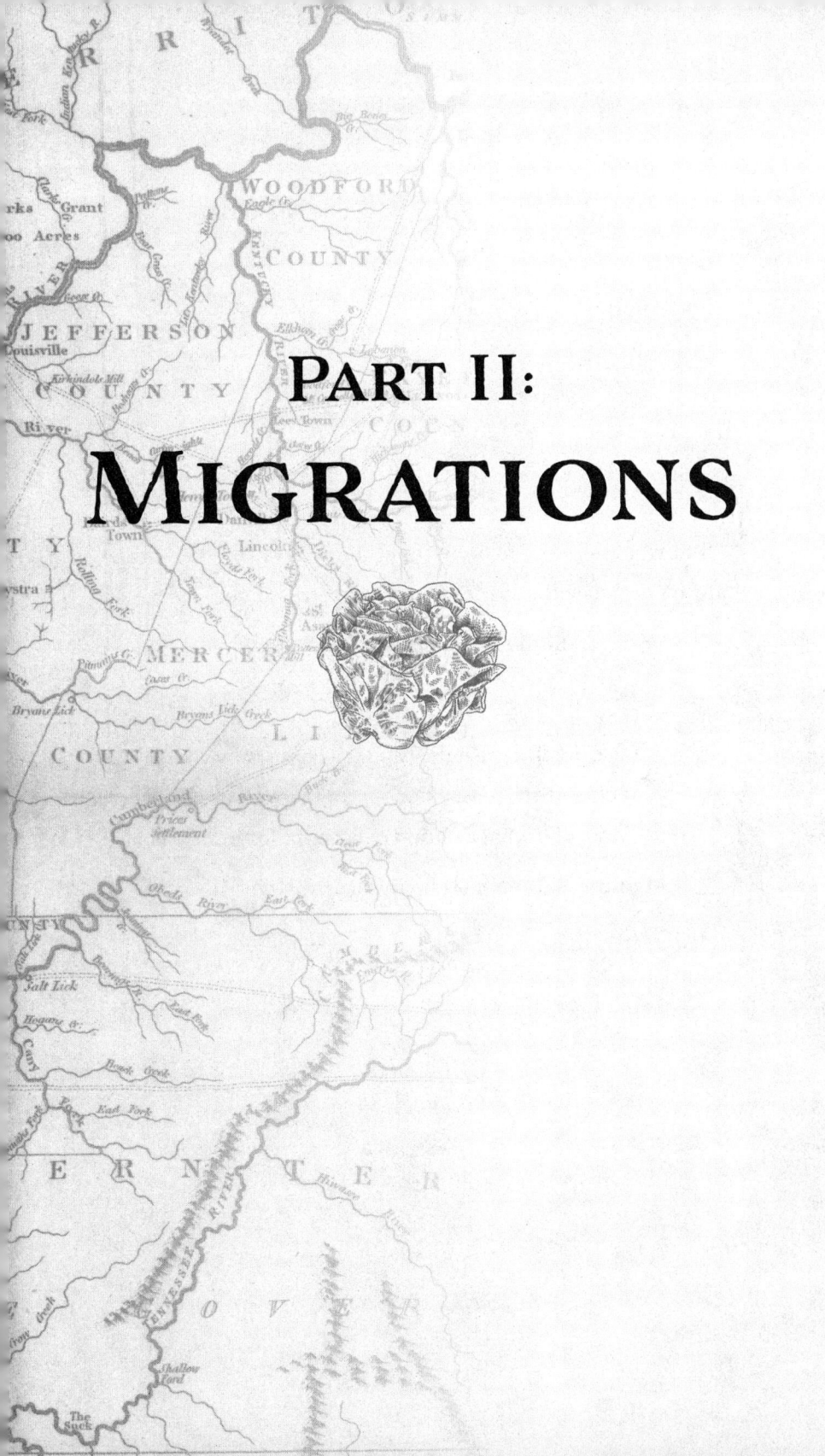

PART II:
MIGRATIONS

"But who we aspire to be, without the safety of the lie, should always organize the stories we tell ourselves about who we are.

—**Eddie S. Glaude Jr.,** *Begin Again*

"One can tell a great deal about a country by what it chooses to remember. . . . One can tell even more by what a nation chooses to forget."

—**Lonnie G. Bunch III in an essay for** *The Atlantic*

CHAPTER 6

CENTRALIA

In 1975, Harold David Bibb Sr., Momma Susie's first cousin, was interviewed about the history of Black Centralia as part of a bicentennial commemoration. In an oral history, he recounts how his grandparents had migrated to Centralia in 1865, from Bibbtown, Kentucky. "It's a small town near Russellville, Kentucky," he reported.

Harold David Bibb Sr. said his grandparents' names were John Bibb and Pocahontas. He added: "They were the proud parents of thirteen children."

Though John and Pocahontas Bibb arrived in Centralia right after the Civil War, they had not been enslaved, Cousin Harold stressed. As to their lives in Kentucky, he explained only that "efforts were made by the people that they worked for, named Bibb, to keep the entire family unit together. Of course, when they came here, to Centralia, Illinois, the family was together in a unit."

If Cousin Harold knew more to their story, he didn't offer it up, and the young interviewer didn't ask.

John Bibb had arrived in Centralia with a head start that began more than two decades earlier. Twenty-five years of freedom had allowed the Black Bibbs to straddle the color line that separated most Black people from their horizons. The Black Bibbs could read and write, they'd been quasi landowners (since it took decades for John Bigger Bibb to deed them the land they lived on, left to them by Major Richard Bibb), they were light skinned in a nation where skin color blocks, tackles, and confers privilege, and they aimed to put every bit of that to use.

In 1865, Illinois became the first state to ratify the Thirteenth Amendment, banning slavery. That same year, it repealed its Black Codes prohibiting Black migration. A decade earlier, the Illinois Central Railroad had completed its Chicago to Centralia charter line linking the industrial Midwest to the South, and the railroad began expanding westward. It all spelled possibility for free people, and the migrants from Russellville were part of a population explosion that saw the numbers of African Americans in Illinois grow from 7,628 in 1860 to 28,762 in 1870. (The state as a whole added more than 800,000 people during that same time, going from 1,711,951 in 1860 to 2,539,891, giving it the largest growth in the country.)

I had hoped Cousin Harold would detail some of this context. I'd wanted him to share everything he knew of the physical, racial, and economic journey that occasioned his grandparents' nearly 230-mile migration.

John, Pocahontas, and other family members had left western

Kentucky as the smoke of the Civil War gave way to its char. In 1865 in Centralia, the promise of America felt close at hand, or so Cousin Harold must have heard. But he said none of that.

Because, as it turns out, even when Black voices travel through time, they speak in survival tongue. And that is all about keeping time on the clock for yourself and your children. It's a code we use, especially in front of "company" (white people). You have to break the code before you can get at the truth in the words, which meant I had to listen for answers in the gaps.

The second time I listened to Cousin Harold's interview, I heard historicizing. I heard resistance. I heard the works by which the Black Bibbs, descendants of those enslaved and emancipated by Major Richard Bibb, and who were born in the industrial heartland of America in the first two decades of the twentieth century, the American Century, wanted to be known.

> As far as contributions, we had three [coal] miners, one machinist, three housewives, and one bartender who owned the saloon on Oak Street. John had a brother named Henry Bibb Sr., who was the first Negro alderman in the city of Centralia. Another son [of John Bibb], my father, named David Bibb, owned a store located at 501 North Elm and it was a general store. Most anything could be purchased there. He was a graduate of Centralia High School in nineteen and two. He had two children, Edna Bibb Hodges and Harold David Bibb.

Cousin Harold talked about other notable Black Centralians, including my uncle David Blackwell, the first African American inducted into the National Academy of Sciences, and his own son, Harold David Bibb Jr., who earned a PhD in developmental biology and became associate dean of the University of Rhode Island Graduate School. He could have added William Norwood, who became the first Black pilot to fly for United Airlines, the US senator Roland Burris, and Michigan State assistant coach Herb Williams, who became Centralia's first Black mayor. He could have named my mother, the beautiful Elizabeth Blackwell, a retired Chicago public schoolteacher who once applied for a summer job as a typist for Johnson Publishing Company, and was made a model on the spot, gracing the covers of *Tan* and *Jet* magazines.

My Black Bibb ancestors must have felt perfectly positioned for citizenship. They must have felt that with hard work and ingenuity, the future for them and their children would be wide open. White people might even come to embrace them, they surely imagined, or at the very least, leave them alone. But that is not what happened, or at least not all of it.

"The war settled the question of slavery itself, but it resolved nothing about the future of African Americans in the United States," wrote historian Kate Masur. And that national question was very much in play in Centralia, where the history of race, family, and America worked out to a full measure of grace for some of us descendants.

And a blues song for others.

There was a languid, soft-focus feel to my childhood summers in Centralia, where both of my parents were born and raised. It kicked in after nearly four hours on the road, as my daddy, Lonnie Gerald, made the long, flat drive for nearly 250 miles south from Chicago on Interstate 57. A flutter of anticipation descended on our station wagon before we hit the city limits as the drive brought us close enough to call out the places we would go: the Confectionary! Nina's house! Fairview Park!

Daddy turned onto IL 161 and we rode past open fields dotted with pump jacks, those rocking-horse oil wells, with their slow, hypnotic nods. Especially in the late afternoons, when long stretches of time and road had lulled me into semi-reverie, I imagined they were seesaws in some roadside extension of Fairview Park. Fairview was where that old Illinois Central steam locomotive appeared ever ready to belch back to life, and the annual July carnival served up all the spun-sugar thrills any summertime could hold.

There was also the Fairview pool, where we passed our days eating ice cream, or more often snow cones (much cheaper), chasing boys, and learning to swim, or, in my case, on a couple of occasions, nearly drowning since we were utterly unsupervised, except if you count the cousins, who were only a few years older.

In 1953, the NAACP, along with Momma's sister-in-law Winnie Blackwell, had sued the city to open the Fairview pool to Black children, but generations of white kids still played with their hatreds.

It was Fairview Park where white kids called me a nigger for the first time, when I was maybe five years old. Two white girls walked up to me in the park. They were impossibly big. At least eleven. They smiled at me. "Are you a nigger?" one asked.

By the time somebody else, a white boy standing a few feet away, threw a rock at my head, I had already started to run. I heard the stone whiz past my ear and land in a nearby creek. It was the kind of thing that had never happened to me on the South Side of Chicago, perhaps because there were no white kids. At least not where I lived, or went to school, or visited, or played.

Having to keep a wary eye out for baleful white children had been part of Centralia childhoods since any of us Bibb-O'Neal cousins could remember. Since any Black people in Centralia could remember.

The adults, of course, had their own Centralia stories. You could only catch tiny bits and pieces of them since children were not allowed to even break the threshold of a room in which grown folks were talking, lest we suffer the consequences. None of us could rightly say what those consequences were, since it was a rule of Black childhood that no one ever broke. More precisely, we didn't realize it could be broken. Just to crawl a bit deeper inside this nesting box, with regard to grown folks' rules, they were so authoritatively beyond the mental reach of Black children, there was simply no groove in our gray matter to accommodate defiance or speculation. At least not on the part of anybody I knew.

The Centralia of my childhood was layered with history, memory, and, as I later found out, a whole host of arrangements. When our stories were vivid, or amusing, or inexplicable enough, they stayed with us, such that we still call them up, adding new insights or details whenever two or more Centralia Bibb cousins (who are also O'Neals, Blackwells, Meeks, Fitzhughs, Hills, Franklins, Braswells, Vaughns, and Westbrooks) are together.

These are the stories we are still combing through.

There are other stories we are yet learning to speak out loud.

In my earliest memories of Momma Susie, she is still in the habit of getting dressed for the day. She is wearing a light sweater or a sleeveless blouse and loose-fitting slacks, which were appropriate to the few images I have of her out of doors and in the world, before she took permanently to her pajamas.

Momma Susie used to visit Chicago for weeks at a time when I was very young, and I remember running up to hug her once as she got out of the car. She was very pale, with a smattering of freckles on her face, and veins like blue-green inchworms inside translucent wrists and hands. Her fine, grayish-black hair was absent any suggestion of kinks or coils, and you might mistake her for a white woman. But you better not do it to her face. Momma Susie was rarely given to physical displays of affection, but she swept me into a wide hug on that day, and I remember feeling happy and chirpy around her.

She wore an apron the few times I saw her behind the bar at the restaurant-tavern she owned with my grandfather Papa Lonnie. It was named O'Neal's Place but was known throughout Southern Illinois as the Confectionary.

As a teen, Papa Lonnie had "hoboed," freight car to freight car, from McComb, Mississippi, to the railroad and coal-mining town of Centralia with his twin brother, my uncle Larry, who called himself Tough Titty (his oft-repeated mantra was "Tough titty, but sometimes, you still gotta suck it"). Their mother, Jessie Mae, had shot and killed a white man crawling through a window to rape her, and the family had to scatter before nightfall, but that was a different story. The kind Black Centralia was built on.

My amiable Papa Lonnie, a shrewd, hardworking moneymaker

behind a Louis Armstrong smile, was known as Chef, from his days at Centralia's historic Langenfeld Hotel. This was before he and Momma Susie, whom he married when she was eighteen, opened the Confectionary, along with Papa Lonnie's other brother, my uncle Manuel O'Neal. The Confectionary was home to cheeseburgers juicy enough to disintegrate the bun they were served on. A place for fried chicken, smothered pork chops, rib-tip sandwich platters. Momma Susie's dessert offerings included lemon cake, or chocolate pie topped with meringue swirls two inches high. Crown Royal whiskey was poured from the top shelf, and if you bought the bottle, you carried it out in that purple-and-gold-velvet drawstring pouch that later held the spare change for every home in Black America. Lunch hours drew shift workers and white businessmen from all over southern Illinois clamoring for Papa Lonnie's chicken and dumplings that had everybody wondering, How do they come to be so butter yellow?

Momma Susie could be found sitting behind the counter, drinking diet Tab, smoking Viceroys, and watching *The Young and the Restless*. Since everybody could see she was watching her "stories," she became seriously attitudinal whenever anybody asked her to do anything. She would refuse to wait on people until a commercial break.

At some point, Papa Lonnie pleaded with her: "Baby, you're running my business out. I'd rather for you to go home and look at TV than to sit here when customers ask you for something, and you don't feel like getting it 'cause you're watching your soap opera." Momma Susie stayed home after that, which I am sure was better for business. (However, that did nothing to solve the problem of their oldest child, and only daughter, my glamorous aunt Jackie, who wouldn't wait on you if she didn't like you.)

"Baby" wasn't just a term of endearment for Momma Susie—it was her name. The story goes that her daddy, my great-grandfather Charlie Bibb, named her after one of his girlfriends, so his wife, my great-grandmother Minnie, simply avoided the issue by calling her daughter Baby. Friends called her Baby loudly and often, and it was "Aunt Baby" (pronounced *Aint*) if you were family, which felt like the entire town. (Of course, she was not to be confused with her sister-in-law, Hastleteen Bibb, my uncle Morris's second wife, who we only knew as Aunt Baby Sis.)

After those first hours in Centralia, when word of our arrival always beat us to Momma Susie's house, my parents (and most of the grown folks in their generation) faded into a speculative somewhere else, whether they remained in Centralia, or returned to Chicago, showing up mostly on occasional phone calls until it was time to return home.

That left us nine Bibb-O'Neal first cousins—the children of Jacqueline, Lonnie Gerald, and Ronnie, those living in Centralia, and those who, like us, had driven from Chicago or thereabouts—to make our own summer plans. This always left me at a structural disadvantage. My sister, Lisa, four school years ahead of me, formed a cohort with Uncle Ronnie's oldest child, Traci, and Aunt Jackie's daughter, Lana Sue. They could walk farther, or drive (or knew people who could). They could visit other teenaged relatives or go to parties at Laura Leake Park.

They could go shopping or to the movies or listen to the record player in somebody's bedroom. They could hang with Aunt Jackie's son, Keppen, who played tennis and pool and was considered the smartest among us, especially after he started taking classes at the

University of Illinois extension when he was sixteen. When he was a fourth grader at the Lincoln School, the vaunted principal William Walker, the former Tuskegee-airman-turned-educator, told my aunt Jackie that Keppen had rarely (or never) missed a question on any standardized test and had consistently scored higher than anyone in the school. Much later Keppen learned the University of Chicago had been interested in having him in one of their programs in elementary school, probably at their Lab School. But Momma Susie and my father had vetoed the idea as too far, too foreign, too white, so that was the end of that.

My brother Chucky was always dropped off at the house of Momma Susie's sister Aunt Hilda as soon as we hit town. Aunt Hilda was Chucky's grandmother even though he was my brother, but Centralia was full of opaque or fictive ways to family, so I accepted the rightness of that at face value. I'd always considered my half brother Lance, the oldest of us nine, my cousin. But he was actually the son my daddy fathered by a former high school friend of my mother who Momma Susie and Papa Lonnie adopted, which officially made Lance my uncle.

That left Traci's brother Little Ronnie, who was just a year older than me. But Traci and Ronald had another set of grandparents a block from Momma Susie's. Plus, he was a boy, he was big for his age, he knew his way around town, and he got to walk or ride his bike with impunity.

For a long time, I was sui generis in the Bibb-O'Neal first-cousin universe. I was the youngest girl (until Uncle Ronnie's daughter, Amber, was born when I was eleven) and the one most subject to the oversight of Momma Susie.

By the time I was nine or so, I was old enough to spend most of my summer vacations with my cousin Nina. But until then I could sometimes spend all day in the house with my grandmother, watching the stories or old Charlie Chan movies, or reading books while listening to her yell into the phone (*Well, she ought not have laid down with him, then!*) before hanging up without saying goodbye. At some point, I could walk by myself to the corner store or even the Confectionary, just past the Lincoln School, to pick up lunch, if Momma Susie hadn't already called to make somebody bring it to us. *Lonnae is hungry. Click.* My grandparents lived on a three-lane, one-way street, a main thoroughfare where the speed limit must have been thirty miles an hour or more, and everything seemed to be moving fast. Maybe because I was little. *Watch out for the cars!* Momma Susie would yell out from her chair each time I left the house, and that's what I did.

Sometimes Momma Susie would call me over to get the comb and scratch the dandruff from her head. I'd have to part her hair, grease her scalp, then use the edge of the comb to scratch the parts I'd just greased. My grandmother's hair was straight at the roots and loosely curled at the ends, so layering it with Ultra Sheen felt like a bit of overkill. Also, she never actually had any dandruff, but I do not remember minding too terribly much. It may have been a Southern thing, or an old Black thing, but it sometimes felt like the only piece of caretaking and connection to be had in a family that didn't hardly touch. Unless it was in anger.

Sometimes she'd close her eyes and she'd tell her own stories.

Momma Susie had been a whiz in math, she bragged. She was the only one out of eight siblings to graduate high school, but there was no money for college so she cried hard, married young, and warned us all, in percussive terms, not to do so. I was nearly out of college before I realized college wasn't compulsory.

Keep your legs closed! Go to college! Get your education!

You make your own money; you don't have to ask nobody for shit!

Don't forget, a man will give out on you sessually fore a woman will.

At some point, I figured out what "sessually" meant, but I never figured out what Papa Lonnie made of that advice, as he sat nearby always smiling, never letting on if he'd heard. Sometimes he'd turn to me to ask if I wanted a biscuit, which he called a "cat head." I myself couldn't see the resemblance.

After she stopped working at the Confectionary, my grandmother largely stopped getting dressed for the day. Most of my memories center around her in her pajamas, sitting in a dark green wingback armchair, from where she could see everybody walking in the house and receive her intelligence reports. This was important, given her role in the underground economy of Centralia.

Nearly every day, a stream of visitors passed through Momma Susie's front door, almost all without knocking. The town was small, the people were known, and Black folks didn't have time for all those formalities. Plus, everybody liked to consider themselves in good with Lonnie and Baby.

The front door opened to a series of rooms, each open to the next on one long level, and visitors would holler their greetings on their way back to Momma Susie's throne room in front of the kitchen. I'd often be watching *The Price Is Right* on the big console TV, since people knew not to visit when my grandmother's stories were on. Sometimes, I'd be reading on the sofa, near the velvet rug featuring Martin Luther

Aunt Hilda (Left) and Momma Susie in her infamous green chair (Right).

King Jr. breaking his chains tacked to the faux-wood paneling, across from the painting of White Jesus on the wall. Verily, White Jesus stared out at us, and I was never sure if he considered his role in all of this as a cross section of Black Centralia stood before Momma Susie. They would tell me how much I'd grown and share the latest news—especially who was pregnant—before settling into the business at hand. That would be ardent pleas for short-term loans. Something that would help family, friends, and neighbors make it to Thursday after next, when, at that moment, their chances to do so felt iffy. Folks referred to Momma Susie as the bank because she loaned her money with interest, and plenty of it.

Sometimes it would be youngsters who'd come in with a handwritten note—*Miss Susie, my momma said to give you this*—but the pleas would always be the same: *Can I borrow something for my light bill? For my gas bill? For my automobile? For my rent? My baby needs milk. My kids need shoes. Can I borrow one hundred dollars and I'll give you one hundred fifty dollars when I get paid in two weeks?*

If she didn't like the terms, Momma Susie would sit there, unsmiling. "No, I don't have it today," she would say. But if it sounded all right, she'd get up and go under the cushion of that green chair, or under her mattress, or to the cigar box in that main bedroom I never saw her share with my grandfather, and dig out the cash.

She must have had a half-dozen loans out at any given time. I never saw her write anything down, but my brother said she had a list, always within armchair's reach. People would pay her back in food stamps if they didn't have the cash. Or they'd sell her six hundred dollars' worth of food stamps for three hundred dollars. She'd use the money for the house or send the food stamps to her grandkids in college (or graduate school, or medical school, or law school), which, at one point or another, was all nine of her grandchildren. She gave her great-nephew Patrick money when he was nineteen, with a baby, and trying to stay in college. That belief in higher education was the most enduring way Momma Susie's influence, and that of much of her generation of Black people whose grandparents had known slavery, rippled through our family.

My grandmother loaned money for decades to Black people who had few other options. She never employed violence to aid her debt collection. She'd just leave word that she was looking for somebody if they owed her, and that mostly worked. If it didn't, she simply wouldn't loan to that person again. In later years, her nephews Robert Bibb, when he was still going by that name, or the former Centralia

Township High School All-American football player Morris Douglas Bibb drove her around town (still in her pajamas) so she could call on, or call out to, those with outstanding balances who dodged her on the street. That became more frequent as the railroad, coal-mining, manufacturing, and retail industries of the town all declined, making Black people the first to succumb to the same ills the nation writes elegies for in white rust belt communities.

The opening scenes of the 1997 Michael Moore documentary *The Big One* featured footage from then candidate Bill Clinton's 1992 visit to Centralia, "where they were good people who played by the rules who'd been forgotten in George Bush's America." I remember Papa Lonnie telling me he'd marked the visit by cutting himself a large piece of watermelon and sitting on the tree stump in front of his house to eat it as cars whizzed by on North Elm. He laughed as hard as I'd ever seen him, giving full Louis Armstrong, talking about how *them white folks almost crashed they cars turnin' around to look at me!*

In the documentary, Moore talked to workers who'd been fired by the factory where they'd made Payday bars—the candy factory, as we always called it, where my cousin Nina had worked. One white worker told him: "People are going to go off the deep end that lose their jobs in America. It happens all the time, the suicides will go up, divorce rates, you know people start beating their kids that normally wouldn't. I mean people just lose it when they don't have an income or they have to go from making ten dollars an hour down to five dollars an hour." Everybody agreed.

At some point, Lemuel "Lemmy" Flagg became Momma Susie's driver. He began working at the Confectionary as a teenager, and my grandparents, and most other Bibbs and O'Neals, treated him like family. On a slow night, the Confectionary would only make around four hundred dollars, but that swelled to twelve hundred dollars or more on a good night. Every night after closing, Papa Lonnie would make the five-minute walk across the Lincoln School lot (which the Bibbs and later the O'Neals once owned) with his money box in one hand and his gun in the other. As Papa Lonnie got older, Lemmy closed up, and he was the only other person in the world Momma Susie allowed to carry the money box home to her, where she would wait up, late into the night, to carefully go over the receipts.

I don't remember how old I was when Momma Susie first sent me to the store. We're not talking about Grandpa Richard's, the little convenience store two doors down on the corner of Elm Street, where you could just grab candy and grape "sody," as Centralia folks called it. (That always struck me as just wrong, since everybody in Chicago knew it was called pop.)

My sister, Lisa, and Cousin Traci were there one day when an old white man came from behind the counter to wiggle his hips and gyrate in front of them. This was not Grandpa Richard, who was, himself, the old white man who owned the Grandpa Richard's store and lived next door, in peace, with Momma Susie. This was a lecherous old clerk who stood in front of Traci, not close enough to touch, but close enough to send them running. When they told Momma Susie, she got up from her chair and, with Lisa and Traci trailing behind, stormed into the store and cussed him out. (Traci doesn't remember her exact words, but this was an old story, as Momma Susie was wearing regular clothes.) "These two right here, they'll be coming back and you don't say nothing. You don't do nothing. You don't even look at them," Momma Susie told the man. That reset things such that they had no more problems.

At some point, you had to graduate from Grandpa Richard's if you wanted anything more than corner-store fare. For me, that point must have been when Momma Susie realized that my daddy, Lonnie Gerald, drank sugar-free, caffeine-free Diet Pepsi, and she had none in the fridge. The grocery stores that carried it were too far to walk, and I couldn't yet drive, so I grabbed a bike from my grandparents' backyard and rode off, I think toward the Piggly Wiggly, but it might have been the family-owned Altadonna's. That grocery store may have also had a sign with a pig out front, hence my confusion. Whatever the case, it wasn't more than a mile or two away, but it felt punitively far on a Centralia-hot summer afternoon if you were steering and pedaling while carrying a plastic bag with a two-liter bottle of pop in one hand. But I made it back fine, and I thought that was the end.

It was not. I had gotten sugar-free Diet Pepsi, but not *caffeine-free*, sugar-free Diet Pepsi. Momma Susie gave me back the receipt—she'd probably had me turn it over to her to make sure I wasn't keeping any of her change—and ordered me back to the store. I got back on the bike and pedaled again, back to the store to *get the right one, baby*. My dad had been the prince of Centralia. He was certainly the prince of the family as far as Momma Susie was concerned, and what Lonnie Gerald wanted, Lonnie Gerald got. No matter what.

In Illinois (and Virginia, Kentucky, Alabama, Georgia, etc.), the white Bibbs got in on the ground floor, although it was already inhabited by

Native people. Illinois is a federal land state, meaning the first land purchases were made by patent (the instrument used by government to transfer land into private hands). Beginning in 1814, when Illinois was part of the Northwest Territory, through 1838, white Bibbs acquired sixty-three parcels of land. Of those, fifty-three were purchased by Major Richard Bibb and his sons Richard Bibb Jr. and John Bigger Bibb in 1836. That same year, the state general assembly incorporated the new Illinois Central Railroad company. A congressional representative introduced federal legislation authorizing a land grant for the company that was officially approved in 1851. By 1853, the Illinois lawyer Abraham Lincoln was on retainer for the railroad and given an annual pass to ride.

The white Bibbs' Illinois land speculation had doubtless gotten a mighty assist from Major Richard Bibb's friendship with Ninian Edwards. Edwards, a Russellville lawyer, Kentucky chief justice, and Kentucky state representative, had been one of the first two US senators from Illinois. Edwards was an enslaver, though slavery in the Northwest Territory was illegal. He served as the only governor of the Illinois Territory and later became the third governor of the young state, and in both tenures, he sent the Illinois militia to attack Native peoples in service of the state's "Indian Removal" policy.

I have found no records of where the Black Bibbs lived when they arrived in Illinois, but the land records of the white Bibbs offer some clues. In 1838, land deeds show John Bigger Bibb and Richard Bibb Jr. owned five parcels of land totaling roughly five hundred acres in Marion County. This was one of three counties that later became part of Centralia. Of the five parcels, John Bigger Bibb owned four, totaling 358 acres.

In 1865, when the Black Bibbs left—or fled—Russellville, under threat from returning white Confederates, it would have been John Bigger Bibb, the Bibb lettuce developer and sole surviving son of Major Richard Bibb, with a lifelong responsibility for his father's legatees, who would have directed them to southern Illinois. (It had been dubbed Little Egypt, an Old Testament reference, in the early nineteenth century when northern Illinoisans had to travel to the region for grain after a series of harsh weather events, although other explanations for the nickname abound. This explains why my Southern Illinois University mascot was an Egyptian dog called a Saluki. Who knew?) It is unclear if the Black Bibbs settled on some parcel of John Bigger Bibb's land, but in "family" migrations, people go where they have established ties. Perhaps John Bigger Bibb sold his Marion County land and gave the Black Bibbs seed money to buy their own. Perhaps they farmed land owned by John Bigger Bibb until they earned the money to buy their own. Either way, they saw land as essential to their prospects.

My great-great-grandfather John W. Bibb and his brother Henry, along with a Jefferson Bibb (who'd been enslaved by Richard Bibb Jr. and family and fought for the Union) started buying land shortly after their arrival in Illinois. From around 1870 to 1880, they bought five parcels of land totaling $1840, mostly in the northeast section of Centralia where Blacks were being steered, east of the railroad tracks. Some of the land was apparently purchased for speculation and decades later was sold to Pittenger and Langenfeld and McClelland—developers whose names became synonymous with hotels, theaters, and opera houses in the rise of downtown Centralia.

From 1901 through 2007, Black Bibbs were involved in hundreds of land transactions. They bought, sold, and leased land. Thirty-three times, they transferred land from one Bibb to another. And, at least once, from a Bibb to an O'Neal. The records demonstrated a sophistication, or at least a broad familiarity with the tools of wealth and instruments of land conveyance within lived memory of the time when most Black people had just gained title to their own bodies. And like most migrants, Black and white, the Bibbs availed themselves of the opportunities to work all around them.

Centralia, chartered in 1859, was named for the Illinois Central (or *that place down Central,* as upstate railroaders called it), which had opened its Centralia-to-Chicago line in 1855, giving Chicago a gateway to the South. A year later, all Illinois charter lines—stretching 705 miles, from Cairo, in the southern tip of Illinois, to Chicago—were complete. Centralia was considered the halfway point between Chicago and Memphis, which meant ailing railcars that could make it to the Centralia shop wouldn't have to backtrack a couple of hundred miles to be fixed. New trains assembled at the Centralia car shed helped supply the railroad's expansion. Other railroad companies, including the Burlington, the Southern, and the Missouri and Illinois rail lines (through its Missouri Pacific connection), added Centralia lines as they began crisscrossing the nation.

The power of those coal-fired steam locomotives, engines of industry that shook the ground in the making of America, was the most muscular story Centralians told about themselves. It was woven through the settlement of the state, the history and economy of the region, and up and down family histories like mine. In 1920, the Centralia city directory lists a Herman Bibb working at the Illinois

Central shops. James Bibb worked for the Burlington Railroad shops along with a Ciciah Bibb (alternately McKie Bibb in census records).

My maternal grandfather, Grover Blackwell, a railroad "hostler," worked at the roundhouse to turn locomotives around and literally kept the trains running on time. He'd blow the steam whistle daily to let Grandma Mabel and my momma, his beloved daughter, Betty Lou, know he'd be home soon for supper. He and his son, my uncle Johnson "Skee" Blackwell, short for the Skeezix comic-strip character, both worked for the railroad for more than forty years. Harold Bibb began as a laborer with the Illinois Central at nineteen, servicing the steam engines, loading them with sand for the rails that helped the train cars maintain their traction. Momma Susie's brothers, my uncle Robert "Bobby" Bibb and Uncle Morris, assembled and repaired trains in the car shed. It could be dirty work, but Uncle Morris, the good-looking Bibb playboy, still managed to keep his reddish-brown hair waved like the matinee idol Errol Flynn and his nails neatly manicured. A host of businesses depended on the railroad—hotels, boardinghouses, and general stores catering to travelers. Churches and housing were built for the influx of workers—European immigrants, German mostly—and the newly emancipated African Americans, who were concentrated on the north and northeastern sides of town.

Those who weren't railroaders were coal miners or farmers. Beginning in the late nineteenth century, the Illinois Central provided passenger service, shipped produce and manufactured goods to market, and served the transportation needs of sixty-five coal mines throughout southern Illinois, including Centralia, whose first vein of coal was discovered in 1874. Freight locomotives would haul coal cars and boxcars from Centralia and surrounding area mines. Later, drilling for oil and natural gas and manufacturing became features of the Centralia economy.

The 1870 census lists John as a laborer and Pocahontas a housekeeper, with their six-year-old son, Robert, born in Kentucky, and two-year-old Elizabeth (Lizzie) and three-month-old James born in Illinois. The census taker initially marked the family *M* for "mulatto," but it is later overwritten with *W* for "white." There is no telling when or why it was changed. White census takers were vulnerable to not knowing what they were looking at when they were looking at Black people but thinking that they did. Or perhaps John Bibb himself had something to do with it, in which case the former would still apply. Either way, by 1880, John is a coal miner, Robert and Lizzie are in school, the couple have three more children, and the census taker has again classified the family as "mulatto."

John Bibb worked the twenty-acre family farm that later became Centralia's Elmwood Cemetery, which was never segregated and where more than fifty Bibbs are buried. Land records show seven Black Bibbs owned twenty-one plots of Centralia land, totaling 130 acres. Of those totals, John and/or Pocahontas owned the majority—eleven plots equaling 90 acres. At some point, my great-great-grandparents John and Pocahontas ran a general store, which the family lived above for years. It feels like an origin story, perhaps telling how my grandparents Momma Susie and Papa Lonnie first met. I was delighted to find out that by the late 1920s, John Bibb's store became the site of the precursor to the first O'Neal Confectionary.

Throughout the latter half of the nineteenth century, Black Bibbs are getting married, having children, and actively testing the extent of universal freedom and enfranchisement. They are customizing their lives. In 1886, a Willie Bibb and a George Bibb are members of the newly formed Negro League baseball team the Centralia Colored Giants. (By the early twentieth century, the Colored Giants have become one of Southern Illinois's most competitive and entertaining teams, playing to capacity crowds. At one point, the Giants' catcher warns the opposing team's base runners with the words "Thou Shall Not Steal" emblazoned across his chest protector.)

John Bibb also worked as a janitor who kept the bellows going at the white First Baptist Church so the pipe organ would have air. In 1869, "a group of Colored citizens feeling the need for greater spiritual outlet" established their own Second Baptist Church, according to a 1971 Second Baptist souvenir book. You can almost hear the Black gospel choir singing between the lines of type. You can almost see the usher (*ursher?*) board in their white gloves and feel the breeze off the cardboard fans, with ads for whatever business provided Black people with funerary services.

The book commemorates one hundred years of church history, which is town history, and names from both sides of my family rise from the pages. "On a rainy afternoon in 1917, the late Mother Leake slowly turned the first spadesful of earth for our present church

Uncle Morris in the Confectionary.

home, while Rev. Carter read the scripture. Mother Martha Bibb held the umbrella over Mother Leake and Rev. Carter." And here I thought Laura Leake was just the park where the teens went to party, attend concerts, and make out when I was a girl.

In his later years, John Bibb was a truck farmer, and I sometimes wonder what would have happened if he'd been given a strain of that "particularly good" limestone lettuce from John Bigger Bibb, on the advice to keep it safe, keep it close, *because I think we're onto something.* I wonder if, instead of the Genenwein family, Black John Bibb and his family, Momma Susie's family, couldn't have been the first to commercially produce Bibb lettuce and watch it catch on. Wouldn't that have been something?

Especially since some of the next generation of the Black Bibb family had a change in fortunes.

By the late nineteenth century, the Black Bibbs were full participants in the civic and political life of their new Illinois hometown. They fought for some of the last gains secured under the 1866 federal Civil Rights Act and the Fourteenth Amendment, as the politics against racial equality solidified.

Both John and Henry joined the Republican Party, the party of Lincoln, and ran for alderman. John was defeated, but Henry won and was reelected by a large majority in 1894. That same year, he served as treasurer of St. Luke Lodge #34, a religious or fraternal organization where his nephew Joseph Bibb and a George Bibb, both listed in census records as "mulattos," also served as officers.

In 1870, Illinois established free public schools for children and, two years later, forbade the exclusion of Black children, but gave school boards leeway to decide if they'd integrate. And "everywhere,

Black parents and community groups pushed state legislatures to provide their children with schools and went to court when they did not," wrote Kate Masur. The Black Bibbs were part of that push.

In 1870, Centralia opened a segregated Black school. By 1873, Centralia had 50 school-age Black children. By 1895, there were 343 Black school-age children and the city built the larger, segregated Lincoln School in Northtown Centralia to accommodate them. But that September, it opened with no students. Black children who lived in Southtown Centralia, where my mother grew up, simply continued attending their local school. In October, the Centralia school board ordered all Black students below seventh grade to attend the new Lincoln School. The following month, Henry Bibb sued the Centralia school board for its failure to integrate. The court "found against the defendants for cost. The colored people gained all they were contending for," in 1896.

Except by then, the school board had instituted a racist workaround. They ordered a redistricting of school attendance boundaries, "without reference to color. However, as most Blacks lived in the north-northeastern part of town, lines were drawn to effect virtual segregation. The exception was the few families living in south town."

This violated the spirit of the court's desegregation ruling.

(In 1908, about eighty miles northwest of Centralia, Scott Bibb, who came from a Missouri branch of Black Bibbs, won an eleven-year fight to return the city of Alton to the desegregated public schools that had been in operation from 1872 to 1897. When the Illinois Supreme Court finally ruled in favor of Bibb, ordering the city to re-desegregate, the city simply refused to comply. This violated the letter of the court's desegregation ruling.)

Centralia Township High School, which opened in the late 1890s and has one of the winningest high school boys' basketball programs in the nation, was never segregated officially or unofficially, however. The ability to utilize the talents of the town's entire high school population over more than a century likely contributed to the success of the Centralia Orphans. And perhaps it allowed Centralia to avoid the racial violence that plagued surrounding communities. When Cousin Harold told the interviewer that his father, David Bibb, graduated CTHS in 1902, he did not mention he was the first Black student to do so. (In 1912, my mother's aunt Ella Johnson was the first Black girl to graduate from CTHS.) After graduating, David Bibb was hired as a teacher at the Lincoln School, though he was a laborer for the railroad when he died at forty-eight, in 1931.

The Black Bibbs had put down roots, made tracks, and made gains in Illinois, but they'd taken some hits as well. By the time my great-great-grandmother Pocahontas died in 1916, she'd outlived more than half of her children. And some of the survivors were starting to fall on hard times.

The population of Centralia rose steadily for the first half of the twentieth century. Fueled by railroading, coal mining, and agricultural production (especially fruit) able to be transported in some of the first refrigerated railcars, the population grew from 6,721 in 1900 to a high of 16,343 by 1940.

In the 1920s, the Rotary Club spent seven hundred dollars to erect a large wooden sign atop a downtown building facing the railroad tracks. It beckoned newcomers with the words: CENTRALIA YOUR OPPORTUNITY. In 1935, my cousin Lana Sue's grandfather, the newly minted Dr. Percy May, took the train from Chicago to Cairo looking for a good place to hang his shingle. Not having found it, Dr. May was returning to Chicago when he saw the YOUR OPPORTUNITY sign at the Centralia stop and took it as a harbinger of good things. He grabbed his bag, disembarked, and for decades practiced medicine as the town's only Black doctor. In 1959, when Uncle Morris's first wife, Dolores, died during what was supposed to be a routine surgery to remove a benign uterine tumor, it was Dr. May who came to see him. "They are going to tell you it was a heart attack," he told Uncle Morris, "but she had an allergic reaction to the anesthesia." There was nothing they could do about it, he said, but he wanted Uncle Morris to know. Uncle Morris understood and thanked him.

Inside the myriad stories of Centralia growth and opportunities were deeper, more layered sagas. They reveal the entropy of places where Black people are deprived of sufficient operating space by the white people who benefit—culturally, politically, economically—from that arrangement, so they fold in on themselves in ways that some do not survive. And some who do are scarred. They are stories suffused with serpentine relationships, complex power dynamics, hidden truths, and lurking deceptions twinned in Black and white. Violence begets violence. As above, so below. The perils come from within and without.

In the early twentieth century, Black Bibbs were growing in numbers, but also losing people to the hardness of the times. An 1894 mining accident claimed the life of Grant Bibb, "a young Centralian" who was labeled "mulatto" in census records, as was his father, Amos, who had been born in Logan County. A contemporaneous account said he was "instantly killed" and another man seriously injured when "there seemed to be a misunderstanding of the signals and the cage was hoisted when it should not have been."

By the time John Bibb dies in 1913, he has outlived seven of his and Pocahontas's thirteen children, a number of whom show up briefly in records before vanishing, presumably dying before adulthood. Many were infants or young children, but in 1893, Hattie Belle Bibb, just the second surviving girl in a family of boys, fell ill and died at sixteen, and even on paper, with time stretched like the arms of Jesus between us, the sadness of her death pulls at me. Robert Bibb, the oldest child of John and Pocahontas, and the only one born in Kentucky, died of consumption in 1896 at age thirty-two.

Decades later, in 1938, John Edward Bibb, another son, a "colored miner at No. 5 mine" according to the *Centralia Sentinel*, died from injuries suffered when a rock fell on him and another miner. He'd been a member of the local Masonic lodge, and the funeral was at Second Baptist. Nearly a decade later, 111 miners were killed when the No. 5 mine exploded. The 1941 Woody Guthrie song "The Dying Miner" was taken from the last words the doomed men scratched out to their families. "Goodbye Centralia, goodbye."

John Bibb had left his property to his wife, Pocahontas, "for the term of her natural life." Upon her death, all land was to be managed by their son James, with the annual proceeds from his management to be divided equally among John's remaining heirs—his six surviving children, Lizzie, Joe, James, John, David, and Charles (known as Charlie), and his grandson Theodore. John Bibb's will instructed James to divide the land equally between them twenty years after his death. But they went through some things in the intervening years.

In 1914, six Black Bibbs, excluding Momma Susie's father, Charles Smith Bibb (who I'd only ever heard of as Charlie Bibb and whose full government name I heard for the first time from Michael Morrow at the 2019 Bibb House reunion), show up on a Marion County delinquent-tax list. The next year, Joseph Bibb died. By the time Pocahontas died in 1916 at age sixty-nine, she'd outlived eight of her thirteen children. In 1919, Charlie Bibb quitclaimed the land left to him by his father to his surviving siblings, indicating perhaps that he was beginning to sell some of his land for money.

By the early 1920s, Charlie and Minnie Bibb and their three oldest children are living at the McKee Street address where I used to visit their two youngest, Aunt Ellen and Uncle Morris, in side-by-side trailers, nearly seven decades later. The family managed to hold on to that land. But almost a decade later, the Great Depression devastated millions, and Charlie Bibb and his family, including a teenaged Momma Susie, were not just poor, like much of America; they were hungry. Businesses and banks failed, farmers lost their farms, unemployment reached as high as 25 percent, and those who were working saw salaries and wages plummet—40 percent for the former and 60 percent for the latter—in the early 1930s.

According to the Library of Congress, "By 1932, approximately half of African Americans were out of work. In some Northern cities, whites called for African Americans to be fired from any jobs as long as there were whites out of work." For decades, Charlie Bibb and other southern Illinois Black coal miners had braved the hazards of the job while earning less than their white counterparts, who saw them as threats to their all-white unions and their livelihoods. The Depression, coming after years of accidents, explosions, and violent and sometimes racialized conflict between union workers and mine owners, hastened the industry's downturn. In 1930, Charlie Bibb was a general laborer rather than a coal miner, and work was hard to find. By the late 1930s, only two of Centralia's five mines were operational.

Railroads, which had begun losing passengers to automobiles, hemorrhaged jobs. Black workers, who had long faced pay inequities and discrimination, were replaced by white workers who belonged to unions closed to members "of African descent." It reminds me that Charlie Bibb once wrote "African" for race on a World War I draft registration card between two decades where he's "mulatto" in census records. I now believe that was some form of resistance, or at least that these things might be in some way related. "Hobos," dozens at a time, "rode the rails"—jumping onto slow-moving freight cars and searching for work. Illinois set up "transient" camps throughout the state.

"There was no work to do," said Centralia native Charles S. Bunch in a 1974 oral history at the University of Illinois in Springfield. "Some of the people were so destitute." He told a story that sounded eerily familiar. It was about the time a crowd gathered outside the general store at the Marion County Relief just north of Centralia.

"One day, they come up there, a crowd of them, and said, 'We want groceries. Take a list of everything that we need.'

"The man said, 'But you can't just take my groceries off my shelves.'

"They said, 'No you just stand over there, you're going to get your money when we get some money, and you won't get hurt.' And they take it. Everybody. Taking what he got and everything.... They would have put that man out of business that day, but the Marion County Relief paid the bill. But they was just that desperate."

This sounded very much like the story I heard from my cousin Marvin years earlier, who heard it from his grandfather, my uncle Morris, the youngest of the eight Bibb siblings who lived to adulthood. In that telling, there was no crowd. It was just Charles Smith Bibb (Charlie Bibb, everyone called him) and the grocer he hit, knocking him to the floor before he filled his bag with groceries. But he, too, left a note with his tally and a promise to return when he had the money to pay what was owed.

I do not know if these two stories were the same event, but in the version I heard, Charlie Bibb just couldn't stand his kids talking about how hungry they were anymore.

Every cousin in my generation who heard the name Charlie Bibb heard that he was mean. Usually, that was the only thing we heard.

There were a few more details from Centralians in my mother's generation. Though Charlie Bibb died when they were babies or before they were born, they were raised around people who knew him firsthand, and you could pull from them a few more (heavily caveated) insights.

My mother's lifelong friend and classmate Joel Berkley didn't get out of the house much as a child, so he heard more grown folks talk than most. He grew up with grandparents, great-grandparents, and his mom. His father died when he was a baby, and his mother later remarried my grandfather's brother, another Centralia stalwart and Confectionary great, my great-uncle Manuel (pronounced *manual*, like manual labor). Joel's grandfather J. T. Woods knew Charlie Bibb.

He would say that Charlie didn't want his daughters, or anybody in the family, to marry anyone that couldn't pass the paper bag test. As in, you better be lighter than.

Berkley's uncle Eddie and my great-aunt Hilda were an item. But that didn't last. Berkley's aunt Charlotte Washington doesn't recall Charlie Bibb. But she remembered my aunt Hilda and her brother Eddie "courting." "I'll never know what happened," Washington said. "But it was a shock to everybody. Because she used to come every Sunday after church. When he went into the service she'd always come see us." It seemed Eddie was a little too brown-skinned for Charlie Bibb.

No one ever told me my great-grandfather was color struck. Here's what they said:

"I heard he would beat people's ass."

"He would come outside and say, 'Get out of my yard!' and he meant it. You could tell by the tone of his voice that he was not playing."

"Minnie Bibb was the salt of the earth, but my mother told me Charlie Bibb was a monster."

Then there were the stories that came from those folks who had held their lips in the tightest of lines when it came to Charlie Bibb, and by extension what they had been through. Folks who, toward the end of their lives, began to open up. It still wasn't much by way of precise details. But as with so many Centralia stories, when you listened hard enough, things began to add up.

My father's first cousin Robert Bibb (who became Abdullah Idris Mubarak) and his wife, Rita Westbrook, named their third son Charlie Bibb after his grandfather, Charles Smith Bibb. Everybody called him Charlie B, and my aunt Ellen soon began drawing comparisons between her grandson and her late father—especially when young Charlie B seemed to act overly headstrong (back then it was called hardheaded) or defiant.

"She would often talk about Charlie B being like his great-granddaddy, in a joking way, but also in a way that now as an adult I realize was registering something with her [about how she experienced him]," my cousin Patrick told me. "Because she would never talk about how loving Charlie B was. It was always him being selfish. Being mean. Acting like his great-granddaddy."

I heard Charlie Bibb beat my great-aunt Jeanette, who they called Pocahontas, nearly to death when she became romantically involved with a dark-skinned man. No one alive to tell it can say for true. I never met my aunt Jeanette. She was Charlie Bibb and Minnie's oldest child, married at sixteen and divorced by nineteen, with a three-year-old son. In the few old photos I've seen, she has this distant look, even right up close, when she's smiling. It's like part of her wants to leave with whatever is haunting the camera that captured her image. She reminds me of a character in a Zora Neale Hurston novel, though not one Hurston ever wrote. Jeanette came down with that Black plague, sugar diabetes, as folks called it, and had to have her leg amputated. She was fifty-five when she died in 1965. Her gravestone quotes the old gospel song: "Precious Lord, take my hand, lead me on, let me stand."

Lemuel Flagg, who started working at the Confectionary when he was sixteen, was close to all the Bibb sisters. He lived for a time with Aunt Hilda, who used to talk about Charlie Bibb all the time, he said.

"Excuse my language. She said Charlie Bibb was a big, red, mean motherfucker! She told me about the time that they got in an argument about something. I guess she was a teenager, and they got to arguing and she told him, 'You run over everybody from Momma all the way down to Morris. But I'll go to hell with my back broke before I let you run over me.'

"He hauled off and hit her so hard, she said, 'I woke up and I ain't lying. I swear, I saw stars.' And she said, 'I ran.' She said, 'I went to the police station, and I told them Charlie Bibb was my father, and he had hit me.' I know that she didn't have a good relationship with Mr. Bibb."

Charlie Bibb died at fifty-three, in 1940, although he was sick for years before that. Sick from what, no one can recall. It could have been those decades in the coal mines. Though some think it was some of that mean that finally turned on him. Or maybe he'd had a knowing, a fore-shadowing that took the life from him—that all of his kids, and most of his grandkids, would go on to marry dark-skinned Black people.

Several years after that first Bibb House reunion, I asked my cousin Vicki Wallace Cawthon, the great-granddaughter of John Edward Bibb, who'd died in the coal mines, if she'd ever heard that Charlie Bibb was mean, and she just laughed. "Honey, they all were," she said. "They all had that mean streak."

Cawthon's grandmother Gladys and Aunt Hilda were first cousins who owned adjoining properties across from the Lincoln School, and in the late 1980s got into a land dispute over a shed that Aunt Hilda owned behind her house that partially crossed onto Gladys's property. The two women died having never spoken again.

Early in my reporting career, I was visiting my alma mater, Southern Illinois University at Carbondale (there's an Edwardsville campus in the town named for Ninian Edwards), about an hour south of Centralia, when I stopped by the office of one of the two Black deans I remembered from my undergrad years. I didn't know it as a student, but Dean Harvey Welch was from Centralia, where he'd been a standout high school basketball player, and he had gone on to be an all-conference player at SIU.

Too many Centralia relatives to name had also gone to SIU-C. They'd played basketball and/or pledged Alpha Phi Alpha Fraternity Inc., or in my older sister's case, Alpha Kappa Alpha Sorority Inc., as had I.

My father's older sister, Aunt Jackie, dated comedian Dick Gregory at SIU. I met Gregory when he came to SIU to speak once and he remembered visiting Centralia; he told me he used to go to the Confectionary to chat up Momma Susie. Aunt Jackie would finish morning classes, then hop the train from Carbondale to Centralia to change clothes. She'd catch the next train and be back in Carbondale in time to show off her new outfit for classes that same afternoon. In the 1950s, when downtown Centralia was segregated, when most white women couldn't afford to shop Centralia's priciest boutique, Aunt Jackie was on a first-name basis with the owners. My grandparents' money also blocked and tackled. Aunt Jackie could call the shop owners and they'd send her a new outfit by cab.

I told Dean Welch my family was from Centralia, and he told me right away who my people were. Especially my mother, Betty Lou Blackwell, who was known as the prettiest girl in Illinois, he said. Cousin Harold Bibb had wanted Momma and his son Harold David Jr. to get married, probably ever since they were in a Tom Thumb wedding together at Second Baptist when both of them were five. I was reminded of close circles and long memories in places where those kinds of things could make all the difference in the world. Especially when the world was Black.

For much of its history, Centralia was divided into two parts—Northtown and Southtown. In the 1940s and '50s, you could count the number of Black people who didn't live in one of those two areas of Centralia on one hand and still have fingers left. Joel Berkley contended he was the product of a mixed marriage. His father came from Southtown, his mother from Northtown. The physical distance between the two was small, but the psychic dividing line was nearly geologic.

My momma had grown up in Southtown, along with a smattering of other Black families. Her family owned property and ran a general store. She was almost always the only Black student in her elementary school classes at the Field School, or perhaps one of two. Her older brother, my uncle Skee, once told the *Centralia Sentinel* newspaper he had white classmates who would raise their hands to brag, "My daddy's in the KKK!" For Black families, it was a choice between walking a few blocks to school or walking two and a half miles to the Lincoln School in Northtown, which is not to say the choice was easy.

Charlotte Washington, Joel Berkley's aunt, recalled her mother had to push for her to attend the Field School: "I will tell you what she told us. She said, 'You might not sing in the choir and you might not be in the class play. But all you have to do is sit there and listen, because they're going to teach their children.' That was what she told us. And it was the truth."

On Sundays, Momma's family drove to Northtown in a fancy Buick to go to Second Baptist, which her momma's people had helped build. She was the youngest, by more than two decades, of four children, and the only girl. Her oldest brother, David Blackwell, of the Rao-Blackwell statistics theorem, got a PhD in mathematics from the University of

Illinois at twenty-one. He chaired the math department at Howard University before becoming the first Black tenured professor and math department chair at University of California, Berkeley, which in 2018 named a new dorm for him. Uncle Dave's theorems are foundational to artificial intelligence, which is why the tech giant Nvidia named their revolutionary super chip Blackwell. His appointment to Berkeley had been delayed by a decade because the wife of the then mathematics department chair used to hostess faculty gatherings and didn't want a Black man in her house.

Along with the majority of Black people in Centralia, the Bibbs and O'Neals lived in Northtown, which was also home to the majority of Black businesses, churches, culture, and identity.

My parents' generation grew up in the mid-twentieth century, when Black Centralia businesses constituted a world unto themselves. There was the trucking business of Uncle Skee, the garbage-hauling business of Roscoe Meeks, and the candy stores of Miss Susie Lee Davis and of the Burrises, a son of whom, Roland Burris, was best man at my parents' wedding and later, briefly, a US senator from Illinois. There were tailors, hairdressers (and earlier, the barbershop of Charles Smith, who my great-grandfather was named after), restaurants, pool halls, auto shops, and mutual aid societies that grew up with the railroad town of Centralia as well.

Lawson was one of those Black family names that everyone knows, but then everybody knows everybody in small towns, period, let alone in the Black parts in the 1950s. Rolland Lawson was one of Daddy's best friends. I visited with him shortly before he died. He had his good days and his bad days. We were reading the names of Black businesses long gone when he yelled out: "Big Deal Bar-B-Que?! It might look nasty but it sho' tastes good!!!" Turns out Lawson's grandfather had owned Big Deal.

Black people in Northtown had each other, but Momma felt the sting of segregation alone. In sixth or seventh grade, she and her classmates went to paint the downtown shop windows for Halloween, with the promise of a prize for the best one. They stopped for hamburgers at Walgreens, but after they ordered, the waitress told Momma she couldn't eat inside. She had to take her hamburger outside to eat, the waitress said.

"My little friends just looked at me. And I felt, like, what's wrong with me, you know? I hadn't experienced anything like this. Anyway, I said, 'No thank you.' I didn't take the hamburger and I didn't eat. I just left. I went outside, but I left."

Momma told me this story as an eighty-year-old woman, and I could still hear the hurt and vulnerability in her words. I was reminded that the things we cannot clear from our heads get added to our voices, or even our bodies. Momma's young white friends, who stayed, didn't ask why she'd been excluded. Centralia didn't have those old segregation signs that said WHITE and COLORED, but people obeyed them anyway.

"I don't think they knew why [we were segregated] unless they were coached at home or something to exclude me, or that we were different," Momma told me. "But I certainly wasn't. I was just young and wild and free to play, you know, run, jump, hop, crawl, climb, do anything I wanted to until I found that I couldn't. Or that I was different or whatever, I think that was my first wake-up call."

Centralians of my parents' age and older tell stories of the segregated movie theaters. Fairview swimming pool was off-limits to Blacks, but you could catch a double feature with friends and be at the movies all day. Black people had to sit in a certain section of the theater, and when another theater opened, they had to go upstairs to the balcony in that one.

"I'm not talking about the first balcony. You're up there where the lights are almost shining." Charlotte Washington said she didn't go to the movies much growing up, because her mother told her she didn't want to have to *come up there*. And Washington knew what she meant. Everybody knew what she meant. Knew that Black parents (aunts and uncles, cousins, fictive kin, etc.) only "come up there," wherever there is, by way of trouble with whiteness. So doing anything that required the involvement of Black parents was to be maximally avoided.

Even the State Theatre, the smallest of the three theaters in Centralia, was segregated. Joel Berkley recalled: "And you know, Black people did things to protest. Some things were nice and some things were bad." The State only held about fifty people, with three back rows on one side for Blacks. The floor sloped downward, which gave them the high ground. "The bathroom was next to the screen, which was up front," said Berkley. "If there were no other Black people sitting in front of them, they let it run down." Black boys would pee on the floor so it would run down the aisle to where the white folks, in the best seats, were sitting. It was the mid-1950s, and Northtown was restive.

"You got to pay the cost to be the boss," said Berkley.

At the Illinois Theatre, the Black kids would rain paper or popcorn down on white kids from the balcony.

I don't remember when I found out Momma Susie didn't like white people. If there was an origin story, I never heard it. But it was something everybody knew, and that which was understood didn't need to be spoken. In Momma Susie's case, it was a macro-animus that, without contradiction, peacefully coexisted with the story of one of Daddy's best friends and high school teammates, a white kid named Norman "Junior" Schuchman. He and Daddy met as freshmen athletes, and a few years later, Junior Schuchman was the only white player in the starting five of the storied Centralia Orphans basketball team, on which Daddy also starred. Schuchman was poor, even by the standards of those who viscerally understood the feel of the word. His father was violent, he'd been kicked out of his house at twelve, and he slept, mostly, upstairs at the Meadow Woods Country Club. Then he and Daddy became fast friends, and he would sleep at Momma Susie and Papa Lonnie's house. And even when he didn't, they made sure he was fed. When Momma Susie packed Daddy's school lunch, she packed the same lunch for Junior Schuchman. Every day when Daddy ate at the Confectionary, Junior Schuchman ate at the Confectionary. "I would have starved to death if it hadn't been for Susie and Lonnie O'Neal," Junior Schuchman told me. He went on to become the head of his own engineering firm and the city manager of Centralia before retiring to Florida.

Others had less-accommodating stories of Momma Susie and white folks. My cousin Amber, the youngest of the Bibb-O'Neal grand-kids, took my place in Momma Susie's chain of custody summers. Amber recalled one summer day: Momma Susie was in her pajamas in her green chair, she was sitting on the couch, and they were watching the stories, when a white woman knocked on the door. Amber got up to let her in, and the woman greeted my grandmother.

"Oh, Miss Susie, I just came to bring you some tomatoes from my garden. They're so good!"

Momma Susie smiled at her sweetly. "Oh, thank you. Mmm-hmmm. Yes. Thank you."

The woman visited for a few minutes, then left. That's when my grandmother told Amber, "Go put this shit in the garbage! I'm not eating anything that she gave us. I don't need any tomatoes from a white woman."

"It was clear this woman was trying to be very charitable, you know?" said Amber. "She was well dressed. I could tell she wasn't from right there. I was shocked by two things. One, that Momma Susie felt that much animosity that she wouldn't want to eat something that was so good. But more important to me was the juxtaposition. The way Momma Susie changed. I mean she didn't show that white woman any attitude. She was smiling this, like, syrupy-sweet smile. 'Oh, okay, thank you, mmm-hmmm.' Then the way the smile just dropped off her face when the woman walked out, and she told me to throw the tomatoes away. It was just very impactful to me. Obviously, I still remember it all these years later. I mean if you don't like her, why did you even have to pretend that you did?"

Why, indeed?

❄ ❄ ❄ ❄

The Illinois Central Railroad wound its way through Illinois, birthing small town after small town along its path—towns built as much on racial exclusion as they were on railroad jobs. This nearly forgotten bit of Americana included the "sundown towns," as chronicled by historian and author James W. Loewen, that dotted the exits along our drive from Chicago to Centralia. Effingham and Vandalia, towns for which I can still see the big highways signs, had been sundown towns. Centralia shared an exit with Salem, which once posted signs on all the main roads into town warning Black people to be gone before dark.

The town of Anna, eighty miles south of Centralia, which residents and those in nearby hamlets have long understood to mean "Ain't No Niggers Allowed," expelled its Black citizens in 1909, after a man from Anna was lynched in nearby Cairo. It was part of what Loewen called the "waves of ethnic cleansing" in America and the nadir of race relations. Or one of them, I suppose. All-white towns, hamlets, and enclaves are all white on purpose, no matter what the white people living there tell their children, and Illinois has a particularly grievous history, with tentacles all over the here and now. Of the 671 towns with populations over one thousand, an estimated 472 were sundown towns. "We were surrounded," my mother once told me. "That's why we had to stick so close together." It's a useful thing to think about when white people cry reverse racism.

We were surrounded on slave ships, surrounded on plantations, surrounded in Bibbtown and Black Bottoms, in Northtowns and Southsides, where we were not just surrounded, you understand, we were fucked with, and surrounded in America. Illinois, Goddamn!

When I've talked with white people about segregation, in Russellville; in Centralia; in Washington, DC; and other places, they often invoke those revered Black figures of bygone days that made such an impression on them. They tell me the story of that Black fella who would . . . They get all misty about that Black woman who used to . . . They invoke these folks not only as examples, you see, of what is possible between the races. But, in their estimation, this is what's possible in America if Black people, writ large, would only keep some do-right in their system, so I can see the psychic convenience of it all. Especially if I'm looking through the lens of whiteness, which my country calls patriotism with a fatuousness that makes me choke.

They give name after name of their own beloved Black figures to make racial inferences and suppositions—to draw conclusions that don't stand up to even a single layer of inquiry. It acts as a form of misinformation. White memories of race are always based on experiences that Black people have never actually had, or at the very least saw very, very differently from the white folks doing the telling.

My cousin Little Ronnie recalls how old-timers used to talk about the racist communities in central and southern Illinois. His grandfather Henderson Meeks was one of those respected and revered Centralia figures, who worked for the railroad, farmed his own land in Marion and Jefferson counties, and owned rental property, an ice company, and a coal-hauling business. When he'd finish his coal deliveries in one of those nearby communities, if it was too late to make it back home to Centralia, Mr. Meeks would park outside of town and spend the night in his truck to avoid being caught after sundown.

Cousin Harold Bibb was hired at nineteen as a laborer for the Illinois Central Railroad in 1931 after the death of his father, at forty-eight, who was also a laborer for the company. He stood no chance of becoming an engineer because Black men weren't hired as foremen, which was the first step in becoming an engineer. The Black railroaders had formed a local shop—the International Brotherhood of Firemen, Oilers, Helpers, Roundhouse and Railroad Shop Laborers—to fight discrimination.

It was about 1940 when the "first Negro foreman" was hired, Cousin Harold told the Centralia oral history project interviewer. It's not clear if he meant in Centralia or at another depot, and as of 1975, he still didn't know of any Black engineers. Perhaps there were some in the South, he speculated. When the interviewer asked Cousin Harold how he felt about his inability to advance in a way that was consistent with his capacity and skills, and whether he was angry, he denied that he was. "No, I was not angry. I realized the injustice that was being done, but being angry. No."

Cousin Harold had been active in the union fighting discrimination at the railroad. He was a warden and worshipful master at the local Black Masonic lodge, a member of the NAACP when it sued to desegregate Fairview swimming pool, and a member of the deacon board at Second Baptist. That was a lot of Black solidarity and resistance for a brother who came across so temperate. I knew just what I was hearing when Cousin Harold said he wasn't angry.

Harold David Bibb Sr. was born in Centralia in 1912 and had grown up understanding that you didn't talk freely with white people. His cousin Susie Wylene Bibb, born in 1918, understood the same. Especially not about race. No matter how earnest or well-intentioned they seemed, white people didn't know what they didn't know about what riled up other white people. Not only what could cause Black people trouble, you understand, but what even constitutes trouble when you're Black. I was reminded of that 1897 *Louisville Courier-Journal* article where one of the Black Bibbs told a white former enslaver and reporter how they'd all been moved to tears by kindly Major Richard Bibb shipping their family members off to freedom in Liberia.

White interviewers (visitors, neighbors) could ask their questions and be on their way, leaving Black people to deal with any fallout from their answers. Fallout, by the way, that white people would swear to God could never happen here. Or they refused to believe it had happened when Black folks told them that it did. Our whole-ass truth might make white people uncomfortable, and that's something historically they've enacted policies to avoid. This was why you didn't talk about the vicissitudes of Black life to white people. *There was simply no future in it*, I imagine Momma Susie would have said if someone had interviewed her. Or more likely, she would have just looked at them and smiled tightly.

In another one of the 1975 Centralia oral histories, a former Ku Klux Klansman whose name wasn't recorded talked about a cross burning, between 1911 and 1920, perhaps three or four miles southeast of town, attended by about 150 to 200 Klansmen in uniform. It makes the point about the proximity of ardent racists in this small town, and the power they held over the everyday life of Black folks. It makes the point that Black folks could never tell who they were talking to.

"I never recognized any of 'em, but I found out later that one of them, the chief of this unit, was [name withheld], the Chief of the Locomotive Engineers.... I don't think that this Klan here existed very long. And I don't think they did anything that very much outta the way, or underhanded, as, as the Klan did in other places—some of them that were vengeful in one way or another and did spite work."

This Centralia Klansman didn't pay his dues, he never got a uniform, he didn't like what they were doing in other places, so he was only a member for a couple of months, he said. A casual member.

Of the one meeting he attended, on Fayette Road, he said this: "I think more, it was just kind of a method they had of impressing the Negroes and, uh, making them keep their place, you know.... I think in places where [they were dealing with] Negroes and Southern white women or something, like, that's why they, they took action against them and things like that. They were pretty rough with them for a while . . . just kind of impressing on them. Make them keep in line more than anything else. But I never attended one of their private meetings. And I suppose they had a committee, so I don't know too much about it. But our chief of engineers here was the chief of Klan here too."

Cousin Harold had been clear-eyed about the racism that prevented Black railroad workers in Centralia, and elsewhere, from being engineers. And so too was the Klansman who said the chief railroad engineer—whose name he had spelled out—had also headed the local KKK.

The Klansman was another voice that traveled through time and revealed a specific code. The Klansman's formulation, that Black people were giving whites a hard way to go, contended that any demand, action, and advocacy for fair treatment while Black was subversive. This is why being Black and doing anything is always doing two things.

It explains the brick wall white people sometimes hit when their affections toward particular Black individuals, or classes/castes/ teams of Black folks, are undone by any signs of Black self-interest. Especially as that self-interest challenges white cultural, economic, or political hegemony. They are not good at sharing the world or managing their discomfort when they are compelled to. It explains why some white folks, tens of millions across the nation, are so aggrieved, even as they'll claim all the Black folks they love. And I believe in some narrow ways that's true. That aggrievement and love can coexist.

It's just that Black people are like that old Flat Stanley cutout from childhood to some folks. As long as we keep smiling and keep our mouths closed, white people can take us, more or less, wherever they go. It's not an affliction of the heart; it's more of an indexing problem. You only have to read a couple of entries in the United States Census Slave Schedules to recognize that when you've built a whole system and an entire self based on plunder for nearly 250 years, it can rearrange you in lasting ways that can be difficult to unwind.

It is why nothing meant more to white people's sense of themselves than Black people. It was so meaningful to be white, according to the government of the United States, because it was so very important not to be Black.

White people who don't know this history may not recognize this telling, especially not the parts predicated on race, which is over and around it and woven throughout. They are too busy talking about how they don't see color. This is why there are those who could scarcely imagine someone like Momma Susie, or so much of the subterranean backstory of places like Russellville, Kentucky, and Centralia, Illinois. It is why there are those who can scarcely imagine the Bibb family, in Black and white, who were capable of such great and terrible things.

CHAPTER 7

THE STORIES

Cousin Nina and Freedom Summers

From the moment we hit Centralia, I could hardly wait for somebody to drive me to my cousin Nina's house. It was different for all nine grandkids of Momma Susie, but for me, every summer, Nina's house, and all it stood for, was, indisputably, where it was at.

Nina was the daughter of Momma Susie's baby sister, my aunt Ellen Louise Franklin (née Bibb). Nina was just two years older than me, but far more knowing in all kinds of ways that made sense for young girls coming of age while Black in small Southern-feeling towns deep into the twilight of the industrial Midwest.

Sometimes, it would take days for me to get to Nina, but there was simply nothing for it. My parents, Betty Lou and Lonnie Gerald, my uncle Ronnie and his wife, Aunt Carolyn, and my aunt Jackie scarcely figured into my June and July logistics. When they returned to the town where they were born and raised, or where Aunt Jackie still lived, they had their own preoccupations to see about. There were old haunts and old haints that required visitation. There was family to see, or avoid, wounds to salve, or inflict, scars to pick at, and duties to line up for. Who could tell the shrouded inner workings of grown Black lives? Eventually, one of Momma Susie's drivers, or Aunt Hilda's store boys, got me to Nina—or perhaps Aunt Ellen and Uncle Simon picked me up—and that opened a whole wide expanse of summer happenings.

For a time, Aunt Ellen, Uncle Simon, Nina, and her brother Daniel lived in a big house, in a neighborhood with wide streets at the west edge of town. This was before Aunt Ellen and Uncle Simon divorced and Aunt Ellen moved to a trailer on McKee Street, in Northtown on land that had Black Bibbs for generations. Nina was Malibu Barbie brown with sandy-brown hair that curled all down her back. She had connections. That is to say, she had her big brothers—Aunt Ellen's sons Doug and Robert—and older cousins or women Robert was familiar with or had children by, who Nina often babysat. Somebody in that constellation could be counted on to take us where we wanted to go.

Nina would figure out our cash needs to go swimming at Fairview Park, rent lockers, and buy snow cones. And she always had an extra $1.50 handy, in case one of us younger cousins came up short. She could ride me on the handlebars, or later the back seat of her bicycle, past all the cute boys, without falling, or even seeming to notice they were there.

One July afternoon, we walked from the Fairview Park to Dairy Queen, along a four-lane stretch of road, as passing drivers laid on their horns, whistling out their windows, and hollering our way. Even white boys. Especially white boys, since the town had so many of them. We'd gone swimming and we were both still wearing our bikinis. I was maybe thirteen years old.

"Take a picture, it might last longer!" Nina yelled back, and we kept walking, casual as you please. I didn't know why, but I felt giddy. I felt a powerful undertow pulling on me that summer. This was one of the things I wouldn't have been allowed to do, or even thought to do, if I wasn't with Nina. If we'd been seen by the wrong Black folks during our walk, they might have pulled over. Might have made us get in the car. Driven us back to Momma Susie's house and called my parents.

If that were to happen, Nina would have gone in with me. She would have pleaded for me not to get in trouble, and claimed the walking and the bikinis were all her fault. Nina was my protector. And the protector for a lot of other cousins as well. But absent my involvement, I don't think anybody would have been scandalized enough to call my aunt Ellen about us walking around in our bathing suits. Or, they may not have wanted to make Aunt Ellen mad, knowing that would have gone badly for Nina.

Nina was her youngest, her only daughter, adopted at five years old, along with her older brother Daniel, from a white woman Aunt Ellen used to work with. Nina's white biological mother was poor, and undereducated, with dirt prospects. She was about to marry a man who wanted nothing to do with two half-Black kids, she told my aunt Ellen.

Her family was embarrassed by her, or more specifically by her two biracial children. "We used to have to duck down in the back of the car because they were ashamed of us," Nina said. "One day a car came to get us. We got in the car and looked back, and [my mother] was gone."

They might have been on the verge of being "state kids," which is what Momma Susie used to call children who were caught up in the child services system. But Nina's biological mother had an arrangement with Aunt Ellen, who, along with Uncle Simon, adopted them.

I spent weeks at a time with Nina, Aunt Ellen, and Uncle Simon Franklin, who owned a barbecue restaurant and, in the mid-1970s, became Centralia's first Black chief of police, and they treated me fine. Nina called them Mommy Ellen and Daddy Simon (pronounced *Day Simon*), so at some point I called them that as well. I didn't have to do many chores, if any at all, and nobody said a cross word to me. But Nina and Daniel were a different story.

Nina! Niiiiina! Niiiiiinaaaa!!! Aunt Ellen would yell out from every part of the house. *Yes, ma'am*, Nina would say, as she ran to attend to Mommy Ellen. *Clean this room, put up these groceries, sweep this floor! And you'd better be quick about it.*

Perhaps it was the same for all children of the 1970s and 1980s, but it was usual and customary for grown people to treat kids like servants when I was a child. Friends my age joke that grown people would call you to change the channel in a room where they sat just a few feet from the TV, whether you were in another room, another part of the house, or outside across the street: *Change the TV. Bring me some ice water. Throw this in the garbage. Scratch the dandruff out of my head.*

But that thing between Aunt Ellen and Nina (never with Day Simon) was different. Aunt Ellen didn't treat Nina like a servant; she treated her like a slave. There was violence in Aunt Ellen's voice. Violence in the timbre of her constant, barking commands. I was there. I saw it. I didn't know what to make of it, so I didn't make anything of it at all, except perhaps to be secretly glad it wasn't me. Some of us Centralia cousins were protected, and nobody would dare touch us. And some were not.

"I remember one time I was so embarrassed. Uncle Morris was there and she [Mommy Ellen] wanted me to make some spaghetti. I asked her how do you make it and she was like, 'You know how.' I put the water in the pot and I didn't let it boil. She got a gallon of milk in the refrigerator and hit me in the head with it. I was more embarrassed than hurt. 'That's not how you do it!' she said. I was probably, like, ten years old, cooking dinners, cleaning chitlins. I put toilet paper up my nose to cut down the smell. Picking greens and string beans, while she laid on the couch."

"I'm sorry. I didn't know," I told Nina when we were both middle-aged.

"You knew," she said quietly.

But I did not. Mommy Ellen didn't hit Nina when I was there, and I was not constituted to recognize warning signs. Trouble was a personal binary; you were either in it or you weren't, based on something you did or didn't do. To the extent the cohort of children I belonged to had language to understand abuse, it was all just wrapped around meanness. We heard Charlie Bibb had been mean; Uncle Bobby, who lived with us in Chicago and babysat us, was mean; Aunt Ellen was mean to Nina and Daniel. To more than a few people, Momma Susie was mean, but that had to be different, right? Though I can scarcely hold the thought.

Nina didn't tell anybody when Aunt Ellen hit her. But how would she even open her mouth to speak it, before Oprah, before social media, before awareness? Who, after all, would she tell? And what possible difference would it make? The whole of Black life was constituted to keep us away from white people—away from their arbitrary rule-making and racist or self-serving views of justice, and the layers of ruin they carried with them everywhere they treaded. In that context, for those times, what folks did with their kids was treated as those folks' business.

Nina always babysat her younger cousins. Mostly the kids of Aunt Ellen's son Robert Bibb. Robert had that mean gene too. Aunt Ellen checked him into a mental hospital when he was younger. He was taking drugs, he shaved his head, he started screaming at Aunt Ellen. Nina felt better keeping an eye on his half-dozen children by two different women, with more by others.

One day Nina told Aunt Ellen she was taking Robert's daughter, her four-year-old niece, Malynda, to McDonald's, but when she got back, Aunt Ellen accused Nina of leaving without telling her and raised her hand to strike her. But Aunt Ellen had blinked. Nina had grown older and stronger and tired as fuck of getting hit.

"I grabbed her arms. I would never have hit her, but I grabbed her arms and I was like, 'You . . . will not . . . hit me . . . no more. You can't move.' I said, 'You realize my strength. You realize you're not doing this to me NO MORE.' And I held her, but I wouldn't have hit her, because I'm not a disrespectful person. I know you're not supposed to hit an adult or your parents or somebody that's taking care of you. But I held her to let her know that you're not going to touch me ever again. It's over."

Nina's oldest brother, Douglas, walked in. He had to take Nina's hands. He, too, told his mother she wasn't going to hit Nina anymore. Told Nina to pack her things so she could go stay with Day Simon. She was sixteen years old. I wasn't there, and I never heard about it. Or if I did, it didn't register.

As we got older, Nina and I spent less time together. My parents divorced. My trips to Centralia dwindled, then stopped. I remember hearing about violence following Nina. Or just following Centralia. But actually, it had always been there. Girls wanted to fight Nina. "Jealous bitches," she'd call them. She carried a switchblade.

"My looks were deceiving. I could fight," she said.

I remember hearing there'd been a fight after a party one day in the mid-1980s, and one of Nina's friends had been stabbed. "She fell into my arms and died," Nina said. "I carried her to the hospital."

In 1985, my father, Lonnie Gerald, killed himself, and I largely stopped going to Centralia. Nina got married and worked at the candy factory. Aunt Ellen changed after Nina had her first child. She wanted to see her granddaughter, and Nina and Aunt Ellen got close. Aunt Ellen had "that sugar diabetes," and Nina would go over to her house to help her clean and cook and take care of herself. She visited her in the hospital. They never talked about the past. I didn't attend Aunt Ellen's funeral, although I told Momma Susie that I would be there.

It was more than three decades before I saw Nina again. She got divorced, left Centralia when the candy factory closed, and moved to Orlando. We had much to catch up on. Unlike in childhood, when my cousin Nina represented everything good summer had to offer, this time, tears and wine were involved. "I broke the cycle," she told me.

Silky and Dr. Westbrook

As we got older, hanging with Nina in the summer meant being around a bunch of little cousins she was looking after, especially Chad, Patrick, and Quentin. Quentin was a cousin by declaration, although by whose, I could not say. He was a lean, brown little guy with Coke-bottle glasses and a cloud of thick black curls that battled each other when it came to which way they should curve around his head.

Chad and Patrick—I can't swear that I always knew which was which—were the oldest sons of Robert Bibb (who later became Abdullah Idris Mubarak), my dad's first cousin and Aunt Ellen's youngest-born son. When I visited Abdullah at the long-term rehab facility in Phoenix where he'd lived for a few years before he died, he was much diminished, but he could still recount a few stories. *He's a real one*, I remember telling his roommate

By that time, Robert had been Abdullah for nearly three decades, but I'd also known him by other names. For a while when I was young, he rented the pool hall / arcade / game room owned by my grandparents known as the Little Place, which was tucked behind the Confectionary, so I'd see him often.

Every summer we pulled up to the Confectionary straight off the road, and my daddy, athlete that he had been, bounce-stepped right

Abdullah Idris Mubarak (formerly Robert "Silk" Bibb) with Baby Satchel in Lonnae's home.

back in time. In his senior high school yearbook, the quote by his picture read "I'll have a hot time in the old town tonight!" and Lonnie Gerald was quick to reprise his starring role as prince of the city: both dutiful son and the life of the party, or the one to get it started just as soon as he began pouring the drinks. Maybe that was because his parents owned a restaurant/tavern, and that fact had given him the keys to a home-court, late-night, after-the-game party place. Maybe he had a bent for alcohol, or a thirst he couldn't satisfy, but Lonnie Gerald had started drinking young. He often started early and kept going for a very long time. Daddy grabbed an apron to help Papa Lonnie, or Papa Lonnie's brother, my dear uncle Manuel, serve up smothered meats and laughter. I made a production of going behind the counter, to show off not only that I could, but that I could also get candy or a bottle of soda pop for free. I would beg Momma or any nearby relative for quarters for the jukebox, aka the Venda, as Papa Lonnie called it, referring to the name of the high-end model.

Grown people, family, folks who grew up with my parents, folks whose dirt-doing days were behind them, or mere hours into the future, would always give us a dollar on the spot, just because they hadn't seen us since last summer, and *just look at how you've grown!*

They were always asking about our "lessons," our grades, about how we were doing in school. There was a town consensus about education, and that was amplified to us because folks knew that Momma Susie put such stock in it, and what else are you going to ask the O'Neal kids when you're sitting in the Confectionary? If I'd gotten straight As, somebody, Jack O'Neal or maybe my aunt Jackie's boyfriend, Boogie, gave me five dollars. Nothing in Centralia brought you more immediate praise, attention, and love than good grades, not even long hair.

Folks would often ask, or maybe it was just me always volunteering, what I wanted to be when I grew up. It seemed everybody was in on the grades, education, future plans bit—perhaps a residual of the vaunted, all-Black, all-excellent Lincoln School. Everybody except for my daddy's first cousin Robert.

He was on some different shit.

I once told Robert I wanted to be a doctor, and he was real convict about the implications. "That's good, that's good. That means you can get me some drugs," he said approvingly. Robert was six foot four, lean, cool, memorable. He was light skinned, though more brown than yellow, with those Bibb baby freckles and a tilt to his head, but perhaps it was just that he was so tall and always looking down. He had a half-shuttered look about the eyes. Like he was always measuring people from a distance. Like he was always sizing up their angles.

He called himself Silk or Silky when I was a kid, which was short for the Silk Nigga. Friends would come over to his house to party, and reliably at some point in the night, he'd stand up and yell out, *Smooth as silk, baby! I'm smooth as silk!* And that he was. He used his smarts, his charisma, all his considerable charm to talk himself into situations and out of them. There was the time he talked himself out of getting killed in Chicago when he was kidnapped on a drug buy.

These niggas was holding him hostage for, like, two days. They were getting ready to kill him, but you know he talked his way out of that shit.

Or at least that's the story that got out. TSN was always an active participant in the shaping of his legend. That partially explains why he had so many children by so many different women. That's why it took all those years for his long-suffering wife, Rita, who everybody loved and who so loved Robert, to leave him. And why his longtime girlfriend

Geraldine, the mother of his children Malynda and Ahmad, only broke free of him at great cost. Though Robert and Rita married when Chad and Patrick were still in elementary school, the brothers kept their last name Westbrook, because that was who they'd been, Patrick said, and they wanted to honor their mother's side of the family. Their younger brothers, Charlie B and Rashid, are Bibbs, as is Malynda, while Ahmad followed his father when he converted to Islam and changed his last name to Mubarak. Patrick's younger sister by three years, Corrina Maines-Johnson, grew up in Centralia, but they didn't meet until he was a college freshman.

One of Robert's two, ever, government jobs was as a prison guard in Vandalia, about a half hour north of Centralia. After he lost the prison job, he started hustling in addition to running the Little Place, which is where he sold most of his drugs. "The first time my dad went to prison was because Uncle Danny [Nina's brother] came into the Little Place and, according to my dad, he was talking greasy about my mom," said Patrick. "My dad went out to his car and got my mom's pistol, a little twelve-shot Beretta. He came back inside; Danny was still talking shit and my dad pistol-whipped him to within an inch of his life."

The police picked Robert up that night. Robert spent the next three or four years in prison, landing back first in Vandalia, where he had been a guard years earlier. Perhaps it was a form of retribution for some secret beef or some underground infraction lost to time, since everybody knows you don't put a man in the same prison where he once worked as a guard. After a few months, he was transferred to the maximum-security prison Menard, which was the hardest time you could do in Illinois.

When Robert got out, he was selling marijuana and working

construction, doing concrete and rebar. There were two starting times for the concrete crew. The early shift started at eight a.m., and Robert's shift started at nine. He sold weed to guys on his crew, but at some point he got tired of using up every morning on his side hustle before work. One morning, when Rita had left for her job at the phone company where she'd worked since she was sixteen, and Chad and Patrick, who were both under ten, were having cereal before catching the school bus, Robert sat down with them to explain some immediate operational changes with his business: "It's two, five, or ten. If they give you two dollars you give 'em one of these. If they give you five dollars, you give 'em one of these."

"And so, guys would show up and they would knock on the door in the morning and, you know, hand me two dollars. I'd go in and get a joint out of his little cigar box and bring the joint to the dude," recalled Patrick. "Or if he handed me five dollars, I'd go in and get a nickel bag. If he gave me ten dollars, all right, here's a dime bag. And so we were, you know, like his junior sales force in his drug enterprise to his coworkers."

Rita knew Robert sold weed, but she didn't know he'd had their young sons helping him. When Robert lost his job working with concrete, he started selling weed full-time. And pills. Although he was using cocaine, it's unclear if he was also selling it. There were always drugs around, Patrick said. There were always guns.

Like Aunt Hilda, Aunt Ellen sold tips, a pull-tab gambling game, from off a master tip board, which meant she always kept cash on her. She had a pistol for protection and she kept it close. She'd have her .357 Magnum on the kitchen table next to the sugar is what I've heard, but I don't distinctly remember seeing it. Although maybe I did once. She'd have it out when she was cooking, and I have a fleeting impression of it in my mind's eye. The theory was that if somebody wanted to run up on her and rob her, they would think twice, because everybody knew Ellen Franklin was holding. When the gun wasn't in the kitchen, she kept it in her bedroom. If kids were feeling adventurous, and Mommy Ellen was preoccupied, you could lift up the mattress and find it right there.

Even though he was a felon, Robert had a pistol and a shotgun. He was out driving one day when he turned into the public housing neighborhood of his drug supplier and friend who folks called Johnny Blaze. He had spotted Robert from the end of the block. "My dad owed Johnny Blaze money for some dope. Johnny Blaze decided he needed to send my dad a message," said Patrick. Blaze ran into the house to get his shotgun. It was loaded with buckshot, and he fired into Robert's car—it was actually Rita's station wagon since Robert had crashed his Grand Marquis six months earlier—making the windshield look like a spiderweb. Johnny Blaze lowered the gun when he saw Chad and Patrick in the car. The next day, Patrick recalled, his dad and Johnny Blaze were getting high again together. Rita was furious. Shortly after that, she left Robert for good.

One summer, my cousin Ronald, who was always Little Ronnie even though he grew to be six foot four, was visiting Aunt Ellen when Robert came by high. This was when Aunt Ellen and Uncle Morris lived in neighboring trailers on McKee Street, which had been Black Bibb–owned land since at least 1920.

Aunt Ellen and Robert started arguing, and it began to escalate. Robert stood at the door of the trailer, Aunt Ellen stood in the hall-way off her kitchen, "and with my own eyes I watched as each one of them pulled out a pistol," Ronald said. "Robert pointed his gun at Aunt Ellen, who pointed hers back at him, and I'm standing in the equivalent of the cross fire. And it wasn't like I was afraid I was going to get hit, but I can't believe this is my auntie and my cousin and they literally had loaded pistols pointed at each other! And at first, when you see something that's so jacked up, you think it's a joke. So, I kind of thought at first they were joking, but then they were 'muthafuckin'' and 'Goddamning' each other, and 'I'll bust a cap,' and 'bitch!'"

Ronald never told that story to his parents, or Momma Susie, because they'd have been furious. "And I just knew I would never get to go back over there and visit. Rightly so, by the way," said Ronald. "But even as a teenager, I remember thinking this is some toxic-ass shit. I was shook after that for a long time." It's especially hard to be shook and have to be silent about it. But this was family, and Ronald didn't want to be the one to get family in trouble.

"Robert ended up closing the door. And Aunt Ellen put her gun down, and I shit you not, it's going to sound funny but after he left, I was like, 'A'ight, well, you know what, Aunt Ellen, I'mma see y'all later.' I kind of made my way out and walked back to Susie's house and I'm like, what just happened? And I can't even ask or talk about it"—because at some point, you come to understand it's not the family who will get in trouble, it's the person who tells the story.

It was all redolent of a pervasive violence. Though I didn't see it physically and wouldn't have known what to call it as a child, it was there, nonetheless. I would hear of it in shards. In sentence fragments and whispered words, over and over through the years such that even when there was no discernible story, I was left with the feel of one. With the offal, spray, and free-floating residue of beatdowns, child rapes, shootings, and killings all shrouded in an interlocking silence. In 1976, when my father's half sister, Marion, killed herself, apparently succumbing to grief over the murder of her sixteen-year-old son, Cleve, three years earlier, I was sad because everybody around me was sad.

But I hadn't even known my father had a half sister. (That was probably Momma Susie's doing, since Papa Lonnie had fathered Marion before she and Papa Lonnie got married. Everybody else just went along with it.)

Our understanding of this violence was different from how we felt living in Chicago, where the scales were bigger but more remote. Perhaps because we were not blood relations to half the town and fictive kin to the other half.

That deep history in small places came with an overlay of, if not always respectability, at least a kind of mutuality as folks lived their Black lives, in social and physical relation to one another. The land and home ownership, though tenuous for some, represented a staging area for Black people who had somewhere to go and someplace to be, even as whiteness was all around them, collecting taxes, controlling jobs, commanding labor, sealing them off in specific parts of the city but always trying to reach in. Black people had ties to each other that engendered a kind of permanency and rootedness that got passed down generationally, even as the trauma and dysfunction of disinvestment and interpersonal grievance unfolded around them.

And that got passed down too.

Patrick was trying to learn how to play solitaire one night when Robert came home drunk. Said he would teach his son. Said: "'You are going to learn how to do it right tonight.' So, he took off his belt, and every time I made a mistake," said Patrick, "he would slap me with his belt on my knee, on my legs," which were bare since it was summertime and Patrick had on shorts. If he cried, Robert hit him again. "He didn't see anything wrong with it. He was teaching me how to play the card game. Right?" said Patrick.

In the winter of his life, when memory and time had folded in on him, if you asked the former Robert Bibb about a female cousin he'd grown up with who got routinely beaten, he'd say this: "I used to see ass whoopin' all the time. I used to get an ass whoopin' every day. Did I raise my hand [to speak up or fight back]? Ellen would've smoked that ass. She used to whoop my ass."

And if you asked him if he'd known about a relative who'd been sexually abused by a friend of the family, he said: "That could very possibly have been. Momma was getting ready to get in his ass one time because he assaulted me. I was eight, nine, ten, something like that. You ain't gotta do nothing. I take care of that business. It ain't to where I can't defend myself. I ain't got that old or that young where I can't defend myself."

The worst beating of Patrick's life didn't happen to him. It happened to Quentin. Aunt Ellen treated Quentin and his older brother, David, like grandsons. (Although only David, who was the son of Aunt Ellen's late nephew, Charles O'Neal Sr., was related to her biologically.)

There was a line of trees and bushes between Aunt Ellen's and Uncle Morris's trailers, and one day, Quentin thought it would be a good idea for him, Chad, and Patrick to set them on fire. But the fire got big. Bigger than they thought it would, such that they had to run and tell Aunt Ellen. Uncle Morris came out and sprayed it down with a garden hose.

"Mommy Ellen took Quentin inside," said Patrick. "It was the most violent beating I'd ever witnessed.

"First, she grabbed an extension cord, and she was whipping him on the legs. I don't know if that just wasn't satisfying enough or what it was that escalated it to where she grabbed a curtain rod, literally ripped the curtain rod off the wall, and began hitting Quentin about the legs and in the thighs; she didn't hit him in the head or anything. But I just remember Quentin being curled up on the floor while she was beating him. He was probably eight. We were just standing there frozen, watching and wondering if we were next. And I don't know why she didn't whip us and beat us. I have my theories as to why—but she didn't. She finished with Quentin, and he was just lying on the floor for what seemed like a half hour. I don't know how long it was in reality, but he laid there on the floor in the hallway right by that window. He laid there for a long time. He was apologizing and crying. Saying, 'I'm sorry! I'm sorry! I didn't mean to do it,' and all of that. Like I said, violence was sort of always around."

In a violent world, everybody gets touched. But since Chad and Patrick were Aunt Ellen's grandchildren by blood, they were treated a little better. And sometimes that's enough to make a difference in life. It did in Bibbtown, where the light-skinned formerly enslaved—long understood to be the sons and daughters of the white Bibb men, or to have children whose fathers were white Bibbs—got more and better land, among other things.

This is a different legacy than what was presented and preserved for the white Bibbs, I imagine. The history is newer for those of us who don't have family papers archived in universities or access to genealogical research, but it's a story just as old. Slavery was a crime of violence and abuse. Slavery was a crime of sexual trafficking. (And we already understand that trauma is generational.) Our Bibb family birthright is every bit as American as the emancipating Major Bibb, the old Chancellor Bibb, the Governors and Senators Bibb, John Bigger Bibb, and all those who, for more than two centuries, have had a hand in chronicling and curating their side of the Bibb family in America.

Our stories are simply the other side.

In the early 1990s, after Robert's brother Doug, a musician and army veteran, Nina's protector, died of AIDS, Robert went on a yearlong drug binge such that Chad and Patrick had a gallows bet about when he'd die. He was homeless and destitute when he went to the Islamic Center in Centralia, where the brothers in the mosque allowed him to clean up, cut grass, and live in the basement as long as he stayed clean.

Robert became a devout Muslim, changed his name to Abdullah Idris Mubarak, and kept living. He connected with his kids, some who had especially missed him and adored him, though all of them had struggled to one degree or another with some form of addiction. And day-by-day overcoming.

Quentin's brother, David (he and my brother Chucky had the same father), took me to see Abdullah at that nursing home in Phoenix. Abdullah had a hand in all their lives growing up, and it was David, who he'd moved to Phoenix to be near, who found him on the floor three days after he'd had a stroke. At seventy-one, Abdullah, who needed help to sit up, was not so much a shadow of his former selves, but rather an aggregate of them all.

Abdullah popped up unexpectedly at my house outside Washington, DC, in 2002. He'd had trouble finding it, so he just walked my neighborhood with a few of his Muslim brothers for a bit. He was a thin, six foot four, bearded, light brown–skinned man wearing a full thobe and a kufi. He looked for all the world like Osama bin Laden, but my neighbors pointed him in my direction.

That must have been some smooth talking.

Smooth as silk, baby, I'm smooth as silk.

(I also lived in a mostly Black neighborhood, which often comes with more attenuated powers of discernment about the range of Black people in the world and in our families. About what constitutes danger, and who is simply somebody's cousin Robert who now goes by Abdullah. It's a useful skill to have in a diverse country, in a public world.)

Abdullah stood in my living room and I asked him how in the world he'd been allowed to fly, allowed to board a plane. "I bet you'll clear an airport, won't you? How did you even get here?" I joked.

At the nursing home, Abdullah talked a bit about my daddy, and Momma Susie's brother Uncle Hickey and the Chicago Police Department, where both my dad and Hickey had been officers. He talked about his seven children and said he'd just finished talking to Malynda Bibb, his youngest daughter (by one month), who served time in prison for selling drugs and now runs her own financial services company. Abdullah was close to her and her younger brother Ahmad, though one of Malynda's earliest memories was seeing her father beat their mother nearly to death when Malynda was four. "I think to myself all the time, I was born into trauma, dysfunction, addiction, manipulation," Malynda said. "Like, I was born into this ball of mess."

As we were leaving, Abdullah called out to David: "Hey, don't be tardy with those visits."

Months after my visit, Abdullah Idris Mubarak died.

People go different ways with their pain. But even when they go far in life, that doesn't mean the trauma didn't happen. That it doesn't cost still, and always.

In 2001, my cousin Quentin, whose curls, and glasses, and laughter were part of my summer reel-to-reel, died at twenty-nine, of a heroin overdose.

My cousin Patrick has a PhD in education policy from the University of Illinois.

When Patrick visited his father in Phoenix, there were things Abdullah could no longer recall, but he remembered to introduce his son as Dr. Patrick. That was the former Silk Nigga, late in life, claiming his part in his son's education. And who is to say it wasn't so? Part of education is condemning a path that you've already walked so your children, and their children, don't have to. And even if Dr. Kyle Patrick Allen Westbrook, who folks from back in the day still call Patrick, didn't carry the Bibb name, everybody knew the former Robert Bibb's son was an educated man.

I visited Patrick one night, and he cooked me salmon with the fresh basil he'd grown in his garden, outside the house he'd rehabbed himself in Chicago. Huge maps of political and geographic regions of the world covered many of the walls. Later we went downstairs to his music studio, where he'd taught himself to play the keyboard and drums during the covid lockdown. (A few years after that, he released his first album, *delicada*.) "Did you get more than your fair share of gifts, my cousin?" I asked him.

I called him a Renaissance man, but it was Blacker than that, and I'd seen it before. It was a bent toward achievement, and especially education, that runs up and down Black time lines. That comes from people who drilled into their kids you have to be twice as good as white people at everything you do. It is a manifestation I saw in our Bibb (O'Neal, Blackwell) family tree. The lawyers, the reverend doctor, the ER doctor, the double degreed. The educators and entrepreneurs. It was a hedge against all our historical and family odds. It was a nearly primal desire to take our Black cards and run a Boston. Or die trying. And folks did both.

"People can be predisposed to addiction, but if they're not in the right conditions and circumstances, that predisposition can go a lifetime without ever expressing itself," Patrick said. "If you're not in a family that represses, represses, represses, and then has these fits of rage, if you're not in a family that has some . . . *dysfunctional* views of sex and sexuality . . . then that seed doesn't have fertile soil to sprout. But if you're in that world, then there's all kinds of seeds that can sprout."

None of his brothers have been violent, Patrick said. But "Charlie struggles with addiction, I struggle with addiction. I've learned to channel it into productive addictions, which is why you described me as some sort of Renaissance man. I just know that I have this addictive side of me and I need to feed it with cooking, or I need to feed it with music. I need to feed it with home improvement. I need to feed it with writing. I need to feed it with building a company. I know enough about myself to know that if I didn't, I would feed it with alcohol and I would feed it with cigarettes. I've experimented with all the drugs in high school but grew out of that really fast. Whatever that thing my dad has, I have it and Charlie has it. I've just learned how to express it in ways that aren't going to be counterproductive," said Patrick. In ways that don't haunt children.

When Abdullah was Robert, he promised his wife, Rita, he'd sell the car his friend Johnny Blaze shot into. But he never did. They kept that car for years. It was the family car, the one Patrick learned to drive in. When his mom finally got rid of the car, the windshield was still broken, with lines in the glass going everywhere, like a spiderweb.

Traci and Uncle Ronnie

Nearly eight years after my father killed himself, I asked his brother, my uncle Ronnie, to walk me down the aisle. I hadn't seen him, or any of Daddy's people, much since Daddy died. I'd hear about Bibbs' and O'Neals' comings and goings and doings sometimes, but I was in Washington, DC, making my own way, trying to reconstitute myself, find community, and heal. I was not yet a reporter, but about to be a wife.

I had last seen Uncle Ronnie and Aunt Carolyn a year before at their home in Elgin, Illinois, a far-northern Chicago suburb, where both were educators. Education was the family business, as far back as David Bibb, teaching at the Lincoln School in the early years of the twentieth century. It was, historically, one of the few professions open to educated Black people, who taught, guided, and advocated for Black children before the 1954 *Brown v. Board of Education* Supreme Court ruling desegregated public schools. Just like my parents and my sister, my aunt and uncle were teachers and administrators. As his son, my cousin Little Ronnie, puts it, Uncle Ronnie had a genius for school management. In 2014, Sheridan Elementary School in Elgin, Illinois, was renamed Ronald D. O'Neal Elementary School in his honor.

At my last visit, my grandfather Papa Lonnie had made a batch of his famed chicken and dumplings, and when I went for seconds, a watchful Momma Susie warned that if I kept it up, I was going to be a fat bride. This was the way in our family. Take something good and find a potential peril. If nothing comes of it, fine. If calamity (however problematically defined) comes to pass, folks who take satisfaction in that kind of thing could say they warned you. That they saw it coming. Could claim special insights. But distance had given me perspective, and I was just happy Momma Susie was paying enough attention to tease me.

It hadn't been terribly long since he had seen me, but I had probably changed to my uncle Ronnie's eyes. Or, at the very least, grown up. I wore a fitted, mermaid-style dress, with the sleeves off my shoulders and my hair upswept, and when Uncle Ronnie opened the door to the bride's room at Beth Eden Baptist Church in Chicago, he saw me standing there young and happy, looking forward to seeing the uncle who looked so much like my daddy. To my surprise Uncle Ronnie started pumping his fists.

"All right! All right!" he cheered, and he broke into a little side-to-side shuffle. I'd call it a happy dance, but few who knew Ronald D. O'Neal would believe it. Uncle Ronnie didn't say anything else, but he didn't have to. Uncle Ronnie made me feel like he was happy to stand in for my dad. That he was proud of how I was turning out. He made me feel like I was every bit my mother's daughter, which was the

Lonnae with Uncle Ronnie.

highest compliment anyone could give me. I imagine it is the way a father's approval would feel to a daughter on her wedding day, and perhaps over many moments of their lives, but I'm only speculating. Not because I didn't have a father, but because if your father kills himself on Father's Day when you are eighteen, then obviously he was unavailable in all kinds of ways for years before that.

My next Uncle Ronnie moment came more than fifteen years later, a year or so before he died. He had been ill, and I decided my then husband, three kids (who were teens and tweens), and I needed to make the drive from suburban Washington, DC, to suburban Chicago for Thanksgiving. Uncle Ronnie had made breakfast with griddle offerings galore, reminding me of those big Sunday morning meals my dad and dads everywhere seem to specialize in.

Afterward, I grabbed a broom to join everyone else cleaning up. I wanted to show myself to be a quality niece, with good home training. To show that I was down-to-earth and grounded in good scrubbing, wiping, and sweeping techniques.

Uncle Ronnie was watching old Westerns in the family room but paused it when he saw me. "Girl, that broom don't even look right in your hands!" he told me, and I instantly stopped sweeping.

"I know, RIGHT?! Uncle Ronnie, oh my goodness! You are the only one who gets me!!!" We laughed a good while before I picked the broom up again. That visit was the last time I saw him.

I have many memories of Uncle Ronnie, all of them fond, if remote. But those two meant the most. Those two made me feel like I had a father, or something close, when the father I had was long gone. When measured against a lifetime of absence, it was not a lot to go on. But then, some people don't even get that.

I was often wistful about the stories I heard from Uncle Ronnie's kids. Especially his oldest, Traci O'Neal Ellis. It seemed Uncle Ronnie was always having to get between Traci and some troubled white folks. Would that my daddy ever paid close enough attention to engage anybody about me for any reason, I told Traci. And here Traci was, "wishing that my dad would go get some business other than mine."

One story I well remember happened near the end of one of those long Centralia summers. Traci;, my sister, Lisa; and Traci's cousin Felice were at St. Clair Square mall with Aunt Carolyn and her best friend, Felice's mom, Eunice Garrett (this makes Felice not a blood cousin, but never underestimate the power of fictive kinship with Black folks).

I was at Momma Susie's house when she got word something had gone wrong. I remember the way the air changes when the trouble call comes and there are white people involved. Traci had met up with my sister, Lisa, and Felice at Burger Chef.

Lisa told her some white kids stuck their fingers in the salad dressings, tasting different ones.

"I looked over at them and I'm, like, that's super unsanitary," Traci said. "And then I went back to minding all my own business."

Later, as they were leaving, one of the white guys grabbed Traci's arm. "I saw you talking about us," he said.

"Nobody's talking about you other than you stuck your fingers in the dressing and that's nasty, but let go of me," said Traci.

He wouldn't let go. "You fucking nigger," he said.

"I hauled off with my free hand and smacked him and that became the brawl. All four of them jumped on me. The manager came over and grabbed me and started holding me from behind, but while this woman is holding me, one of the kids is wailing on me. Like I'm getting the smack beat out of me because I'm being held."

The police came, arrested Traci, and let the white kids leave the mall.

The police officers didn't explain to Aunt Carolyn why they'd let the other kids leave. And when she told them she was parked on the other side of the mall, that she didn't know her way to the police station, and begged *Can you wait to take her, so I can follow you?* the police officer refused.

A random Black man who happened to be nearby told aunt

Carolyn that he knew where the station was and she could follow him. "Just some angel dropped into the middle of this story," said Traci. "I didn't see him before, I haven't seen him since."

At the police station, one of the white teens saw Traci in an empty waiting room. Told her he was going to kick her "nigger bitch ass." She stood up and a police officer entered, with his hand on his gun. He ordered her to sit down, and started laughing with the white kid.

I remember the phone call to Momma Susie's house, trying to find Uncle Ronnie. She tracked him down, instantly, probably at the Confectionary, and he hopped in the car to make the hourlong drive to the police station where Traci was being held. I was intrigued by what it meant to be track-down-able, because I've often known men who simply were not.

"I know exactly when my father arrived," Traci said. "I heard him before I ever saw him. I heard, 'I want to speak to the police chief,' with a booming voice. He did not show out. He wasn't cussing him out but he showed up as an angry Black man and 'I want to talk to the chief of police. I want to talk to somebody in charge.'"

The white officer in charge told Uncle Ronnie that Traci assaulted four teenagers, by herself. That they had scratches. Uncle Ronnie repeated that story back to him, and the policeman started stammering. Uncle Ronnie posted bail and they let Traci go, "and I got yelled at all the way back to Centralia—what was I doing, and why was I fighting in the mall, and tell me again what happened!"

They stayed in Centralia an extra week for Traci's court date. Momma Susie snapped at me when I tried to make a joke, so I stayed quiet. Uncle Ronnie made Traci plead guilty. He said he didn't want to have to take off work, to come back to court.

Decades later, it's something that still doesn't sit well with Traci. She had to answer for it when she applied to take the bar exam. Had to tell a board of examiners whether she had a problem with anger and violence.

I fantasize sometimes about incidents like this, or others, involving me or somebody I love. I want to get the incident report. I want to find those white kids to ask them what they remember. And what they think now. But, of course, that's not how Black people do. Because that would be all we do. We wouldn't have time for much else. And even if the white folks don't remember it, whatever *it* was, it would probably be just one little incident to them. But that's legions of them, doing their one little thing, and that math, for us, is nasty.

When Traci was grown with children, my grandfather Papa Lonnie and her uncle Rick would still tell the story of how Traci fought off four white kids and went to jail. "Traci don't take no stuff!" they joked, but the staying power in that story makes sense. Because it means something to fight back. No matter the odds. You know the game is rigged (they know it too), but it feels better to fight and claw and stand up than to lie down. Uncle Ronnie never talked about it again, Traci said. It is a reminder of forces that are bigger and older, and even more powerful than your big Black daddy. They are those of white people bird-dogging you. Come to exploit you. Come to underpay you. Come to deny your account of things, your truth, the proof of your eyes, common sense; it can all be a casualty when we get into these kinds of difficulties with white folks.

That's why even white people who scream loudly and often that there is no racism, would be apoplectic if they were treated like us when it comes to the police.

When my father died, Uncle Ronnie called my sister, my brother, and me together to talk to us, and hand us checks from the estate.

We could come to him if we ever needed anything, he said, even though he wasn't trying to replace our father. I took that to mean *Don't bother me, don't lean on me, I am not your daddy.* My sister kept in close touch with Uncle Ronnie, but I never did. It was not until Uncle Ronnie was near death that I told my cousin Little Ronnie what I took from what his dad had said, and Little Ronnie told me I had been mistaken.

By the time I realized that it was too late. Uncle Ronnie was beyond me. It had made sense to me that Uncle Ronnie wouldn't want to be my father, so I never reached out. It makes sense to me now that Uncle Ronnie would never risk being seen as trying to compete with Lonnie Gerald, so he never reached out either.

But I do have those two fondest of memories. And for that I am grateful.

Aunt Hilda's Music Box

The *Centralia Sentinel* said the road was wet the afternoon of October 17, 1967, when Charles Allen O'Neal and his wife, Jacquelyn, both nineteen, were driving home from classes at Kaskaskia College. It is unclear if that was a factor in the accident, but what is clear is that Charles and Jackie slammed into the diesel engine of a Southern Railway freight train at an unprotected railroad crossing. Both were thrown from their car and died instantly. Their infant son, Charles Allen O'Neal Jr., Chucky was six months old.

Charles Sr. was the youngest son of my great-aunt Hilda Jean O'Neal Scott (née Bibb), Momma Susie's younger sister, and sometimes foe. An Aunt Hilda sighting meant you were squarely on vacation, in a room, perhaps, full of beer and cigarettes, where conversations got loud and talk would invariably turn to the scourge of "*these* motherfuckers" who, apparently, were lurking everywhere. Three years before Charles Sr. was killed, Aunt Hilda's oldest son, Stevie Anderson, was shot and killed by his roommate at what is now Colorado Mesa University in Grand Junction, Colorado. Aunt Hilda had begged Stevie to go to school closer to home. But he wanted to be in Colorado with his stepdaddy, Aunt Hilda's ex-husband and my grandfather's brother, Alexander "Cut" O'Neal. Stevie's roommate, James A. Hollowell, pled guilty to involuntary manslaughter and received one year of probation.

After the car accident, the custody fight for baby Chucky divided the Bibb and O'Neal family. Some, like my uncle Hickey (Hickman Bibb, a Chicago police officer) sided with Aunt Hilda, who wanted to keep Chucky. Others sided with Momma Susie and Daddy, who painted Aunt Hilda as a woman made unstable by grief. My momma didn't have any say in the family's decision-makings, and adopting Chucky was no different.

The judge decided: Chucky became Momma's and Daddy's third child and only son, and since he was just six weeks

Aunt Hilda with Charles (killed in train accident) and Stevie (killed by his roommate in college).

younger than me, for all intents and purposes, I gained a twin brother. How all of that worked out in terms of that railroad settlement money, reportedly roughly $200,000, was not for me to know.

Centralia was a town full of cousins, and play cousins, aunties, and uncles, some twice removed, which could be a term of relation. But it could also stand for those folks whose story, or spirit or curse, still seemed to linger overhead, playing misty for us, picking sides, pulling strings, long after they'd left or died. Sometimes those two went together, but I do know of people who left without dying. That is to say, they were truly gone, whether or not they still drew breath. It might mean they'd needed to get out of town before settling down to die somewhere else. But it could also mean they were simply "on vacation, in Hawai'i," which is what Aunt Hilda told my brother Chucky when he'd ask to go visit our big cousin, the former Robert Bibb, when he was in jail.

While I spent summers at Momma Susie's house, Chucky always went straight to see his grandmother, to my aunt Hilda's house. Aunt Hilda made Chucky essential to processing the overlapping cruelties of her life.

I used to see her behind the bar at the Confectionary when she was working, or she'd walk through the dining area holding her tip board, going table to table collecting a dollar or two or maybe even five, for the chance to pull open the folded paper tabs and find yourself a winner.

I sometimes still think about that last visit with Aunt Hilda. I think about the through lines of money, control, and violence that striated her story. I've heard variations of these themes in stories about Centralia Bibbs, about their descendants, and in my own family my entire life, though I did not recognize them as such. It took a long time before I thought to myself, *Now where have I heard this shit before?* I remember the last thing Aunt Hilda said to me and, sometimes, I still wonder what of it was really real.

It had been many years since my childhood when I'd spent the longest weeks of every summer in Centralia and everywhere my legs carried me felt hotter than July.

My parents divorced when I was fifteen, and my father shot himself three years later, early on Father's Day morning, a week after I foretold that someone was going to get killed. I don't know who I said it to, or even if I spoke it out loud. I just know I knew. I was in summer school, in college, an hour south of Centralia, and I gave my roommate and sorority sister the phone number to my boyfriend's house. In case she needed to reach me. In case somebody died.

After I stopped visiting Centralia, I didn't call anybody, I didn't write, there were no weddings to attend, and I didn't go to funerals. There was no place in the family where I made sense to myself without the corporeal clarity of Momma and Daddy. Without Lonnie Gerald and Betty Lou to situate me, or just be there, around, even if only for the drive down I-57. There was no family architecture that could hold me. No place where I wasn't sad and scared, where I didn't feel myself falling all the time.

My father's death only added to the pall of grief that hung over us like cobwebs in rooms long shuttered. It added to the compound losses that no one talked about. At least not to me. There was no respite, even with close relatives, only tragedy and bitterness and regret oozing, like sap, from a family tree I no longer felt attached to.

I don't know what returned me to Centralia several years later, but distance, time, and accomplishment, perhaps, had made me stronger.

Made me feel safe to be there by the time I visited my once formidable Aunt Hilda. She'd had a stroke in the late 1980s and moved across and down from Momma Susie and Papa Lonnie, into one of the houses they owned. It may have been Momma Susie who told me to go see her. But perhaps she simply pointed the way (in her pajamas from her green armchair, of course).

Aunt Hilda was sitting at a kitchen table, a Formica half-moon propped against the wall, smoking Virginia Slims, or on second thought it was "Mores," which were just as long and slim (and conveniently well suited to the Black-people convention of adding an *s* to proper names that did not technically have one. Like the Jewels in Chicago). Her long, straight black hair was still pinned up, as I had only ever seen it. She may have been wearing that red lipstick that she'd possibly been born with, which let folks know that she knew that of all the Bibb girls, she'd been the most beautiful, and still laid claim to the title. But I cannot say for certain. I do know she squealed when she saw me, which was perfectly Aunt Hilda. She used to scream when she saw my brother Chucky, especially if a few months, or even a few days, had passed since the last time she saw him. A piercing, high-pitched sound such that people nearby would whip their heads around to see what was happening, as if they could have understood.

Aunt Hilda rushed up to me, animated, sticking her tongue out between her teeth as she squinted and smiled, something she did when she was delighted. The words tumbled from her mouth.

"Music, music, music, muse. The muse. Muse. Music, the muse. Music, music, muse, the muse, the muse, the muse, music, muse. Music, muse."

I matched my aunt Hilda's smile. I nodded, I hugged her, my face gave nothing away. But my insides bubbled. *Fuck*. Centralia had caught me unawares once again. I knew Aunt Hilda had had a stroke, but I hadn't known what that meant in terms of the woman in front of me. No one warned me that she could no longer talk. Of course, who would have thought to do such a thing? I'd been gone a long time. Besides, in Centralia, you opened the door, you got what you got. Weren't those the rules?

"I just graduated, Aunt Hilda," I told her. "I know it's been a long time. How are you? I'm moving to Washington. I'm going to graduate school. I'm going to be a reporter. I'm so happy to see you."

"Music, music, music, muse. The muse. Muse. Music, the muse. Music, music, muse, the muse, the muse, the muse, music, music. Music, music, music, muse. The muse. Muse. Music, the muse. Music, music, muse, the muse, the muse, the muse, music, music."

Aunt Hilda stood up. She gestured widely, urgently repeating herself—everything about her seemed to be in motion.

She smiled her trademark smile, half sticking her tongue between her teeth to grin.

"Music, music, music, muse. The muse. Muse. Music, the muse. Music, music, muse, the muse, the muse, the muse, music, music."

"I'm sorry, I don't understand what you're saying," I finally told her, gently. I never looked from her face. My smile never faltered. Aunt Hilda grabbed my hand and kissed it.

After twenty minutes or so I stood up to leave and began saying my goodbyes. I hugged her tight for a bit, then I pulled away. "You look so good, Aunt Hilda," I chirped, and she became very still. Or perhaps it was simply her words that had finally stopped moving.

"Oh, but baby, I feel so bad," Aunt Hilda told me.

I don't remember what I said after that, or if I said anything at all, but I'm sure I kept smiling. I do know she didn't speak legibly again.

"Music, music, music, muse. The muse. Muse. Music, the muse. Music, music, muse, the muse, the muse, the muse, music, music," she said before I left.

My legs were quick about it on that short walk back to Momma Susie's. It felt as if I had been caught up in some bit of magical realism. In the closing chapter of a very long story. Sometimes I wonder if I imagined the whole thing. But I know I did not, because who could make up such a thing? Especially that last part, where there was so much life, and death, behind her words.

Decades later, I recounted this story to my brother Chucky for the first time. Aunt Hilda had doted on him. Though she had other grandchildren, everybody of a certain age in Centralia will tell you she only had grandmother eyes for Chucky. And every summer when he got dropped off at her house, she'd whisper that poison in his ear. *They don't really want you. They just want the money.* "My grandmother went from talking all day, every day, to one word," my brother told me. The "music" may have been the memory of a musical jewelry box she got as a gift when she was young and hopeful.

I was in high school when my mother remarried, and my brother went to live with his grandmother in Centralia. Aunt Hilda finally got control, or at least influence, over whatever was left of the settlement money from that deadly train accident all those years before. She bought Chucky a moped and a car. She let his girlfriend spend the night and let him smoke weed—reefers, the grown folks called it—in the house. A Division II football coach once called to offer Chucky a full scholarship to play in college, but Aunt Hilda told the coach Chucky was too distraught over my father's suicide to go off to school. She didn't tell my brother about that call until years later. Even after Chucky went away to school, an HBCU in Oklahoma, Aunt Hilda was still trying to talk to him, to baby him, to whisper her internecine theories of family into his ear, but he was no longer listening to her. Or anyone, really.

We grew up hearing that Aunt Hilda allegedly had our house in Chicago burglarized when I was a child. I vaguely remember the incident. We walked in to see drawers thrown open and clothes strewn about the house. Aunt Hilda must have been babysitting us while Momma and Daddy were somewhere else, and she warned us not to say anything when they got home. She wanted to be the one to tell them about the break-in.

When Momma and Daddy pulled up, my sister, Lisa, recalled, "We all ran out to greet them. They hadn't even brought the luggage in, and I said somebody had broken into our house. Aunt Hilda had a big ring on. She punched me in the chest. She said, 'I told you not to say anything!' Why didn't Mom or Dad say anything to Aunt Hilda? I wondered. Why did they let this crazy woman punch me dead in my chest?"

After Stevie was shot, and Charles was hit by a train, Aunt Hilda's last remaining child was a darling girl named Little Hilda. (Little Hilda was long-rumored to be the daughter of Uncle Cut and a white woman he got pregnant while stationed in Germany. Uncle Cut and Aunt Hilda adopted the little girl and brought her home to Centralia after his tour of duty.) When I heard Little Hilda had died as a middle-aged woman in 2013, I didn't know the cause of death. I just remember thinking she died from having lived as Little Hilda.

Those old enough to remember said Little Hilda cowered around her momma. Widened her eyes or lowered her gaze. That she was always trembly, always bracing for the blow to come. She was very light and you could see the imprint of Aunt Hilda's cocktail ring on her cheekbones and forehead. She'd show up places with black eyes and bruised arms that were also dotted with cigarette burns.

One day Little Hilda was lying across the top of the bunk bed at our uncle Morris's house. Aunt Hilda walked in and grabbed the child by her arms, my cousin Cathy O'Neal-Windom remembered. Little Hilda was maybe eight or nine, just a few years older than Cathy. Aunt Hilda snatched Little Hilda from the bunk and she hit the floor. "Go find my house shoes!" Aunt Hilda spat. "I felt so sorry for Little Hilda," said Cathy.

I was at Momma Susie's house one day while Little Hilda was there. She was a teenager, or perhaps a young woman, to my child's eyes. She'd always had a wide smile for me, but not this time. The particulars have faded, but some things I still remember. Momma Susie was in her armchair. Little Hilda was sitting nearby, silent, as tears streamed down her face. My grandmother held the phone an inch or so from her ear, and I could hear Aunt Hilda yelling and cursing symphonically, in crescendos and waves you could hear above the TV. I was looking at Little Hilda's close-cropped, curly hair. Why did she wear it so short? I wondered.

Long after she died, I found out Little Hilda used to have hair down her back. Aunt Hilda had grabbed her one day in a fit of rage and cut it all off. I only ever knew Little Hilda with short hair. I knew her as a young wife and mother with four beautiful children, three of them little girls who would crowd around Momma Susie, who they called Aunt Baby, and scratch the dandruff out of her hair with a comb, much as I used to do as a child. My grandmother was their surrogate grandmother since Aunt Hilda didn't claim them. After a time, what I knew of Little Hilda was that she had troubles. I heard she had substance use disorder, which at the time I heard as "Little Hilda's a drug addict." I heard she was a lesbian, at a time when I didn't even know what that was. I heard she'd left her children unprotected in many ways, and they had fallen into harm.

Why did no one ever stop Aunt Hilda? I wanted to know years later. Why did none of her siblings stop her? Why didn't my father or any of the O'Neals stop her? Why, Lord, was she allowed to torture this child in full view of everyone? I've never gotten a simple answer. I've never heard any answer that wasn't bound up and compacted in race and trauma, spread over time, rooted in place and the Bibb last name.

When Aunt Hilda told the police her daddy, Charlie Bibb, hit her, they didn't do anything either. It was the 1930s in a small, segregated town where everyone knew everyone, and no one, Black or white, was inclined to take the side of a child.

"I heard it from her own mouth that she would run away as a teen because her father would beat her ass," my cousin Ronald told me. "She would get beat and I suspect all of [the Bibb siblings] did, because all of them had issues. Hickey was mean like his dad, Bobby was an alcoholic, Morris was a womanizer. I loved Uncle Morris, but he was a womanizer. Ellen was abusive to Nina and Daniel, and Robert and Doug." And of course, Momma Susie had to control the lives (and money) of everyone around her.

Save once when I was very young, Aunt Hilda never spoke a cross word to me. Perhaps because I was the sister of her adored grandson. (She had two other grandsons she had less use for until the years before she died. I've heard it was because she didn't want their mommas coming after that train settlement money.) My momma said butter dripped from her lips if she liked you. She made her store boys and errand fellas buy us food and candy and take us for ice cream. She bragged loudly and often, "I got Lonnae's hair to growing, by combing it with beer." And Lord, maybe she did.

I didn't know the extent of her abuse when I went to see her before she died. But I also don't know if it would have made a difference. I knew only that she was mean, like I knew Aunt Ellen was mean, but not to me. I was not prepared to know anything more, then. Now I'm inclined to draw a wider circle.

These are also through lines, the themes I've seen reflected in tax records that valued my fourth great-grandmother at three hundred dollars in Logan County, Kentucky, and her children at under a hundred dollars. I've seen the iron shackles found in the yard behind the Bibb House. I've seen the heartache between the lines in every will that left Black people to white Bibbs, to "dispose of however you please," and advertisements of ten-year-old "likely negro boys" offered up for sale.

Violence in service of wealth ordered the labor of my Centralia Bibbs' ancestors. It ran them out of town, upon pain of death, and kept them in other parts of towns where they could be exploited. The healers say trauma is generational, and who, now, would say that it isn't?

So are scars, ghosts, and memories, and also, sometimes, so is hope, forgiveness, and grace. At least in my observation.

Little Hilda reconciled with her mother, Big Hilda, and helped take care of her before Big Hilda died in a nursing home not long after I visited. As far as anyone alive remembers, my aunt Hilda continued to talk about the music, some say from a jewelry box, long lost, that only she could hear and speak of until she died.

Six of the eight Bibb siblings at Momma Susie's house, mid 1970s.

CHAPTER 8

CHICAGO:
A BLUES SONG FOR
LONNIE GERALD

For years, I thought my daddy killed Fred Hampton.

I would periodically google Lonnie O'Neal and the Chicago Police Department, where he'd been an officer from 1966 to 1971, and every time I did so, articles about Hampton came up. The revolutionary young Black Panther, who'd been deputy chairman of the party's Illinois chapter, was murdered along with fellow activist Mark Clark during a predawn CPD police raid in 1969, while he was asleep with his pregnant fiancée.

I couldn't bring myself to click on any of those articles. I didn't want to accidentally learn the truth, so I averted my eyes and quickly exited my search. For a long time, I simply harbored this vestigial fear that I was too reluctant to confront. Or let go.

That was how things had long gone with me and my daddy, Lonnie Gerald. Everything about him was too much. Too deep. Too sinister. Far too complex and sad to be engaged with except in tiny doses over extended periods of time. He overwhelmed my nervous system, more in death, but during his life as well. For much of my own life, I could only nibble at the edges of the story of Lonnie G.

One day, I worked up the courage to ask my mother: "Momma, did Daddy kill Fred Hampton?" She said no, though she didn't wonder why I'd asked. And I was still afraid. My father invested a lot of his identity in his authority. I was not surprised to learn that he'd been on the front lines in 1968 when the Chicago police cracked heads at the Democratic National Convention.

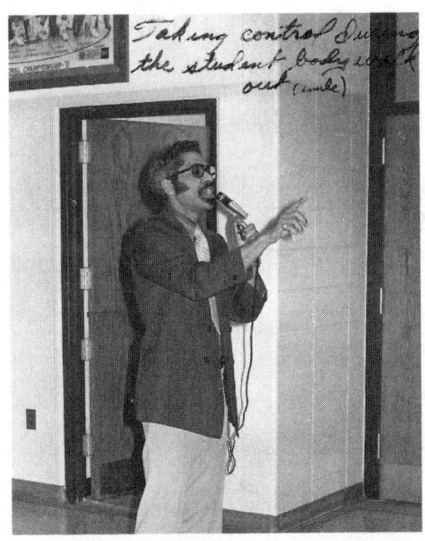

Lonnie Gerald with mic in hand "taking control" at West Side High School.

Plus, I knew he'd killed somebody. We all did.

A few years before my father's death, my brother Chucky was sitting in the passenger seat as my dad was driving. My parents were still married, we lived in a southwest Chicago suburb, and Dad was an assistant principal at West Side High School in Gary, Indiana. They stopped at a traffic light not far from the house.

Suddenly, Dad turned to face Chucky. "What would you have done if it was you? What would you have done?"

My brother just looked at him. He had no idea what Dad was talking about. He thought my father might be joking.

"What?"

"It was either him or me! What would you have done? It's either him or me."

Daddy's whole body was tensed, and he sounded untethered.

"Him?" my brother blurted out. He still thought maybe this was a joke.

"What?! It was him or me! It was him or me!!!"

"Me!!! Me!!! Me!!!"

By then, Chucky knew exactly what my father was asking.

When my newsroom colleague Soraya Nadia McDonald reviewed the 2021 movie *Judas and the Black Messiah*, I forced myself to read the review. That's how I learned my daddy had not killed Fred Hampton. Undercover FBI informant William O'Neal betrayed Hampton to his death, and that's why a search for "O'Neal" and "Chicago Police" always came back with Fred Hampton stories.

I was relieved. Trembly, perhaps. I emailed Soraya my heartfelt thanks. She urged me to take deep breaths. Sometimes you don't know the weight of something until that weight is lifted.

But you don't always feel lighter, because there's plenty more where that came from.

One night, late in my dad's tenure as a Chicago police officer, Dad and his partner had drinks with his former best friend and high school teammate, Norman Schuchman, a former Centralia city manager. Schuchman would recall decades later that they told him they knew a guy who was planning to rob a jewelry store on the South Side the next day. They were then going to rob the guy who robbed the store. A day or two later, Schuchman got a call from Uncle Simon, the Centralia chief of police who he had hired, saying my dad had shot and killed the jewelry store thief.

Not Fred Hampton. But I doubt that made any difference to my father.

When my parents moved from Centralia to Chicago in the early 1960s, it represented a kind of chain migration in the broader context of the Second Great Migration of Black people from South to North. For my dad, it widened the aperture of possibilities that had first opened with the migration of John and Pocahontas Bibb from Bibbtown, Kentucky, to southern Illinois a century before.

Like many in that second wave, my mother and father were prepared for the trip. They weren't going from farm to city like the first

Lisa, Lonnae, and Chucky in Chicago.

wave of Black migrants who moved north before the Great Depression. They had been fortified by the hard work, smarts, and resources of their Centralia parents. And they'd been raised with an ambition to make their mark on the wider world and strike a blow for the race, just by living and loving while Black. They were educated: My mother was in college; my father had just graduated from the University of Illinois. They could take advantage of public sector jobs that were opening up more broadly to Black people. They could demand higher-skilled positions in managerial and administrative occupations. But for my parents, just as in prior generations of Black Bibbs and Black people everywhere, each migration occasioned a custom negotiation with whiteness that would tax their emotional bandwidth, their interpersonal relationships, and their natural Black minds.

In 1900, more than 90 percent of African Americans still lived in the South, and Black people comprised less than 2 percent of the

Lonnie Gerald and Betty Lou at a Chicago nightclub.

population of Chicago (a city founded by Jean-Baptist-Point Du Sable, a Black man, on the banks of the Chicago River in the 1780s).

In 1905, Robert S. Abbott founded the *Chicago Defender* newspaper, and its pages urged Black Southerners to flee to the North, as they had done during enslavement. The *Defender* articles, editorials, and cartoons painted a picture of a better life away from Southern sharecropping, lynching, and second-class citizenship (that still required them to pay their full freight in taxes). It extolled the growing opportunities in great American metropolises north of the Mason-Dixon Line and listed Black churches that would help with housing and employment. The Illinois Central Railroad cut the path and provided the soundtrack with its steady *clackity-clack* from the Mississippi Delta to Chicago's Grand Central Station.

Hundreds of thousands of Black people were persuaded by Chicago's reputation as a manufacturing mecca, with work opportunities in iron and steel, garment manufacturing, agricultural and electrical machinery manufacturing, commercial printing, railroading, and meat packing, among other jobs. The city's Black population increased from 30,574 in 1900 to 278,538 in 1940, making them 8.2 percent, and rising, of the city's total population of 3.4 million.

The Second Great Migration (1940–1970) brought another wave of Blacks into northern and western US cities. Increased farming mechanization hampered sharecropping in the 1930s and 1940s, and Black workers again looked north, hoping to become part of the World War II defense buildup, and then the postwar economic boom. Roughly three thousand people a day hopped off their trains to join established Black communities—with churches, businesses, newspapers, nightclubs, and political organizations that created fertile ground for Black life and Black culture. For a telegenic young couple like Lonnie Gerald and Betty Lou, who could still feel the heat of the Deep South in their hometown of Centralia, Chicago was a place to repot themselves and grow.

I imagine my momma and daddy side by side as they take in Chicago's massive proportions and aggressive vitality. As they cross the distance from southern Illinois to Chicago, they are tethered by affection and hopefulness, at least back then, and unencumbered by the bondage that Momma Keziah had faced more than 160 years earlier. But I also feel Momma Keziah imagining the possibilities her forced march through the Appalachian Mountains to the Kentucky wilderness had birthed.

Chicago's total population peaked at 3,620,962 in 1950. By the time my parents arrived in 1961, there were around 813,000 Black folks in Chicago, representing nearly a quarter of the total population, with more coming. By 1970, there were a million Black people in the city, representing a little over 34 percent of the total of 3.3 million. A decade later, the Black Chicago population peaked at 1.1 million, making them nearly 40 percent of the total population. But all of this was happening against a backdrop of white flight. Chicago's overall population decreased steadily from its peak to just 2,783,726 in 1990, with the white population comprising just about 38 percent of that total.

In 1940, newly arriving Blacks were "redlined" (a color-coded Federal Housing Administration system that indexed housing valuations to race) into three South Side community areas (out of a then seventy-five total community areas constituting a Black Belt, with white majorities in the rest of the city. According to a Chicago news station report: "after World War II, whites began moving to the suburbs, and the restrictive covenants that had prohibited blacks from living in most neighborhoods were struck down by the courts. By 1950, the Black Belt had expanded.... By 1980, it was no longer a belt. It was a crescent encompassing most of the city's West and South sides.... This was total ethnic succession. In one generation, a third of the city's community areas went from monolithically white to monolithically black..."

These majority Black areas, then, became a problem, and a target, for policing, which, writ large, had made it an ongoing concern to control Black bodies, consistent with its historical beginnings as "slave patrols." In 1946, Momma Susie's brother Hickman Dwight Bibb, who we called Uncle Hickey, went to work for the Chicago Police Department. No one alive now can say how he got there, but the Bibb family, or their ghosts, always seem to leave a trail of breadcrumbs.

By 1940, the family circumstances had changed. Charlie Bibb—Momma Susie's father, who would die that year, at fifty-four, having been in ill health—was living at the family home in Centralia with

Lonnae's great-aunt Nellie Bibb Fields, in Chicago.

a "May" Bibb, who is listed in the census as his wife but is actually his daughter-in-law. (Census records, I have learned, sometimes got ages, names, or spellings wrong, transposing letters or numbers.) I didn't think anything of it until I saw, in another census document, my great-grandmother Minnie Bibb, Charlie's wife, living with her sister in Chicago, along with their daughter, my aunt Nellie, that same year.

(When my siblings and I were small, Aunt Nellie was a great big woman, at least five feet eight inches tall, who used to greet people with a high-pitched, singsongy "How do! How do!" She lived on the South Side, too, at at Seventy-First and St. Lawrence Avenue, where she owned a big brick two-flat. We used to jump off the high steps and stone walls around her porch as children. But we mostly saw Aunt Nellie during visits to our Black, female, South Side pediatrician, Dr. Walker, where Aunt Nellie moved around waiting rooms and exam rooms in a crisp white nurse's uniform and ran the office with a full-throated authority that made her seem even bigger. When she got older and sick, I remember thinking she wasn't big anymore, which frightened me. She slept on the let-out couch in front of Momma Susie's green chair. I saw her rise only to go to the portable commode a foot from her bed. The last time I saw her, she met my gaze evenly and I looked away. Aunt Nellie died in 1986 at seventy-three. None of the Bibb siblings made it out of their seventies.)

In that 1940 census, Uncle Hickey at twenty years old is listed as both Charles Bibb's son and the head of the household. He has dropped out of high school to be a café car porter for the railroad, working sixty hours a week. Aunt Hilda, seventeen, has dropped out of high school and is working as a maid. I don't know if this was the period Aunt Hilda talked about when she told people how poor they were growing up. "We didn't have nothing. We were just poor little church mice."

Besides Aunt Nellie, Uncle Hickey's two other older sisters, Aunt Jeanette and Momma Susie, are married by that time, and out of the house. But Uncle Hickey's younger siblings, Ellen, Morris, and Robert, along with Hilda Bibb, ages nine through seventeen, are living at the family home on McKee Street, as is Jeanette's son, Elroy, thirteen.

The discrepancy over who was head of household could be explained by the fact that Charles Bibb is recorded as not having worked at all prior to the census, making Uncle Hickey the imputed head of household, at least to the Ancestry.com program that has digitized the record. And perhaps according to Uncle Hickey himself.

In 1941, Uncle Hickey was an army private at the Savanna (Illinois) Ordnance Depot, a railroad town about a two-and-a-half-hour drive west of Chicago, which is where he spent part of WWII becoming a technical sergeant until his 1944 discharge. (His younger brothers, Uncle Bobby and Uncle Morris—who lied about his age in order to enlist—also served as army privates in WWII. My uncle Roy (Elroy Calendar), Hickey's nephew, served in the navy.) After his discharge, Uncle Hickey landed a postal service job in downtown Chicago, which was most often the result of political patronage. By 1946, he was a Chicago policeman. There's a Bibb history clue to how that might have happened.

It is powerfully intriguing to think that Uncle Hickey's job at the post office and later with the police department (first temporary, then permanent) may have been aided by the prominent Black Chicago lawyer, editor, and activist Joseph Dandridge Bibb Jr. That it was connected to a network of Black activism that predated the modern

Civil Rights Movement, and a network of Black people who are tied in ways that have historically been, and continue to be, invisible to white people. And sometimes to ourselves. Especially since often those ties wound through slavery.

Joseph D. Bibb Jr., who was born in Montgomery, Alabama, in 1891, looked like one of the Black Bibbs in my family, which is to say he was a Black man who looked like he might be white.

His father, Joseph D. Bibb Sr., was a renowned Atlanta educator. His grandfather Price Bibb, who was formerly enslaved in Mississippi, moved to Montgomery after the Civil War. John Dandridge Bibb—who is likely the great-grandfather of Joseph D. Bibb Jr.—was the nephew of Major Richard Bibb. That John Dandridge was part of the branch of white Bibbs who migrated from Virginia to the Deep South, where they continued to enslave people, usually in the family groups wealthy enslavers could afford to keep together. (This Deep South branch of the white Bibbs included a US senator, who was the namesake for Bibb Counties in Alabama and Georgia, and was the first governor of Alabama, with his brother being the second. A later descendant, David Bibb Graves, also an Alabama governor, was a grand cyclops in the Montgomery chapter of the Ku Klux Klan.)

Joseph D. Bibb Jr. graduated from Atlanta University, an HBCU, and attended Harvard, where he received his law degree. He was a columnist and editor for the *Chicago Whip*, a Black weekly newspaper best known for its 1929 "Don't Buy Where You Can't Work" campaign, urging Blacks to boycott white businesses that didn't hire Black workers. It is unclear whether Joseph D. Bibb and my uncle Hickman D. Bibb knew each other. But at the time of Uncle Hickey's migration to

Chicago, where he immediately began his job as a mail carrier, Bibb was a prominent advocate for Black people with city employers, and he "obtained thousands of jobs for colored [*sic*]." Joseph D. Bibb, a Republican, also worked closely with the well-connected Republican Oscar De Priest, Chicago's first Black alderman.

In 1953, Joseph D. Bibb became the Illinois director of public safety, the first African American appointed to statewide office, and his tenure was marked by an increase in the number of African American state police officers. So, it stands to reason he would have helped Uncle Hickey secure those Chicago public sector jobs. But what is also true is Uncle Hickey had his own way of getting things done.

While I've never heard of Uncle Hickey passing for white, it's not clear if folks in the CPD always knew he was Black, according to family lore. Any clues as to his race are redacted in the Chicago police records. After Uncle Hickey died, we heard the only time he'd pulled his gun was on a fellow police officer who'd racially insulted him. We also heard he liked to swing his billy club at folks, and that he had been on the take.

Abdullah Idris Mubarak—who, when he was Robert Bibb, would go back and forth from Chicago to Centralia and later Springfield, Illinois, on drug (and gang) business—said Uncle Hickey started out as a "door shaker. Literally what it sounds like." In police parlance, it referred to making sure doors are locked, thereby protecting merchants from petty thievery. But it also might involve having said merchants pay the same police officer for said security. In Uncle Hickey's case, it seemed to mean protecting people involved in illicit activity from other people involved in illicit activity who might want to steal from them. It meant giving criminals a heads-up about impending police activity, or other violence coming their way, all for a percentage of their earnings.

I remember Uncle Hickey as a large man who would pick me up and swing me, until his health started to decline. Uncle Morris's daughter, Sharon, remembers visiting her adoring uncle in Chicago as a little girl. Uncle Hickey would take her around to local shops and merchants, tell her to pick out whatever food, candy, or toys she wanted. Then they would leave, and the store owners, who were so friendly with Uncle Hickey, would smile as they waved goodbye. And Uncle Hickey never paid for a thing. He died in 1975, at fifty-five.

When my parents first arrived in Chicago, my dad taught school in Gary, Indiana—home of the Jackson 5—a half hour drive from the South Side. By the mid-1960s, they'd moved into a building on South Sangamon Street, owned by Uncle Hickey and his wife, my dear auntie Eleanor. She did hair out of her beauty shop in the basement, and I can still see the hot comb sizzling over the open flame as I held my ears so they wouldn't get burned. Uncle Hickey used to lord over, and yell at, Aunt Eleanor. My sister saw him get angry and break all Auntie's plates. He followed her to Texas once, which was where she was from. She had some canaries, but in a fit of rage, he opened the window and let them all go.

Momma hated Uncle Hickey's influence over my father. She hated that Uncle Hickey persuaded Daddy to join the police force.

The origins of modern policing are rooted in the antebellum "slave patrols." This was especially true in the Deep South, where terror and violence were used to enforce slave codes, extinguish uprisings, and intimidate the enslaved from resisting. These patrols were empowered to pursue and capture runaways and act as the security forces that protected the interests of enslavers. They ended with the passage of the Thirteenth Amendment, but they were replaced by militia-like groups, including white supremacist groups in Kentucky, which was the only non-seceding state with a significant Klan presence during the early Reconstruction period when the Klan was founded. These groups menaced and victimized newly emancipated Blacks and helped enforce state and local laws, known as the Black Codes, restricting their rights and dignity. Slave patrols begat militia groups, which begat police forces.

Though Illinois was admitted into the Union in 1818 as a free state, enslavement had been practiced within its borders for over one hundred years. The Chicago Police Department, which began in 1835, before the city was even incorporated, is one of the world's oldest police forces. It has a long history of protecting the interests of the powerful and wealthy, which codes white. The department grew in size as the city grew, not chiefly to keep residents safe, but to stifle labor organizing and unrest and to control immigrant populations and formerly enslaved Blacks.

The first full-time police force in Chicago was organized in response to the Lager Beer Riots of 1855. This was a brutal conflict between German and Irish immigrants and Anglo nativists (some of the first "America First" xenophobes) over the enforcement of a liquor ordinance—which raised license fees and closed taverns on Sundays—that targeted the German immigrant community. The CPD was initially composed exclusively of native-born white men. Its recruitment expanded to include white immigrants even as the force repressed the immigrant-led labor movement, most notably in the 1886 Haymarket Affair, where striking laborers and members of

Chicago Police Officer Hickman Bibb on patrol.

the anarchist movement organized demonstrations and marches in support of an eight-hour workday. The CPD, which was tasked with disrupting the demonstrations, fired into a crowd of striking workers, killing as many as six people. The following night, rally goers set off a homemade bomb that killed one officer and injured several others. More officers died in the subsequent cross fire (though historians posit much of that was police firing on their own in the chaos and darkness). In the end, seven police officers and at least four workers were killed, with scores of civilians injured.

The Haymarket Affair spawned the earliest incarnation of an arm of the CPD ultimately called the Red Squad, an intelligence unit that used overt coercion and covert manipulation to root out and undermine labor radicalism. It wasn't until a court decision in 1985 that the modern version of the Red Squad, the CPD's Subversive Activities Unit, was finally ended, along with its long-standing practice of unlawful surveillance of political dissenters.

In the 1937 Memorial Day Massacre, Chicago police shot and killed ten steelworker unionists. During the Prohibition era, the CPD met a violent enemy in organized crime: Al Capone and his gangster contemporaries were not afraid to mix it up with the police, and the experience only made the CPD more brutal, and increasingly involved in the kind of gangland criminality—bribery, kickbacks, violence—it was ostensibly constituted to protect against.

By the late '50s, the Summerdale Scandal had revealed that Chicago police officers, operating out of the North Side, had teamed up with a professional thief as part of a yearslong burglary ring that, according to a 1960 article in the *Atlantic*, stole "television sets, draperies, radios, furniture... everything from automobiles to gumball machines" from city businesses. Eight officers were eventually convicted in the scandal.

In 1960, a young Mayor Richard Daley instituted reforms, including hiring Orlando Wilson in the newly established role of superintendent of police. Wilson recentralized power downtown, lessening local ward influences and old patterns of political patronage. He recruited more Black and Latino people into the CPD's ranks and prioritized the protection of civil rights demonstrations. At the same time, a crackdown on South Side gangs continued a pattern of hyper-policing Black neighborhoods.

This was the history and culture my father walked into when he joined the police force in 1966 at the urging of and perhaps with the help of Uncle Hickey. He was stationed at the old Fifth District station on South Michigan Avenue in the Pullman neighborhood on the city's South Side.

A man named James B. Conlisk Jr. took over as police superintendent after Wilson retired in 1967. Conlisk's tenure was marred by his inability to quell the riots in Black neighborhoods following the assassination of Martin Luther King Jr. in 1968, and the excessive actions of his department in response to protesters at the Democratic National Convention in August of that same year. A national television audience witnessed Chicago police officers using Mace, tear gas, and billy clubs against peaceful protesters at the convention. My father and his partner, Ivan Jefferson, who was also from southern Illinois and married to my mother's cousin Gail Pang, worked at either the nearby Chicago Civic Center (later named the Richard J. Daley Center) or in the streets during that protest. The US National Commission on the

Causes and Prevention of Violence called the incident a police riot, blaming the CPD directly for the chaos.

The following year, Chicago police shot and killed Fred Hampton, in what the Equal Justice Initiative has called an assassination, and others called a summary execution. Meanwhile, the Red Squad kept on doing what it did best, behind the scenes, gathering information on civil rights leaders and leftist activists, or just about any voice raised in political dissent in the '60s.

It was around this time that my dad crossed paths with a young police officer named Jon Burge. Burge was sworn in in March 1970 at the age of twenty-two, after serving as a military police officer in South Korea and Vietnam, where he received training in interrogation and perhaps developed a taste for it. He was assigned to the South Side and promoted to detective after only two years on the job.

I once asked my mother, who retired to North Carolina in 2003, and who had never searched the internet, if she had ever heard of Jon Burge.

"My God, where did you hear that name?" my mother asked. "He was your father's watch commander. Your father said he was a horrid man."

In a town notorious for police brutality, Burge was a different kind of monster. Federal prosecutors contend that in 1972, he began a nearly twenty-year rampage of beatings, torture, planting of evidence, and forced confessions, ultimately leading to his suspension from the force in 1993 and his 2006 conviction in federal court for obstruction. The effort to bring Burge and his team to justice culminated in 2015, with what became known as the Chicago Police Torture reparations case. Burge used, and at times openly displayed, what he called a "nigger box" to administer electrical shocks to detainees' limbs and genitalia.

"Between 1972 and 1991 [Burge] either directly participated in or implicitly approved the torture of at least—and this is an extremely conservative estimate—118 Chicagoans," according to a 2019 *Guardian* newspaper article. Nearly all of Burge's victims were Black. Some were killed, some wrongfully incarcerated and later exonerated, and others simply scarred for life.

When this history is considered in the aggregate, over nearly two centuries, the CPD operated as part of a continuum of white control, rage, and violent depredations.

My dad left the force in September 1971 after my mother begged him to quit, promising that she would finish her degree and get a job as a teacher—both of which she did. I don't know how close, or how often, Daddy came to working with Burge before he resigned. What is true is Burge was only twenty-two when he joined the Chicago Police Department and levitated through the ranks. I wonder if my father knew what he was looking at when he looked at Burge—or if he ever tried to stop him. Or could have.

Burge supposedly didn't implement his "enhanced" interrogation techniques until he was promoted to detective in '72, after my father had already resigned. But what is clear is that his tenure in the Chicago Police Department overlapped with my father's by more than a year, and it was enough to haunt my father. And my mother, who called Burge racist and violent, said, "Your daddy hated him."

My parents moved out of Uncle Hickey's house and moved to the far South Side neighborhood of Washington Heights in 1969, where we lived for nearly a decade and which is the only Chicago home I ever knew.

They bought a three-bedroom bungalow with a big picture window, across the street from Mount Vernon Elementary School and the twelve-acre Jackie Robinson Park and baseball field. Jackie Robinson Park was home to the 2014 US championship Jackie Robinson West Little League team that was later disqualified for fielding out-of-district players—a rule that at best had only been casually observed prior to JRW's championship season. (That ruling failed to consider the racial and socioeconomic factors hindering predominantly Black and urban Little League organizations, as well as the decentralized nature of Little League districts. Also, according to *Chicago* magazine, the boundary rules invoked to disqualify JRW had been bent or even ignored for years. That is, until JRW won, and won big. It doesn't mean JRW didn't break the rule. It simply makes it a rule that was unequally enforced, or rather only enforced when a Black team won.)

A third of the children in my sister's kindergarten class photo were white. By the time I was in kindergarten four years later, there were no white children in the entire school. At least none that I ever saw. When I was a child, white kids were strictly a vacation phenomenon. I only saw white kids when I saw white shoes, after Memorial Day and before Labor Day.

From 1961 to 1971, including the entire time my dad served as a police officer, he taught math in the Gary, Indiana, school system. He went to night school at Roosevelt University, where he received his master's degree in education supervision and administration in July

1971. Two months later, he resigned from the police force and accepted a job as an assistant principal at Tolleston High School, and later West Side High School, which, at the time, was the largest high school in the state. No doubt with Momma Susie on his mind, he kept educating himself. At various times in the early-to-mid 1970s, he took classes at Illinois Institute of Technology, Purdue University, and Indiana University, all while working as an assistant principal in Gary. He considered pursuing a PhD.

In addition to taking us on our annual Centralia vacations, my parents piled us in the station wagon and we drove the country visiting Uncle Cut in Colorado and going to see Pikes Peak. We went to Niagara Falls and Disneyland. We have old eight-millimeter film of Dad training the camera on seagulls outside a motorboat in Northern California, and on some woman in a bikini running through the sand. On our way to Mississippi to see Papa Lonnie's people, we stopped at a motel (with a swimming pool right there!), but when my daddy went to check us in, the manager said there were no vacancies, even as Daddy pointed out the parking lot was nearly empty. As a parent, I find the thought of having to explain a banal racist incident to my disappointed children abhorrent. Then again, nobody explained anything to children when I was a child, so I remember Daddy just driving away.

In many ways, that half decade in the Chicago Police Department was a brief stint compared to my father's decadeslong work as an educator. Everything that followed in his life post-police can be read as an attempt to outrun those five years. But just like that Haunted Mansion ride I remember from that childhood trip to Disneyland, a ghost, or perhaps more than one, followed him home.

There's an image of my father that fills my waking mind.

It is a photograph, though I have vivid memories of my dad around the same time: the 1970s, when he was a young man and I was simply little. I was the daughter he dubbed FiFi because even as a preschooler, I was finicky about food, and he thought I was acting fancy. In one of those life images, my father is holding my brother Chucky and me, one to a shoulder, as he's walking across a stream, skillfully navigating the rocks. At one point, he slips, but he does not fall. He had been a star athlete for the Centralia High School Orphans in football and basketball. The Orphans were so named, local lore has it, because the basketball team once showed up to the state tourney in mismatched uniforms, prompting a quip from the play-by-play announcer, or because some fans thought the team looked "as sad as a band of unwanted orphans," or possibly because a coach, early in the school's history, named them after his favorite silent movie, *Orphans of the Storm.*

But Daddy was no shabby street urchin. He had been nimble, fleet of foot, and so my brother and I barely even registered a dip in altitude when he slipped. Daddy's shoes got wet and he cursed though. He was particular about his look. In any case, we were secure, and it was probably more about his pride than any worry for our safety.

In that way, my memory of my dad is of a piece with the agility, the strength, the sheer physicality of the boys, the young men, and the grown men around me. I could say Black men, but when I was a child, there was no other kind. The boys popped wheelies past our house and rode their bikes back tire only, beyond the point where I could see down the block. They smoked cigarettes hands-free when it came time to take their turn at bat during sixteen-inch softball games, catching the bad throws one-handed and tossing them back to the pitcher with a little bit of shit talk.

They were shirtless, cornrowed, with knee-length shorts fashioned from blue jeans and sliced into thick, ribboned denim fringes that swung past their thighs as they made moves to the baskets, all of which had chains or nothing for nets. Men were always strong, until they weren't, or they got old. Which sometimes felt disconnected from their trips around the sun. Which happened suddenly, with stoops and slurs. With lapses and vague apologies for not being able to hold their pee in the car anymore, particularly after too much beer. But even in a world where physicality was the norm, it still registered that Dad had carried my brother and me across the water, and that clearly took some doing. My father had already begun feeling remote to me, or perhaps he'd always been remote but I was getting old enough to feel it, so I was surprised, and maybe worried about being a burden.

Almost all those action images of my father are from the South Side, which makes sense since our house was small, and we were in close—not just my family, and extended family, but the whole Black world before our move to the Chicago suburbs gave me a different, less boundaried sense of proportion and space.

That move to a south suburban town more closely mirrored the proportions of Russellville and Centralia, in that we were more proximal to white people than we'd ever been on the South Side. I was around ten when I had my first conversation with a white child. I learned that in schools outside Chicago, white children said stuff like *"Timmy acts just like a nigger."* It let you know they had internalized their new proximity to us as well. But they hadn't learned any helpful words from their mommas and daddies to express their discomfort, so they taught their own children *"We don't see race,"* which is a lie. And still leaves white folks without tools to make sense of the world, which is why so many of them revert to, or continue to use, the old ones.

In another mental snapshot, my dad's cheeks are puffed and he is holding both hands to his mouth. He is rushing toward the bathroom before he vomits in waves, after a night of drinking has met the dry dawn, and my young eyes, as I stand in my bedroom doorway, are watching him stumble. A piece of onion has escaped his lips. I've always hated onions.

Those are memories of my dad in motion, but in the photo in my mind's eye, he is still. Hazy. Metaphorical, perhaps. It acts as a portrait. Daddy is standing in front of the mirrored floor-to-ceiling panels that cover our living room wall, to the right of our picture window. He is facing the camera but reflected in the glass. Or perhaps it is the other way around. He is facing the mirror and the camera captures him in full.

Daddy wears a full-length gray leather coat with black fur lapels that reach for his shoulders, and thick fur cuffs accentuate his sleeves. He's got the muttonchop sideburns and a full mustache that blends into a well-trimmed goatee. I cannot see his thick, curly Afro for the wide-brimmed black hat that silos everything underneath in a cone of urban cool. He is tall, to my young eyes. At least six foot. Black, unsmiling. Perhaps it's 1971 and *Shaft* is in the movie theaters. Maybe Daddy is Richard Roundtree. Handsome, authoritative, with a bespoke moral code. A complicated man, and no one understands him but his woman, my momma, Betty Lou. Some elements of this composite sound right on, but I do not think my father is approximating Shaft in that picture.

Maybe it's 1972 and *Super Fly* is in movie theaters. Ron O'Neal is Youngblood Priest. My dad is Ron O'Neal. And this is true even given the fact that he had a brother, my uncle Ronnie, who was actually named Ron O'Neal, though Uncle Ronnie had nothing of the Youngblood Priest, the *Super Fly* character, in him that I ever saw.

Dad is intense and brooding, but that could be just the in-house version I saw in the picture. Outwardly, he's smiling, quick to laugh hard, such that the high notes rise up to fill in the sound of it. A smart brother, a smooth talker. Your money was no good with my daddy. At least not when Lonnie Gerald was paying for the drinks, the food, pulling twenty, fifty, or hundred dollar bills from a wad of bills, straining, sometimes, the shiny silver money clip he kept in the pocket of his Flagg Bros. pants. Of course, sometimes, he'd just loud talk about how he was going to pay, and slip out without doing so.

Rise On Fashions. That was the Flagg Bros. catalog, where the ultra-Black men got their vines, their velvet, their sateen fabrics and platform shoes. "For the outspoken few." What was it that Momma used to call him? Dark Gable. *I know that's right!*

This is where my daddy's stop on the Black Bibb migration train had taken him. Off the plantation, out of Bibbtown, up from Centralia. It was the 1970s, Lonnie Gerald was in Chicago, and he was all the way live. At least on the South Side, which, along with the West Side of the city, was where Black folks were allowed to live. The white folks he worked with, at the Chicago Transit Authority, at the Chicago Police Department, at the board of education in Indiana, wouldn't have known this side of my father. He was trying to make himself into something he didn't have a template for, and America didn't have the tolerance or imagination for, but he authentically wanted to be. A smart-ass, badass, pretty-ass, family-having-ass, church-going-ass Black man. With money.

Daddy liked to argue—*Fish is NOT a meat*; also, *Your good works alone will not get you into heaven*—which is to say he liked to be right, especially since he had his master's degree. "Fifi, a BS degree means *bullshit*," he explained to me once when I was in third or fourth grade. "And an MS just means *more shit*." I think he had been drinking, which was a steady state, or at least much more often than not.

He radiated a kinetic disquiet, or at a minimum an ability to escalate very, very quickly, even as I can see him gesturing widely, slapping backs, and grabbing arms when he's laughing in the room where grown folks are partying. But like Ron O'Neal in *Super Fly*, he pimps it. Daddy is light cocoa brown, with curly black hair, so it makes sense that he is in the mirror or has just turned from it in the photo. It's like when O'Neal stops in front of the mirror to tell himself that, in addition to his prodigious pusher-man gifts, "I'm a pretty nigga, too."

Uncle Morris's daughter, Sharon, used to carry Dad's picture in her wallet and tell her friends he was her fiancé, if she wanted to impress them. Perhaps Daddy was already a schoolteacher, or a bus driver, or finishing up his graduate degree during night school. Maybe he was already an assistant principal, or maybe my perception of time was off. Things can get compressed but still make for a clear composite in your mind's eye as a child.

For instance, this was around the same era Lonnie Gerald drove a sky-blue convertible Cadillac. And the William DeVaughn song "Be Thankful For What You Got" was playing on WVON-1390 AM. I later found out that the call letters stood for "Voice of the Negro," which sounded about right.

Diamond in the back, sunroof top, diggin' the scene with a gangster lean

Ooo-ooo-ooo-ooo

Sometimes Daddy would pile Momma, me, my sister, and my brother into that Cadillac and we'd go for a drive. This was before power steering, when it took two full revolutions of the wheel, using one finger, to make a single left turn. He'd drive the South Side, with the top down and the radio going. But sometimes, we'd go as far as downtown, Grant Park, and the light show at Buckingham Fountain, which, in toto, might have been the best thing about my childhood.

Ronald O'Neal Jr., Little Ronnie, drew a contrast between my father and his father, Dad's younger brother. Uncle Ronnie and my dad would rib each other over who was better looking. Both were educators. But that's where the similarities ended.

Little Ronnie said: "When we would go into the city and see your dad, and I would look at the way he was dressed and see pictures and I was like, 'I can't believe this dude and my dad are siblings.' My father worked very hard, I think, not to be seen as flashy or having any swagger or anything. He just wanted to dress appropriately and look a little cool. Uncle Lonnie Gerald was straight out of central casting. He didn't look like he came from small-town southern Illinois. He looked every bit the city dude."

I thought Daddy traded in the Cadillac for the station wagon at some point after the photo was taken. But it turns out his Cadillac, which he parked in front of our house, had actually been stolen.

He went outside one morning, the car was gone, and Daddy started hollering.

"Oooh, they took it! They took it! They took my car."

The police found the Cadillac, stripped of the radio, stripped of his gangster whitewall tires, and maybe his eight-track cassette player as well. That thievery seemed to take the fight out of him and initiated our station wagon era. First brownish green, as I recall. Then a later model, fire-engine red, down to the leather interior, which always seemed to me to be sending mixed messages.

As I got older, I began to appreciate the ways people responded to my dad. How he could walk into a room and fix all eyes on him. As an assistant principal at West Side High School in Gary, he worked football and basketball games, school plays, and concerts, and would often take us kids along. During the school day, he'd often take control. Any assistant principal could handle the routine one-on-one fights. But my daddy had a talent for the melee, the gang fight, multiple individuals throwing down at once, such that the police might have to get involved. But my father was the police, and although his students didn't know that, they responded to it just the same.

According to dad's former student Jose Newell, who knew him from West Side High: "Mr. O'Neal was always well dressed. He was always, as we say, suited and booted. He had a head full of hair, with some sheen, and a goatee. But it almost seemed like he was young. Mr. O'Neal was the one you could feel comfortable going to say 'Look, this is what's going on down there in the mini-*Casino Royale* bathroom,' where guys were throwing dice or getting shook down. The bathroom that had lookouts with symbols and whistles. Sometimes you'd go just to learn. Just to witness it all. With [one principal] they'd wait until he was ten feet away, then they'd pick everything up, rush out, blowing smoke. He'd never catch anybody.

"With your dad, it was like, 'O'Neal's coming. O'Neal's coming.' Guys were just chill. They'd be like, 'Okay, we gotta wrap this up, man.' Your dad would walk in and say, 'Okay, you guys know you're not supposed to be in here,' and the bathroom would be EMPTY in ten seconds. The guys in the school, the guys who were holding the contraband, seemed to respond better to him than they did the other administrators. And these cats were thugs for real. I was like, If you got that kind of juice from the thugs, there's something going on with you. I don't know if he approved something before I got there, but they knew: Don't mess with him.

"I never saw him worked up. I never saw him lose his cool."

Whatever it was students sensed about him warned them off, and that often carried the day. Mostly it meant he could stop fights before they even got started. When that didn't work, he might grind a knee into some kid's back, like my brother saw him do during a basketball game scuffle to let the kid know, this ends here. He might have to kneel on somebody's head like he told me he'd had to do to this boy who I'd said was cute. (It was an incident that happened before I'd said he was cute, to my understanding. Though I never told Daddy I thought any-body was cute again.)

Dad took my brother and me to a West Side faculty talent show once. There was one skit with the principal and two or three other assistant principals. Daddy came out strutting, wearing a polyester suit (possibly from his closet) and platform shoes, he did a little rap about the tardy bell, and the crowd erupted into cheers and whistles. My brother Chucky says Dad was Chester Cheetah. He was just that cool.

I saw that old photo of my dad in the living room in detail and metaphor, at least the parts that felt known to me, even when I was too young to language them. I see him in the leather and fur, and the wide-brim hat, with little hint of his identity as a math teacher or an assistant principal. There's no sign of the station wagon he drives, but it's all in there. He's the man who carried me across a creek on his shoulder, with a look, an aesthetic, an attitude, perhaps, that makes sense to him as a young Black man in Chicago who came of age before the Civil Rights Movement had crested. He is a man, like Youngblood Priest, like Super Fly, who doesn't have enough elbow room. The kind of elbow room the white Bibbs set out to find on colonized land with the human beings they trafficked. And like Ron O'Neal in *Super Fly*, he is hungry for more than the leftovers of something appreciably more big-time. He was a man who may not have had the emotional band-width to fully match who he was trying to be. *Two warring souls in one dark body.*

I understood Daddy was trying to be a Black man in full, but by the time that picture was shot, that door had already closed on him. It just took another decade and a half or so for him to play out his options. I don't know precisely when the picture was taken, but I know he had quit the police department, which means he had already killed a man. Which means he was already fighting himself over that fact. He was drinking and he was losing. I can see him in my waking mind. I can see into his eyes.

Or perhaps it is his reflection.

It wasn't until 2024 that I committed to memory the actual date in 1985 that my father had died. I had never focused on the precise date in which he shot the white woman he was with—his girlfriend, Kathy (the bullet grazed her head, but she survived)—and then killed himself. I just knew it was early morning, Father's Day. I was in summer school at Southern Illinois University trying to make up for a bad second semester, largely due to pledging a sorority and meeting the boyfriend I dated throughout college.

I was living with a sorority sister but spending most of my time with my boyfriend. The one time my father met this boyfriend, he threatened him. Said he'd already killed one man, and he'd think nothing of killing him if he messed with me. I gave my sorority sister the boyfriend's number. "Let me give you this number in case of emergencies, in case somebody dies," I said. Or, if I didn't say that last part, I thought it.

It turned out, I was not the only one.

A week before Father's Day, Dad called Gailey May, which is what he called Gail—my mother's cousin—when he'd been drinking. He started crying. He said he wanted his family back. Something in Dad's voice scared Gail. Made her tell her boyfriend that she was worried "Lonnie Gerald is going to commit suicide." The boyfriend thought Daddy was just drunk.

Gail called my father the next day: "I said, 'Doc, are you okay?'" She called him Doc because he'd wanted to get a PhD. "He said, 'Gailey May, I'm okay. I promise you I'm okay.'"

She had her ex-husband, his ex–police partner, Ivan, call, but Daddy never picked up the phone.

A few months before he himself died, Rolland Lawson, Daddy's devoted high school friend, told me how he'd had a premonition and gone to see my dad: "I don't know why God lets me see these things," Mr. Lawson told me. He'd urged Daddy to get back with Momma, saying Daddy wouldn't be able to handle it if she married somebody else. He wept softly as he spoke to me. He was in declining health. He had his good days and bad days, his son, Calvin, said, but he'd been talking about my dad a lot. I thought the story might be apocryphal, a figment of one of his bad days, so I asked Calvin when his dad had first told the story of his premonition, of going to warn Lonnie Gerald. Calvin said 1995.

The afternoon before my father shot himself, he called Aunt Hilda. Lemuel Flagg, who was living with her at the time, said Daddy called the house first, but she'd already left.

"He said, 'I'll call down to the Confectionary.' And then he said, 'I want to apologize for the way I acted when I was home last week for Chucky's graduation,'" Lemmy recalled. Chucky had gone to live with Aunt Hilda during high school after Momma had gotten remarried. After the graduation, everybody went to the Confectionary, including Momma and her new husband. Dad's girlfriend wasn't there. Dad had gotten angry and started hollering at Lemmy, *Can't you get the food out any faster? These people are hungry!*

"I said, 'Lonnie Gerald, I didn't pay no attention to what you were talking about. I know you'd been drinking and you were really emotional and everything.' And he said, 'Yeah, just seeing Betty and the kids. I just really want my family back. I just really want my family back.'"

He reached Aunt Hilda after that. He told her that he was sorry for what he had done to her by taking Chucky and said that it wasn't his idea. That it was Momma Susie's. He asked for her forgiveness. She said, "Lonnie Gerald, I forgave you a long time ago."

Three weeks before Dad died, Chucky and his girlfriend took a road trip to Dad's apartment in Hammond, Indiana. Dad had given him a key, but Chucky hadn't given Dad a heads-up that he was coming. When he walked in, he startled Daddy, who put a gun to Chucky's head. A week before Dad died, Chucky went to visit him and Dad was not sober. If he wasn't drinking, he was high. He broke down and told Chuck that his other son, Lance, the one Momma Susie and Papa Lonnie had adopted, didn't want anything to do with him. He talked about Momma getting remarried and said he still loved her. He wept.

An FOIA request to the Chicago Police Department yielded more than two dozen discreet documents, personnel actions, and salary and retirement records about Uncle Hickey, who had worked for the CPD for twenty-five years. A FOIA request for my dad yielded a single card with a start date, an end date, and his unit and badge number. My dad does not show up in a database put together by the nonprofit journalism group the Invisible Institute, though his former partner, hired a little over a month later, does. According to a data and history archive begun by a Chicago police officer and utilized by researchers, personnel records from 1960 to 1969 were removed from the Chicago Police Headquarters vault and not returned.

Everything about my father's story frightened me, which explains why, over so many years, I kept it so far away from my daily mind. I kept it boxed up, like the place where my dad's files probably exist in some cavernous warehouse in a Chicago police facility, full of secrets and dead bodies, or perhaps secrets about dead bodies. This is why I couldn't even take the five minutes I would have needed to figure out that Dad had not, in fact, shot Fred Hampton. This is why I never knew the actual date of my father's suicide. This is why, by the time I finally searched for his girlfriend—the woman he had shot, a woman who had been kind to me as a girl struggling with all kinds of issues—I learned she had passed away a month before I found her, nearly forty years after the shooting.

Finally, irrevocably, irretrievably, I had to deal with the Chicago police directly. They've made themselves into an organization that you don't want to talk to. That you don't want to get anywhere near. That reminds you of every abusive situation you've ever experienced. Whether or not they even touch you, they are always coming at you with an authority that is unleavened by the things that make various types of authority okay and necessary in a democracy. Like transparency. Like adherence to fair rules. Like respect and accountability.

I felt that way, even with the confidence I had earned in my many years as a reporter. Like on the occasions I had to correspond with the CPD about an unrelated FOIA request, which sat for over a year. They obfuscated and policesplained and subtly bullied, saying that it was mistakenly this or unfortunately that. Fortunately, I had a notebook in my hand and institutions behind my name. So that balanced the power dynamics a bit.

But as a daughter, I felt helpless. My daddy went into the CPD for a relatively brief five-year period, and he did not come out right on the other side. You could argue he wasn't right when he went in, but that falls on the police department as well, because he should never have been sworn in in the first place. And so it was that every email I sent and every phone call I made, every conversation I had, was full of fear and trembling.

But there was nothing for it. And if I felt that way, I bet my daddy felt that way too. As did the people he might have hurt.

"Your daddy never got over whatever happened to him on the police force," an aunt once told me. Others have said the same. I believe that is true. And I believe he never got over whatever it was that pre-dated the police force. Whatever it was that drove him into their arms in the first place. But given our family history, given the whole sweep of Bibb history and American history, I do not doubt that whatever it

Lonnie Gerald O'Neal's high school graduation picture, 1957.

was, it was based in a trauma he could not out-educate. He could not out-cool. He could not outrun.

I don't think my father tried to call me in the days before he died. He probably would not have been able to reach me anyway. I do know that I sent him a Father's Day card and it arrived on Monday. The day after he killed himself.

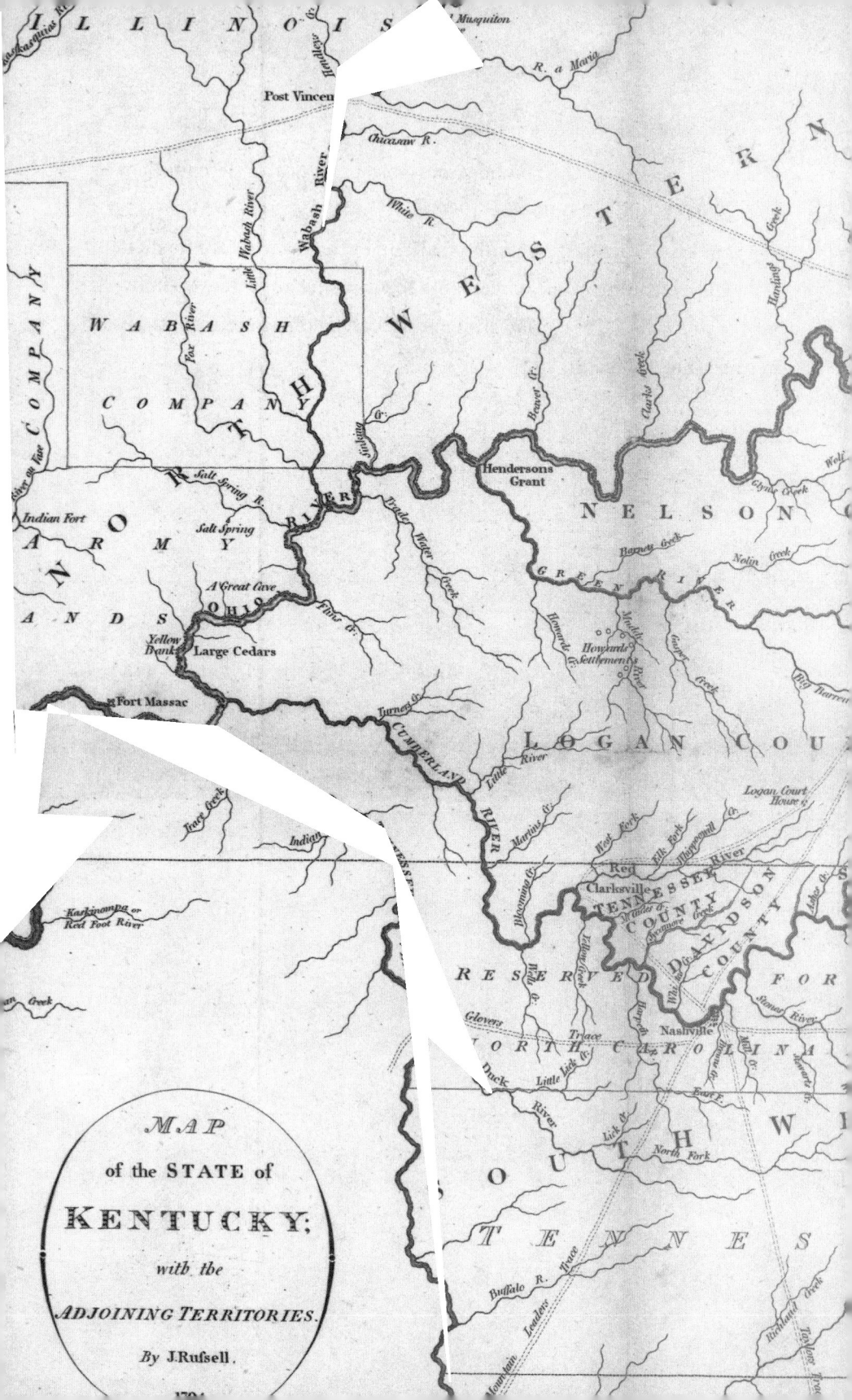

MAP
of the STATE of
KENTUCKY;
with the
ADJOINING TERRITORIES.
By J. Russell.

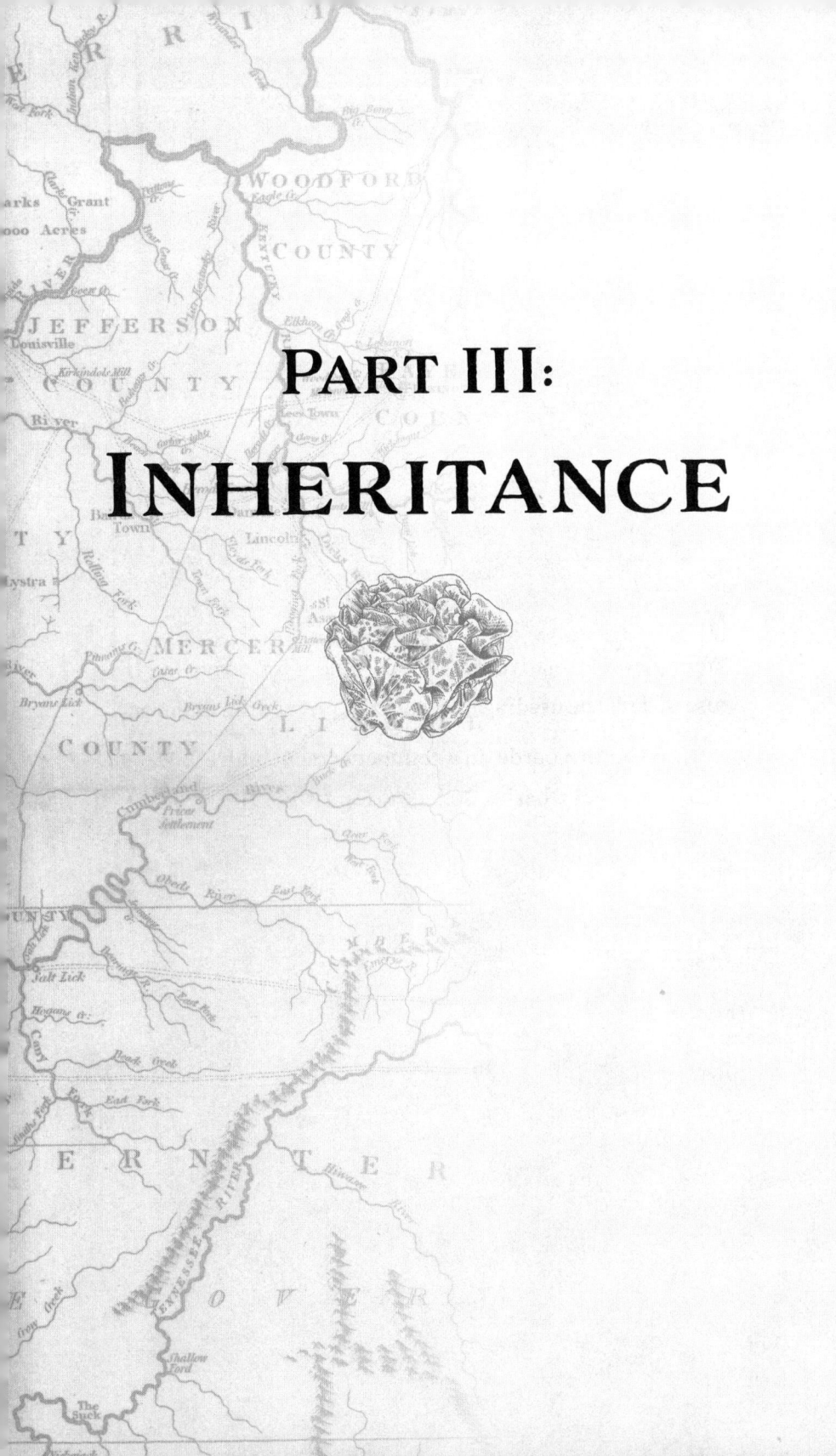

PART III:
INHERITANCE

"Your power is relative, but it is real. And if you do not learn to use it, it will be used, against you, and me, and our children."

**—Audre Lorde, in a commencement address
at Oberlin College (May 29, 1989)**

CHAPTER 9

THE LYNCHING TREE

Michael Morrow is very careful when he tells the story of the August 1, 1908, Logan County lynchings. The story that changed US postal laws to ban the sending of lynching images by mail but left anti-lynching laws for another day.

Morrow had curated an exhibition on the lynching in Russellville's historic Black Bottom in 2008, despite strident local opposition. In 2022, he narrated *By Parties Unknown*, an Emmy Award–winning Western Kentucky University PBS documentary on the lynching. Weeks after the documentary's debut, and days after the first post-covid, in-person Bibb House reunion, Morrow sat for an interview at Russellville's WRUS-AM, and I sat next to him, rapt.

He spun the story out over an hour. He detailed that the labor dispute turned deadly when laborer Rufus Browder, a member of the local True Reformer mutual-aid society, shot and killed overseer James Cunningham, a reputed leader of the local Night Riders militia group who had shot Browder first. Days later, three men from the True Reformer lodge, which had passed resolutions in support of Browder's claims of self-defense, were arrested and lynched. A fourth victim, who was serving a few days' jail time for carrying a concealed weapon, was lynched simply because he was there when the white mob came to seize the other three.

The mob pinned a note onto the body of one of the men hanging from the cedar tree: "Let this be a warning to you niggers to let white people alone or you'll go the same damn way. Your lodges and your halls better shut up and quit."

After three trials, Browder was convicted in the overseer's death, but his sentence was commuted by the Kentucky governor. When Browder's family went to pick him up from the train station, the conductor showed them to a pine box. The death certificate listed tuberculosis as Browder's cause of death, but his family believed he'd been poisoned.

In a 1944 letter to his daughter, Browder's defense attorney, John Rhodes, wrote "not a single soul would help us" gather evidence for the case. "It was as easy to raise a mob in Logan County in those days as to drop a hat, especially where a negro was involved," Rhodes wrote. "Russellville, in Logan County, seemed to be infected, as with a disease."

Morrow layers the story with times, locations, and routes taken. His voice is steady and folksy. It still has some of that dirt on it from growing up in the Black Bottom. His knowledge of Logan County history is intimate and full of viscera. He talks as if he knew the judge; the doctor; the jailer; the jailer's son; and the coroner, Matt Barbie. He conveys the sweep of the terrorism but keeps it close to home.

"Do you believe that there are descendants of the lynch mob still alive in Logan County?" Don Neagle, the radio legend who'd hosted the *Feedback* daily call-in show on WRUS for nearly forty years, asked.

"Plenty of them," said Morrow. "They're just not talking about it. If we are ever going to have any healing, they're going to have to come out of the closet."

As we exited the radio station, we noticed a young white man in a pickup sitting in the parking lot. He hopped from the truck and walked up to us. Michael and I stopped. I shivered. Trembled, perhaps. I wondered what this was about to be.

"I heard you talking on the radio a while ago."

"Uh-huh."

"I found these at my house."

The young man pulled a handful of business cards from his pocket. "I know you know who this is. This is the guy you were talking about!" the young man enthused. He handed Morrow a card from James Matt Barbie, the coroner in the Logan County lynching.

The young man, whose name was Rusty Martin, said he'd found ten of the cards when he redid his house. It was built in 1810. He was the sixth generation to live there. He'd shown them to the Barbie family, but they didn't want them.

"I sho' appreciate this, man," said Morrow, taking one of the cards. He asked if he could have two.

Morrow and Martin exchanged stories about family and ties. About where folks went to church and where they were buried. The afternoon sky was overcast, the air felt heavy, and I was struck by the Southern Gothic of it all.

"I was hearing y'all talk. You said his name and a chill went over me," Martin said. "I just happened to have [the cards] in my hand!"

"You may not believe this," Morrow said, "but this is how this thing has happened to me all my life." He was talking about the Russellville, Bibbtown, Logan County stories and artifacts that always seemed to fall in his lap. Or were given to him by folks who, in the end, resolved not to die without telling him what they knew.

"I heard you talking and I thought, 'Well, I'mma try and get up here,'" said Martin. "I just drove by and I thought, 'Well, he'll probably think I'mma shoot him or somethin'.'" The three of us chuckle at this, or maybe it was just me. I sounded hollow to myself. Morrow's voice was unchanged.

They exchanged information, and Morrow promised to send Martin a biography of Barbie, the coroner who certified that the four victims of the Logan County lynching had died "by parties unknown."

"The Lord works in mysterious ways," Martin called out to us as he hopped back into his truck and drove off. I shivered again.

In the late 1990s, Morrow got a call telling him somebody had finally cut down the "lynching tree," as it had been called for nearly a century. But a lynching tree has deep roots, entertwined branches, untold leaves that fall all over the place.

The US Congress finally took up those lynching laws in 2020. Kentucky Senator Rand Paul initially voted to block the Emmett Till Antilynching Act bill over concerns the language was too broad. He signed on as a cosponsor of the legislation in 2022, and it passed the

Senate by unanimous consent. The House voted overwhelmingly to approve the measure as well, though another Kentucky legislator, Thomas Massie, was one of three Republicans who voted against it.

In the summer of 2024, a white man walked up to Morrow at a yard sale. He handed him one of those banned postcards from the 1908 lynching.

It had been passed down through his family for generations.

By the first post-covid, in-person reunion in Russellville in 2022, I wasn't cursing the invitation to return to the Bibb House plantation, or the paper it was sent on, which I counted as progress. I had already written once about the reunion and I knew I could do so again. I decided it was time for my three young adult children to experience this family history lesson for themselves. Armed with my own autonomous power, I could keep us all at a safe remove, or so I imagined.

We pulled up to our Russellville bed-and-breakfast, tired from our flight and hourlong drive from Nashville, but also a little giddy. Or perhaps it was just me. It was the first time my husband, my kids, and I had spent any non-beach time together in a decidedly Southern town, especially one that held such personal significance. The ascendance of Black Lives Matter in the national racial conversation and the social justice protests following the 2020 murder of George Floyd added to the feeling of uncharted racial territory.

The historic two-story brick bed-and-breakfast on South Main was built in 1857 as both a private residence and home of the Southern Bank of Kentucky, before becoming the Nimrod Long Bank near the end of the Civil War. (On the register of historic places nomination form to the Department of the Interior, the Civil War was referred to by the South-preferred name: War between the States.) The arches, facades, and recessed bays were purported to be some of the finest examples of Renaissance Revival architecture in Kentucky.

But before we even hit the archway and double wooden doors, we noted the historic marker to the left of the entrance celebrating the building's real claim to fame. The old bank had been the subject of an 1868 holdup by the (Jesse) James-Younger gang, in the early stages of their notoriety. Jesse, Frank James, and others made off with more than nine thousand dollars after shooting the bank president, who lived to brag about it. It was an outlaw story that felt exactly right for western Kentucky.

The bank subsequently became a museum, then the the family home of Joe Gran Clark, head of Historic Russellvile, Inc. It now belonged to a husband-and-wife team who were converting it into a bed-and-breakfast. Michael Morrow, who had done some work for the husband, vouched for us, which is how we became their very first guests.

We met the wife first. She was petite, blond, soft-spoken. Gracious in her welcome, if a little nervous on account of how they hadn't formally opened. She gave us a tour, peppering us with tidbits of history about each of the home's many rooms, showing off moldings and anterooms. There was a hidden vault inside a narrow passageway, making me wonder if anyone had ever been locked in.

Our two rooms, one for me and my husband, the other shared by my three kids, each had a fireplace and towering ceilings. Anything we needed, our hostess urged, just ask, and I warmed to her earnestness and quiet vulnerability. The grounds were treed and sprawling, with a giant, buzzing beehive, like something out of a children's book, near the top of one of the tallest trees out back. The finely crafted latticework on the covered back porch helped cast a historic spell we were invited to sink into. The coffee station outside our door was perfectly placed, I told the wife. We met an elderly uncle, who wore an eye patch and joked with us on the back veranda. We met the cat and two dogs, including one that, improbably, carried the same uncommon name as my son, which put me on alert. I nodded to myself, or whatever ghosts might be looking on, to show I'd be paying close attention.

I fell asleep in a high canopy bed trying to imagine the lives of enslaved people who might have once been inside our room. I wondered who'd they'd been and where they'd gone, if indeed they'd left the building.

The next morning, the wife darted from dining room to kitchen, quietly efficient, ferrying homemade biscuits and jams, filling our cups, serving up a savory breakfast in a room filled with sunlight framed in millwork. Her husband and coproprietor came in to greet us, and he was a different story.

He was huge, over six feet and girthy—hard to move, like an offensive lineman, or a young Santa Claus in a Dallas Cowboys jersey. He was burly, bearded, and unbothered by boundaries of personal space. "Bring it in!" he commanded, wanting no parts of any handshake business, wrapping us all up in his hug. He was as loud and rambunctious as his wife was low-key and reserved, but they seemed equally matched in their open arms and welcome. The husband sat with us through most of breakfast, making jokes and football conversation with my college quarterback son. Offering blessings for our stay, until his wife shooed him away into the kitchen. My kids were enchanted. So was I.

Later that night, or the next, the wife and I sat in the dining room for an evening that featured at least one bottle of wine. We spoke of husbands and marriages, her second and mine. Of our hopes for our children and the aches and blessings of caring for elderly parents. We talked about places we'd left, and where we'd unexpectedly found ourselves—how I'd quit my job as a big-city newspaper columnist and she'd left hers as a big-box retail clerk in a small town, both of us staying up for a conversation that felt warm and riveting and ran late into the night.

We each had the feel of gaining a sister, and we said so to each other.

Meanwhile, the elderly uncle was praying for me, he told me. Asking God to bless me and send me an angel who would watch over me for life. The husband insisted I just let him know if I needed to borrow their car, or if there was anything else I needed.

As I walked through the house one day, taking in the books, textiles, and old photos, I came across our hosts' wedding picture. The wife's flowers and cowboy hat set off her white wedding dress nicely. The husband wore a detailed period outfit. A shirt, or tunic of some sort, double-breasted and marked by two rows of gold buttons. He sported a wide-brimmed black hat with two swords crossing in the center. I believe there was some sort of string or tie around his neck. I smiled at the photo, but something nagged at me. I'm not sure if it was in that moment, or later on, looking through a photo album, when I first began to wonder, Wait, who was the blue and who wore gray again?

I waited until I neared the end of the Bibb House reunion to visit the Confederate memorials at Carrico Park Square in downtown Russellville.

It was after I'd toured the Saddle Factory Museum, one of the oldest standing industrial buildings in Kentucky, with Michael Morrow and Russellville resident Charles Neblett. Neblett was one of the four original Freedom Singers, whose voices animated and fortified the Civil Rights Movement and who performed at the 1963 March on Washington. Neblett's wife, Marvinia, an activist in her own right, and I climbed the single-file stairway to the wide-open attic, which had been the living quarters for dozens of enslaved and indentured servants who'd labored at the factory. We could still make out drawings and writings scrawled across the sloped, crumbling walls. This included a name and circumstance lost to time, but whose declaration, for posterity as it turns out, preserved behind glass, read: "[I] will be free two years from now, on May 13, 1848."

We crossed the street to the SEEK Museum archives, which temporarily housed the inventory for Morrow's online Black Bottom Books, one of many businesses he started to create work opportunities for young people in the neighborhood, which was once home to a vibrant business district.

I'd passed the square many times in my two trips to Russellville, and never troubled myself to look at it. Of the park's nine memorials, three were expressly Confederate, and the idea of seeing them was anathema to me. My husband and I ritually give the fingers, one on each hand, to the large Confederate flag and various racist signs that pass as political expression alongside I-95, driving from DC to points south.

I also wondered about the safety of walking the park as a Black woman—visible to passersby—taking notes and pictures to make judgments about town history, and which versions of that history local residents had seen fit to glaze and fire.

It only occurred to me later that passersby may not have thought that's what they were seeing that day on the square, if they saw me at all. They may not have registered my Blackness at a glance, and often white people don't know enough about Black interiority or their own exposure with regard to Confederate iconography to be concerned. Or they simply aren't checking for us, which made me free to go about my own Black business.

The limestone-brick Confederate Soldiers Monument, inscribed in Latin, standing six feet at the base, was topped with a bronzed eagle and arched above a bronzed Confederate soldier facing north, standing armed guard against the forces of historical truth, perhaps. It was erected by the United Confederate Veterans (Camp Caldwell chapter) in 1910. Nearby, the Confederate State Convention marker, erected by the Kentucky Department of Highways, commemorates the 1861 convention where delegates from "sixty-four" Kentucky counties voted to secede from the Union. A few feet away, the Site of the Sovereignty Convention engraved stone, memorializing the same event, honors delegates from "sixty-eight" counties who voted "to set up a newly constituted State of Kentucky," where the "sovereignty of our people found a medium of expression for sympathy with the Southern cause in which there could be no stigma of treason." It was erected in 1949 by the United Daughters of the Confederacy, who seeded the country with monuments, totems, and myths as Black people were pressing for their full rights as citizens. Together, the three monuments approximated a triptych trying to hallow Southern ground and further cement the lies of the lost cause.

That same weekend, Historic Russellville Inc. unveiled a statue of Alice Dunnigan, the first Black female White House correspondent, on the grounds of her sister-in-law's house, which is also one of the SEEK Museums in the Black Bottom, where she grew up. Some local Russellville officials were angry it wasn't erected in Carrico Park, intermixed with its Confederate memorials, "where everybody could see it." *Hell, everybody could see it in the Black Bottom,* Morrow said.

Steps from the park, the historic William Forst House is the home office of J. Gran Clark Jr., attorney-at-law, the SEEK Museum cofounder and head of Historic Russellville Inc. The two-story Federal-style brick building, alternately called the Forst Clark House or simply the Clark House and built in 1820, was the site of that much memorialized 1861 Confederate convention. The great-grandfather of Gran Clark, as everyone called him, had been the convention's doorkeeper. The house was turned into a funeral home run by Clark's grandfather, then partially converted into apartments and his father's first-floor law office before it became his own. For decades, an historic marker sat just left of the front door commemorating the former Convention site and out of towners would prilgrmage to the site, driving by and taking pictures. Joe Gran Clark removed the plaque in 2010 because when he put himself in the place of his close Black friends and the people he worked with, he thought he wouldn't want to walk into a building with a Confederate monument sign. The house is for Clark a place of memory and reconciliation. Home to an adored grandmother with firmly held Southern ideas about race that Clark has held up to the light of reason and modernity to examine many times, from many different angles.

"There was a Black woman who had taken care of my grandmother as a child, and when she became old and sick, my grandmother took her in," Clark told me after we'd toured the house. She thought it was her duty to care for this woman, who had taken such tender care of her, he said.

I understood the power of his grandmother's story because I understand loyalty and human connection. I understand love. But these were my questions: Can I only get that love if I work for you? Do we have to raise you from childhood to get that kind of respect?

What if I come to our relationship with my own agency, self-interest, and assertions? Are you saying when I advocate for a better shake, and a fairer deal for me and mine, I can't get no love?

It was, said Clark, a fair point.

His words acted as a balm, although maybe not in that moment.

Russellville had got me to wondering, not for the first time, about the cost of being in community with white people (as a cohort, not individuals), when even the smallest encounters under the most benign circumstances have the potential to drain our reserves, fray our nerves, and cost us time.

It is not, primarily, that white people say these things, or make political choices that we judge to be harmful. It is that they want us to be cool about it. Or at least silent in ways that go against our own self-interest, which they then take as permission to go further.

They love and welcome us when we entertain or care for them, but so consistently fight our claims of citizenship, equality, or basic humanity when we insist on the same operating space they claim for themselves and their children. They become enraged when our petitions violate their ability to extract labor from our bodies, money from our pockets, and existential meaning from our station relative to their own. For real though, why would they expect us to visit an Alice Dunnigan statue in a park with Confederate memorials?

They become enraged, most especially, when Black people deny them the opportunity to feel charitable, by demanding justice instead.

As travelers and guests, I believe we have an obligation to participate in the local economy. But I'm averse to knowingly spending money in ways that strengthen the hand of folks who vote against Black life. Whether they intend to or not. Whether they realize it or not. My Lord, whether they love us or not.

Later that night, I took a picture of a light outside the Palladian windows at the historic bed-and-breakfast. And I reflected on what that dear, elderly uncle had told me: *I want you to remember my God and I have assigned you a special angel. She will be with you always; you may feel the flutter of her wings every now and then to let you know she is still there and she is yours.* I believed him then. I believe him still.

It is perhaps a marker of my "two-ness," as Du Bois called it. Except from where I was sitting, which was in a beautiful historic building, full of warmth, generosity, and faith in everything but the fullness of Black humanity, it felt more like three-ness or six-ness or *fucking eight-ness*. A house full of contradictions, with questions of America that surpass all understanding.

And don't nobody sing about that old Kentucky home.

CHAPTER 10

COLORISM

The first time I visited the Bibb House Museum, a young man I'd never met had something he needed to ask me. His question was straightforward and simple.

"Are you mixed?" he wanted to know.

It was the morning before the 2019 Bibb reunion. Michael Morrow had been talking about all the late aunts and distant cousins he'd tracked down, when curiosity got the better of the young man, who'd been sitting nearby listening quietly.

At first blush, the young man's question could be seen as an inappropriate thing to ask a complete stranger. But given the circumstances, it seemed about right. I told him I wasn't mixed and he looked confused.

"You're fully white?" he asked.

"Fully Black," I said.

"You're Black?" he pressed.

"And you're about to get beat up," said Morrow, ending that conversation. I was unoffended by his confusion, and I always try to cocoon young Black people in a full measure of grace, but I was also curious. Usually, nobody Black ever takes me for white, particularly not to my face, so our exchange felt striking. But then, we were at the former plantation home of Major Richard Bibb, where these things could get twisted. Where all kinds of things had gotten twisted.

As a matter of safety, self-preservation, or just really wanting to know, that young man needed to hear from me so he could move forward with our conversation. He didn't use these words, but here is what I heard him asking: *Whose side are you on? Who do you claim as your people? And, most specifically, can you be counted on in a fight?*

I don't usually hear the *what-are-you* question so bluntly expressed, but I am not unfamiliar with where it was coming from. And I understood everything that was riding on my answer.

In 1917, my great-grandfather Charles Smith Bibb called himself "African" on his World War I draft registration card.

Not "Negro" like his five brothers, not "Black," "colored," "mulatto," or "white," all of which I have seen on the various papers of his people, who are also my people. He wrote *African* in a neat cursive that started his capital *A* a few notches above the line to fit into a space that was not designed to accommodate that particular notion of self.

But Charlie Bibb was not African, or least had not been for generations. And he had little tolerance for dark-skinned people. I don't know if it was hate, but it was at least a specialized form of fear of what black skin could do to an American life in a system of racial caste.

Darker skin and more Afrocentric features are perceived to be more dangerous, less competent, and even worse, according to researchers. "These biases are held by both Blacks and non-Blacks, the latter of whom may have powerful roles as gatekeepers (educators, police, physicians, bankers, real estate agents, and so on)," wrote Ellis Monk, a scholar who researches social inequality and skin color stratification. Those biases, passed down through generations, result in accrued advantages and accrued disadvantages, meaning "skin tone stratification can quickly take on a deeply structural character."

Charlie Bibb died in 1940, but much of the family remained color-struck. There was not a single conversation about a new baby in the family that didn't begin with a color conference. With an accounting that carried an air of ceremony and command appearance, and enough tactile routine to make it ritual. It began with holding the new baby's hand, for comfort and connection, sure, and also to turn the fingers over and examine the nail bed. Along with the ear tips, this was where you could most reliably determine where the newborn would eventually land on the color line, despite whatever sweet color the baby showed up with.

There is a similar determination about hair, but Black baby hair is notoriously anti-colonial. And starts its resistance early. Many a Black family has been fooled by soft, downy, cooperative curls at week one (this is when everybody says the baby looks Indian) that turn into tight, unreconstructed coils by the end of the child's first year

What qualified as "good hair" was one calculation. But what constituted light skinned, in particular, was another debate. The paper bag test, which was once used as part of membership consideration by Black sororities and fraternities and other social organizations, was always out there as a barometer. But in the oldest extreme calculations, especially the ones coming out of both sides of my family, you wanted to be able to sidle yourself right up to the color line. You wanted, possibly, to be able to pass for white but emphatically choose not to do so.

There's always been an ambient contempt about passing for white among the Black folks I was raised around. I remember my momma's people saying we had a cousin passing for white in Washington, DC, but I couldn't be bothered to investigate. These were people we simply let go of. It was as if they belonged to a tribe of pitiable souls who'd lost themselves blending in, which was both a sin and a foolishness. It was a weighty cousin to the casual disregard we feel for people dressed inappropriately for the weather. The underlying logic goes: No matter the benefits of the outfit, the idea that it outweighs the dictates of temperature, personal comfort, good health, and good sense makes it disqualifying

Maybe it was because they'd been freed from bondage decades before most Black folks, but the Centralia Bibbs had come too far, or were too far gone, depending on how you framed these things, to construct a life on pretending. Who'd want to be a second-class white person losing loved ones, and hiding some of the best and most resourceful parts of yourself, when there was an alternative? Emancipation created more opportunities for all of the formerly enslaved, but the kinship ties of lighter-skinned Blacks to whites often meant more "social, educational, and economic advantages as compared to their darker brethren, giving them "an immense head start," according to Ellis.

"My daddy didn't like whites and he didn't like Blacks, okay?" my cousin Sharon Bibb Vaughn told me. Despite my great-uncle Morris's charm and leading-man looks, Cousin Sharon recalled him often receiving a cool reception from other Black people. "Them high yellows always thought they were something else," Sharon said. "People in Centralia always said the Bibbs thought they were more than everybody."

In the haze of memory and tale, anecdote and lore, details can get lost, but the color keeps in Black stories, like it does in Black faces. Sometimes the color is the story. When Uncle Morris married Sharon's mother, Dolores, some folks were taken aback.

Dolores, the love of Uncle Morris's playboy life, was a beautiful dark brown–skinned woman by the accounts of all those who knew her. Uncle Morris's sisters, especially my aunt Nellie, had a problem with her because of this. Or simply because she'd married their baby brother and the Bibbs were clannish. There may have been more to it, but that is what has survived the telling.

Dolores was waiting for Uncle Morris on the steps of Second Baptist Church of Centralia before heading into the funeral of his momma, Minnie Bibb.

Uncle Morris and his wife, Dolores Crowley, in 1946 on their wedding day.

Aunt Nellie took exception to this. Called her a Black bitch, told her she didn't belong, that she wasn't going to be allowed to go into her momma's funeral.

When my uncle Morris showed up, he walked his wife into Second Baptist, and that was that. The Bibb brothers and sisters didn't confront each other. This was not their way.

Dolores was pregnant with Sharon when Aunt Nellie threw a pot of grease at her on the steps of Momma Susie's house. It missed. But Dolores's mother and sister were hopping mad. "Do I need to come up there and whoop somebody's ass? I'm not that crazy about them yellow niggers anyway."

By the time Sharon married at eighteen, her momma had died. "I didn't want anything as light as my daddy," she said. "I married a dark, dark man. Nobody could think otherwise. I think sometimes we go against our fathers, that's our rebellious nature." When Sharon took her husband to meet her daddy's people, Aunt Nellie sat silent. "The next time I saw them, she told me he was too dark," Sharon said. "I looked at her like she was crazy. I said, 'Well you know, the darker the berry, the sweeter the juice.'"

"Well, baby, that doesn't mean you have to die of sugar diabetes," Aunt Nellie told her.

No notion of beauty is just skin deep when the subject is Black people and skin color. It was not simply preference expressed by my grandmother's generation of Bibbs (not to mention those before and some since). It was a marker of social capital. It was leverage. It was legitimacy, or illegitimacy. Skin color was a proxy for Blackness itself, a valuation of worth rooted in degradation going back to enslavement where light-skinned enslaved women were sold as "fancy girls" and fetched a premium price.

My mother has spent her whole life at the intersection of racism, colorism, and lookism. I have a copy of her picture on a 1959 cover of *Tan,* a pulpy Black magazine that used to sit on the wall at my uncle Joe's house. I've had it sitting on my desk at work and have taken it with me from house to house.

Momma was eighteen, staying with relatives, and had no success job hunting that sweltering summer before college until she wandered into the Chicago offices of Johnson Publishing. Momma asked to be a typist. They made her a model instead, barely even getting lipstick on her or powdering her nose before they started taking photos on the spot.

Momma taught me things about how to walk the world she knew—not just to wear an ankle bracelet so your legs look bigger, which can be a struggle if you're smallish—but about how to put other people at ease with you quickly. How to manage their anxieties about what you, historically, represent and where your loyalties might lie, while at the same time managing your own. For tribal people, the lines are delineated. Especially the color line.

Ask Momma about colorism and she'll put the wide context to it. "Family closeness, skin color, hair, it all went together. Back in those days it was like you have to elevate yourself, you know? And any-thing was better than being Black, by some Black folks in those days. Everybody was trying to move up. Or what they thought was moving up. People were just trying to do better. White people treated you better when you were light skinned."

It strikes me as a data point, a lived history, suffuse with tacit approvals, calamities avoided, benefits of the doubt, and all the smiles

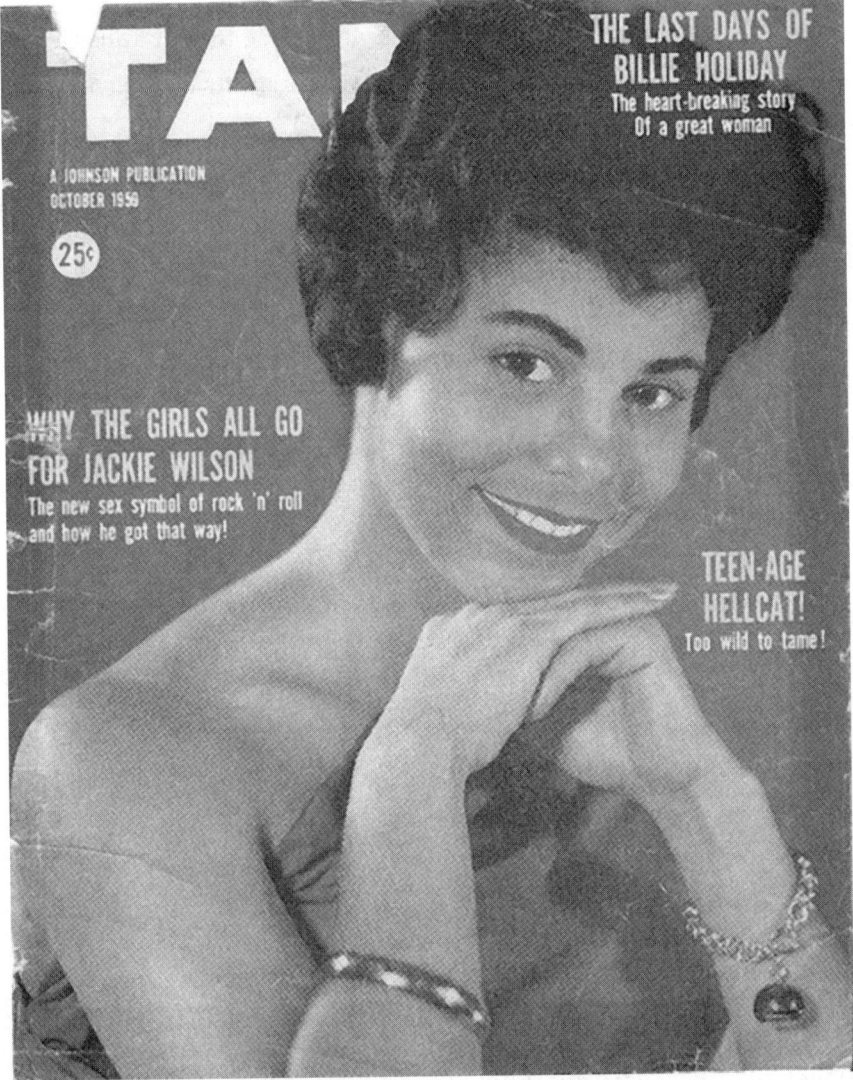

Lonnae's mother, Betty Lou, on the cover of *Tan Magazine*. Black Centralia was scandalized by the "Teen-Age Hellcat" reference, although it had nothing to do with her.

that break your way. By all the subtle advantages stemming from people simply being able to relate to the way you look. In the racial caste system of America, it is the padding of being light that absorbs some of the weathering of being Black. Over time that has positioned some of us to dodge some of the most overt aspects of racism. Or at least have it easier than other Black folks.

My momma, the former Elizabeth Blackwell, was not merely a product of her times, but of all the times that objectified, quantified, commercialized, fetishized, and came after Black people, to control and exploit, or to call for their undoing. Her keen smarts, her understanding of color politics, and her own capacious beauty made her a shrewd, nuanced observer. But even if she was evolving, the culture she was cocooned in was fixed and unmoving on the point. The Bibbs were firmly rooted in that colorism culture. Dug in, even.

> People say I'm trying to bring light-skinned
> back, but I'm just trying to bring back the love.
> **—El DeBarge**

As young girls on the South Side of Chicago, everybody wanted the light-skinned boy with the big, round Afro. The Sylvers, the DeBarges in Switch. Kristoff St. John in *The Bad News Bears* and *The Young and the Restless*. I loved Michi, who played on the Jackie Robinson West Division Little League Tigers with my brother Chucky. Michi was cream colored, with an ice-cream-cone Afro. And he could hit a baseball. Later, was there anything finer than Prince on the poster for "I Wanna Be Your Lover"? Light-skinned boys seduced us. Long before we were having sex, light-skinned boys acculturated us to the idea.

I pined for them, in a class-action kind of way, until I no longer did. Until I started bringing home brown-skinned and dark-skinned and sometimes very dark-skinned boys in junior high and high school. And especially college. It was a product of who stepped to me, I told myself. But I was also doing plenty of choosing. I felt the veiled disapproval from some in my family, the same way my cousin Sharon Bibb Vaughn got an earful when she brought home her new husband, but we were getting just past the time when it was socially acceptable to speak those concerns. And like my generation of Black Bibbs, it wouldn't have mattered to me if they did.

Since colorism is real, with generational consequences, the question becomes: What obligation is conferred on those who benefit from all unearned privilege, and from colorism specifically? Historically, race work was the answer for many. The light-skinned "race-man" or "race-woman" brings to mind a cadre of those who have labored to advance Black progress: This is what Momma Susie's cousin Harold Bibb was doing in all his church, union, and mutual aid society work locally. It is in the tradition of W. E. B. Du Bois, Malcolm X, Thurgood Marshall, Diane Nash, Angela Davis, Rosa Parks, James Farmer, Huey P. Newton, Lena Horne, Harry Belafonte, C. T. Vivian, and Constance Baker Motley, etc. People whose politics distinguished them as among the Blackest people in the room, while their color in a color-caste America had quite possibly opened the door.

It was perhaps work done to counter another Black stereotype—the idea that light-skinned Blacks were not to be trusted.

I watched *The Five Heartbeats*, about a fictitious Black singing group, while visiting my future in-laws once. The main character found out his fiancée had cheated on him with his brother, and he was devastated. "It's always the light-skinned ones," my future mother-in-law said. I was transported back to school, back on the playground, back on my heels, with nothing to say in my defense.

I was fine with having to tell the young man in Russellville I was Black at that first Bibb reunion. Black people have long needed to have these conversations and come to terms with the wary ways we circle each other.

But I resisted the urge to explain myself to people who are not Black—until that urge was no longer there. Until not doing so, not explaining myself, became a point of pride, a way to shift the burden of racial discomfort onto the shoulders it rightly belonged to. I would say I learned that from Momma Susie, but then, she never explained herself to anybody. The legacy of our past is not just in the systems and laws. It's not just in the institutions. It's grafted onto our skin. It tells personal stories and stories of the nation. Even the ones we hesitate to tell because we are quite sure no one wants to hear them.

CHAPTER 11

BEWARE OF BECKY

One weekend when my son was a teen, we watched the three screen adaptations of *The Lord of the Rings* in a J. R. R. Tolkien movie marathon.

We are sci-fi / fantasy fans in my house, and this has often meant LOTR. I've seen the movies, my husband read the books in middle school, and as a matter of habit and course, we talk about the language, lessons, and panoramic sweep of the saga. I sometimes fall asleep to the rhythms of Middle Earth.

Even with transcendent moments in the storytelling, however, I still had to teach my son powers of discernment. I've come to understand the Tolkien oeuvre is framed as a race war, but I'd never seen the mutant Orcs in LOTR as an allegorical threat. (Probably, thankfully, because Black people never occurred to me as Orcs.) Instead, I had to teach my son what he was looking at when he was looking at the movies' white heroines. And the lessons, to my son especially, could not start too soon.

As we watched the trilogy, I noted every scene with Galadriel, Elven queen and the Lady of Lothlorien; Eowyn, a sword-wielding noble of Rohan; and Arwen, the she-elf, the love interest, the brave and intuitive rider, future queen of Middle Earth and all around baddie. Arwen, especially, was bathed in light. A gentle wind lifted her hair. She was beatified by notes of song.

After two or three scenes of this foolishness, I felt compelled to speak up.

Me: [Son], you know white girls aren't all lit up like that, right?

I gave him a few moments. As a thought exercise, it was fascinating to watch my young son try to make sense of what I had just said.

Me: Did you hear me?

Him: Mommmm.

Me: I'm serious, [Son], you know white girls don't come with all that backlight.

Him: Mommmm!!!

Me: [Sonnnn!!!]

Him: Yes, Mom. I know! White girls don't come with their own lights.

Fine. Good. It needed to be said.

It can seem hyperbolic, this talk we must have with our Black sons contextualizing white women, though it is not unrelated to the talk we have to have with them about what to do if they get stopped by the police, in that both are necessitated by white supremacy. Everything you say can seem exaggerated when you're living out loud and Black, but that doesn't make it untrue. It might seem hyperbolic, except what is actually hyperbolic is the savage idea of white womanhood that has gotten Black people killed. It can seem overwrought, except when you understand the stakes, which are rooted in the history of race and sex in America. They are rooted in the money that ends up in your pocket, helping you to take care of your kids and your community. The stakes are informed by the lived experiences of Black mothers, and their mothers and their mothers before them.

And we remember everything.

Everywhere enslavement was practiced, the rape of Black women by white men was central to the institution. It never had the symbolic power of lynching as a visceral totem, but the practice yoked Black women to stereotypes of "illicit sexuality" for centuries, wrote historian Darlene Clark Hine. In a further act of white projection, those stereotypes then became a pretext for why Black men were accused of being so sexually dangerous, which in turn became a justification for lynching.

The 1850 census was the first to include the mixed-race "mulatto" designation, and the term was later characterized to mean "all persons having any perceptible trace of African blood." This taxonomy could refer to Native and Black or Asian and Black mixed-race heritage. But it typically meant a mixture of Black and white ancestry, which also happened to be the only two other racial categories the census recognized until 1870, and in the context of enslavement, that overwhelmingly meant one thing.

"I have rape-colored skin," poet Caroline Randall Williams wrote in the *New York Times*. "My light-brown-blackness is a living testament to the rules, the practices, the causes of the Old South . . . and of my immediate white male ancestors, all of them were rapists."

Williams, a self-described Black Southern woman, called her body a Confederate monument. "My very existence is a relic of slavery and Jim Crow."

In 1860, there were 27 million white people in the US and a little over 4.4 million "free colored and slaves." Of that total "colored" population, 13.25 percent were categorized as "mulatto," up from 11.15 percent in 1850.

Between 1850 and 1860 in Logan County, the total number of enslavers went from 981 to 1,230 (an increase of about 25 percent). The total "colored" population (Black and "mulatto") grew from 5,747 to 6,734 (roughly, a 15 percent increase). The number of enslaved Blacks saw a modest 6 percent increase—from 4,591 to 4,863—while the number of enslaved "mulattoes" in Logan County nearly doubled, going from 791 to 1,501 in ten years. Meanwhile, the number of free Black people in Logan County decreased from 301 to 265, and free "mulattoes" grew from 64 to 105 (a 64 percent increase).

White men elided the rapist implications of that census "increase," and the light-skinned "increases" all around them, and instead wrapped themselves in internally inconsistent arguments—intellectual, legal, religious, and pseudoscientific—to try to make themselves blameless in their own eyes and in the judgment of history.

"Their griefs are transient," Thomas Jefferson opined on the emotional capacity of the enslaved. The founding father, author of the Declaration of Independence, and third US president fathered six children with the enslaved woman Sally Hemings, the half sister of his dead wife. "Those numberless afflictions, which render it doubtful whether heaven has given life to us in mercy or in wrath, are less felt, and sooner forgotten with them," he wrote.

In his famed narrative of enslavement, Henry Bibb detailed how the rapist practices of enslavement played out generationally in Black lives.

"My mother was known by the name of Mildred Jackson. She is the mother of seven slaves only, all being sons, of whom I am the eldest. She was also so fortunate or unfortunate, as to have some of what is called the slaveholding blood flowing in her veins. I know not how much; but not enough to prevent her children though fathered by slaveholders, from being bought and sold in the slave markets of the South. It is almost impossible for slaves to give a correct account of their male parentage. All that I know about it is, that my mother informed me that my father's name was James Bibb. He was doubtless one of the present Bibb family of Kentucky; but I have no personal knowledge of him at all, for he died before my recollection."

My Bibbtown ancestors are part of those Logan County "mulatto" numbers. Bibbtown matriarch Granny Kate, who was understood to be the daughter of Major Richard Bibb, was three when she was emancipated.

He was eighty-six years old when he died.

(Her mother, Nancy, Momma Keziah's daughter, was not listed in Major Bibb's will and had presumably died. Young Catherine was raised with Momma Keziah and her aunts Rachel and Winnie—who is categorized as "deaf and dumb" in the census—and lived with Momma Keziah's oldest son, Frank.)

The US Census of 1860 cited Brace's *Manual of Ethnology* to opine that only "the races most gifted with self-control—those of most moral principle"—could adapt to new circumstances, like those presented by the rigors of freedom, and were best able to survive. It was an argument against miscegenation by and for white people on the eve of the Civil War building to its top-line conclusion that regardless of who's their daddy, "the colored population in America . . . is doomed to comparatively rapid absorption or extinction."

A year after the census that so troubled itself with colored morality was collected, the publication of Harriet Jacobs's autobiography, *Incidents in the Life of a Slave Girl*, offered an unsparing account of female enslavement. Jacobs called her fifteenth birthday the beginning of "a sad epoch in the life of a slave girl . . . when my master began to whisper foul words in my ear. Young as I was, I could not remain ignorant of their import. . . ."

Jacobs once saw an enslaved man lashed to a pulp for arguing with his wife, in front of the overseer, about whether the enslaver was the father of their fair-skinned child. Later, they were both sold to a slave trader. "She had forgotten that it was a crime for a slave to tell who was the father of her child," wrote Jacobs, who spent seven years hiding from her enslaver in a crawl space of her grandmother's house.

"The secrets of slavery are concealed like those of the Inquisition. My master was, to my knowledge, the father of eleven slaves. But did the mothers dare to tell who was the father of their children? Did the other slaves dare to allude to it, except in whispers among themselves? No, indeed! They knew too well the terrible consequences!"

Jacobs would awaken to the mistress bending over her, whispering in the night, to see if Jacobs spilled illicit secrets in her slumber. She lived in terror of the plantation master catching her alone. "I would rather drudge out my life on a cotton plantation, till the grave opened to give me rest, than to live with an unprincipled master and a jealous mistress. [A favorite slave] is not allowed to have any pride of character. It is deemed a crime in her to wish to be virtuous," Jacobs wrote.

There's a further perception—back then, as is the case now—that women invited their own rape. That Black women seduced their enslavers or worked as prostitutes (which is partially why white women, so-called Christian women, who might have shielded enslaved women and children from their husbands, instead targeted them for their wrath). It's the twisted notion that rape victims always face—that they wanted it, a contention that always privileges the rapist. We are simply unaccustomed to thinking about and applying those rape truisms to enslavement, patriarchy, and white supremacy as they relate to the profound vulnerability of Black women during enslavement and Jim Crow.

From the late-nineteenth to the mid-twentieth century, the majority of Black women's work was either agricultural or domestic, the latter taking them into white homes and putting them in constant danger of sexual assault, according to scholars Daina Ramey Berry and Kali Nicole Gross.

"You couldn't be out working 'til you knew how people was raped. You'd know how to run or always not be in the house with the white men or big sons," Weida Edwards, a Black migrant woman, told historian Darlene Clark Hine.

The net effect of this history was to maintain cultural and legal access to women by white men. One caste they took as wives; another they raped with impunity and silenced historically, projecting everything they were perpetrating onto the Black men they lynched and Black women they blamed.

The practice of lynching Black men for rape gained the imprimatur of law in the twentieth century, almost exclusively in the former slaveholding states. Of the 455 people executed for rape between 1930 and the Supreme Court's decision overturning existing death penalty statutes in 1972, 90 percent were Black. And of those state-sanctioned lynchings, 97.4 percent took place in Southern states.

According to historian Kristina DuRocher:

> The high number of white girls and teenagers who accused black men of sexual assault in the Jim Crow South brings into question their motivations for doing so and the reasons why the white community believed these accusations, often despite evidence to the contrary.
>
> Regardless of the veracity of the girls' accusation, the rape-lynch rhetoric gave white southerners a way to unite along racial lines and strengthen white supremacy. Hence, the community often did not doubt the scapegoat's guilt and the victim's innocence in order to reap the social benefits of white unity. In this way, young girls could charge African American men with sexual crimes knowing that the community would regard their accounts as the solemn truth.
>
> This offered some white females the opportunity to circumvent traditional female roles as long as their accounts of their own actions

plausibly portrayed them as maintaining the proper racial boundaries and preserving an ideal of white feminine virtue.

Meanwhile, silence became one of the coping mechanisms Black women used to survive. Because who, after all, was going to save us?

But as Audre Lorde pointed out, our silence did not protect us either.

It is against that brutal history that Black women have always worked, physically, emotionally, intellectually, morally, and politically to be free of sexual stereotypes. In the early twentieth century, a wide swath of Black women buttoned up from their necks down to their ankles. Later they customized and maintained our respectability as they marched, organized, and fought alongside and sometimes against Black men. That last point, we kept to ourselves, as in-house, family business, as if the race depended on it. Because it surely did. Because white men were seizing Black husbands, brothers, fathers, sons, and using us, in part, to justify their violence, with the sanction or even encouragement of white women who dressed for these barbarous occasions. Who packed food and took their children to watch the spectacle of lynchings performed in the defense of white womanhood.

A 2018 *Guardian* newspaper article on lynching stated: "In the 1931 Maryville, Missouri, lynching of Raymond Gunn, the crowd estimated at two thousand to four thousand was at least a quarter women, and included hundreds of children. One woman 'held her little girl up so she could get a better view of the naked Negro blazing on the roof,' wrote Arthur F. Raper in *The Tragedy of Lynching*."

It is against this backdrop that Black mothers, especially, consider the ways white women as a cohort, as a reliable voting bloc for policies that imperil us, as enslavers, segregationists, lynching enthusiasts, and Karens have impacted our lives.

It is against that history that we think about the risk and reward of allowing them into our lives, how close we want them to get to our children, and how eager we should be to consider them family.

And Black women, who are always seeing around corners (which is why we're so often cast as mystics and spiritualists in movies, no?), who are reliably on the side of our democratic republic, which is our best hope to protect Black children, which also happens to save the nation, took note. As we ever have.

Long before the term (not the name) *Karen* became a blanket 2020s shorthand for white women who weaponize their race, gender, and tears to intimidate Black and brown people, racially police public spaces, and act out their anti-Blackness, Black women warned sons known and unknown to us to stay away from white girls. Warned they could get you lost or killed. Warned that they might take you from yourself and put you beyond the reach of your people. Or simply cause you to forfeit all your cool points.

And quicker than a chorus of white women can rise up to say "not me," or "not all white women," it's important to detail exactly what we're talking about. It's important to scan the bone memory of Black people to get at those white women in our hollows. Because that history matters, that complexity matters, that trauma matters, and it is generational.

Put another way, it matters, deeply, how we got here.

In the cultural and historical narratives of slavery, the role of white women has been underplayed. They've often been depicted as bystanders, also victimized by white male oppression. In some conceptions, they participated in slavery, but only insofar as their primary considerations around hearth and home were engaged.

They were understood to resort to fits of cruelty upon finding out their husbands, whom they could not formally punish, were raping enslaved women. But they are not central to the economics or perpetuation of slavery in the wholesale rendering of historians. This limited accounting has been inadequate to the scope of white women's impact on enslaved Black lives and the furtherance of white supremacy.

It doesn't help us figure out how we got here.

Roughly 40 percent of those who enslaved Black people were white women, historian Stephanie E. Jones-Rogers found in researching her book *They Were Her Property: White Women as Slave Owners in the American South*.

She cross-referenced 1930s Federal Writers' Project interviews of the formerly enslaved with United States Census Slave Schedules and other population reports, bills of sale, tax documents, and various documents, and contends historians overlooked white women's centrality to slavery "because their behaviors toward and relationships with their [enslaved] do not conform to prevailing ideas about white women and slave mastery."

No group spoke about white women's "investments in slavery more often, or more powerfully, than the enslaved people subjected to their ownership and control," Jones-Rogers wrote.

I was reminded that in 1742 in Hanover County, Virginia, the father-in-law of Henry Bibb (a white Bibb descendant) left Bibb's mother-in-law, Elizabeth, "six negro slaves, three males and three females, she to take her choice" in his will. Women couldn't own land until the late nineteenth century in Virginia, but they'd owned Black people since 1644, and according to the will, and custom, any "increase" the enslaved females bore was left to Elizabeth's "sole disposing and to her heirs forever."

Major Richard Bibb is thought to have given enslaved people to his six children, including his three daughters, who couldn't own land, to act as their personal maids and servants, before he had a change of heart and began emancipating those he enslaved in 1832. The second wife of George Mortimer Bibb brought enslaved people to their marriage, as did the wife of John Bigger Bibb. She inherited three dozen enslaved people in Frankfort, Kentucky, who passed to him after she died.

White women, who were often gifted or bequeathed Black people, prepared for their roles as enslavers from childhood, learning how to issue orders and mete out punishment. In one such example cited by Jones-Rogers, Lizzie Anna Burwell of Lynesville, North Carolina, became cross with Fanny, the enslaved woman who cared for her, so she asked her father to "cut Fanny's ears off" and get her a new maid. Lizzie Anna was three.

From an early age, white women learned the full extension of their proprietary rights over Black lives. They understood the power that comes with personal wealth, even in a patriarchy, and they owned twice as many enslaved women than they did enslaved men, women who they bred so they could own and profit from Black children, according to the law.

"Only enslaved people could speak about their female owners' profound economic contributions to their continued enslavement with such astonishing precision.... They were the people whose lives were forever changed when a mistress sold someone just so she could buy a new dress. They were best equipped to describe the agony that shook their bodies and souls when they returned from their errands to discover that their children were gone and their mistresses were counting piles of money they had received from the live traders who bought them," Jones-Rogers wrote.

When they married men who had fathered enslaved children, "they do not trouble themselves about it," Harriet Jacobs wrote. "They regard such children as property, as marketable as the pigs on the plantation; and it is seldom that they do not make them aware of this, passing them into the slave trader's hands as soon as possible."

White men realized white women had to be personal and direct beneficiaries of slavery for the institution to survive. And long before feminism hit its first wave, white women found agency, independence, and their greatest equality with white men in owning Black people.

That central role in enslavement sets up the next era of white women in the anti-Black history of the nation. Those of us born after the Civil Rights Movement, without the lived experience of Jim Crow, were taught that like slavery, segregation was mainly a project of white men. They were the rancid, dullard thugs blocking school doors and beating civil rights protesters about the head at segregated lunch counters. White women were the ones standing by, laughing, scream- ing, or sneering in photos, or so we were taught.

But just as in slavery, where the roles of white women were obscured, twisted, brushed over in Southern pastels, so it was with their Jim Crow work as well.

It was white women who were "segregation's constant gardeners," according to historian Elizabeth Gillespie McRae.

By 1920, the Ku Klux Klan was newly ascendant, and white women, in pointy white hats ironed to a crisp, helped lead the way.

Mary Elizabeth Tyler, who cofounded the Southern Publicity Association in Atlanta, evangelized for the Klan, reaching out to white women with appeals that encouraged parity with white men in the pursuit of white supremacy. She founded the Klan newspaper *The Searchlight*, and by 1923, the KKK had upward of 1.5 million white female members, including a third of the white Protestant women in Indiana, according to historian Linda Gordon.

The Nineteenth Amendment, granting women the right to vote in 1920, opened new lanes for women's cultural, religious, and political expression. And the Women of the Ku Klux Klan, the WKKK, became an extension of social and church networks engendering a clubby, Christian confederation of haters speechifying about American rights and "pure womanhood."

They "organized Klan rites of passage, baptisms, graduations, marriages and funerals. Every time the Klan put on a big pageant or lecture, you can be sure that it was women who were doing the publicity and collecting the food," Gordon wrote. They provided organizational scaffolding and tapped into their new electoral power to help elect a broad cadre of local, state, and national segregationist politicians.

In Logan County, white women organized social events for the local chapter of the KKK—picnics, church services, bargain day sales, and games—as Klan numbers outgrew their hall, prompting them to meet at the Logan County Courthouse in Russellville. The WKKK ran newspaper ads inviting more women to join and "Bring your friends." I imagine my Bibbtown ancestors were glad to be self-sufficient enough not to have to venture into town on these occasions, and not to have to work in these Christian women's homes as they planned their first homecoming and Flag Day celebrations.

In 1917, the year before Momma Susie was born, white mobs, angry over the influx of Black industrial workers, shot, hung, beat, and burned Black residents of East St. Louis, Illinois, just an hour west of Centralia, officially killing thirty-nine people and possibly as many as two hundred. The Red Summer of 1919 saw a national frenzy of white violence, with riots and lynchings in more than two dozen cities and towns, including Chicago, where days of rioting left fifteen whites and twenty-three Blacks dead, and hundreds more injured. As my grandmother was growing up in the 1920s, two hundred thousand Illinoisans were joining the KKK (though those were Klan-reported numbers, according to historian Darrel Dexter, and the real figure is likely less), which helped elect candidates across the state, with support from the Illinois governor. According to the 1975 Centralia Library oral history project, Centralia had an active KKK chapter. And as with slavery, this was all work that could not have existed without the promotion of white women who remained stunningly attentive to their most small-minded aggressions. Just like that white wife of the Berkeley math department chair who delayed the appointment of my uncle Dave.

Segregation was another American enterprise that generations of white women threw themselves into with gusto, largely beneath the notice or attention of the media, as was the case with most women's work. "Maintaining racial segregation was not solely or even primarily the work of elected officials," McRae wrote in *Mothers of Massive Resistance: White Women and the Politics of White Supremacy.* It was a system, generations in the making, requiring "quotidian work and organizations that reached beyond the KKK and the Citizen's Councils—far below the legislative halls, judicial chambers and voting booths."

Segregation in "dating etiquette, teacher training, public health policies, sexual customs, civic organizations, and in the stories people told" had to be ritualized, and supported, by formal and informal networks of mutuality. White women preached it in their homes and reinforced it in the streets—or at least the theaters, restaurants, parks, pools, classrooms, and sock hops. At PTA meetings and Tupperware parties. Behind the scenes white women did the spite work of segregation (just like behind the scenes Black women did the dignity work of civil rights).

And they brought a particular zeal to their cause.

Segregation gave white women stature, influence, purpose, and proximal and positional power with white men. And it gave them something else. Something deeper, lower perhaps, that they could feel in their innards. It's a heady thing to think that you are so beautiful and worthy of protection that men would kill for you. Or at least arrange the nation to keep you from having to see Black people minding their own Black business. Or so I imagine.

White women used racial hatred to caulk the seams of American life. It was white women who "were the mass in massive resistance," McRae wrote. They worked inside their spheres of influence, especially public schools, but also religion and popular culture, to tend to the daily, prosaic, often hyperlocal grassroots work of keeping and reinforcing the systems of racial caste that gave their lives meaning. At the cost of their souls.

Nobel laureate Toni Morrison said this in an interview:

During the Civil Rights Movement, there were women who would rush out to the schoolyards when they were trying to integrate schools, and they would push over the school buses that were bringing Black children to these schools. Push them over and set them on fire.

And when I saw that, I was wondering whether I could ever get a group of Black women, under any circumstances, from any walk of life to hurt some white children. To set a bus on fire, full of white children, for any reason. Prostitutes, drug addicts, ministers, teachers, Black women of any level, could I call them all together and say, "We have got to burn these white children?"

And I didn't believe I could ever find that. So, I thought those white mothers, they were not just white women, they had actually had children. They knew what that was like. But they could do that to those children. They could spit at a child. . . . The absence of that shame was so profound that the real victim was not those children, it was those women who had given up everything—their motherhood, their woman-hood, their citizenship—everything to do that nasty thing.

Now that is a true victim of history.

In this context, plus covid and the social-justice protests over the 2020 police murder of George Floyd, the subsequent moral panic over books, authors, and educators who talk about race and inequality across every stratum of American society becomes much more legible.

The ends, the means, and the expressions are different, but it's the same tradition that gives license to the tearful, privilege-hoarding mothers protesting admission changes to elite schools across the country. And to the white woman who called the police on a group of Black men for their unsanctioned barbecuing on a charcoal grill at Lake Merritt park in Oakland. That 2018 incident was turned into the "BBQ Becky" meme, one of the earliest high-profile examples of the "Karen meme genre... that call attention to, and reject, white women's surveillance and regulation of Black bodies in public spaces—making an important connection between racialized surveillance of the past and contemporary acts of 'casual racism,'" according to Apryl Williams, a scholar of gender and race in digital spaces. The memes frame "Karens and Beckys as racist—not just disgruntled or entitled," and call for consequences.

I doubt these women see themselves in each other, or the history that connects them. White innocence is a gossamer cloak, soaked in denial, sprinkled with angel dust, and aged. It acts as a powerful hallucinogenic, and white women's addiction to it (as a cohort) explains both the majority of them who vote for anti-Black and anti-reproductive freedom projects, and the liberal white feminists who are so repetitively shocked, *shocked*, by that outcome. One of its components is not knowing the history of white women in anti-Blackness because you don't want to know the history. Because the facts are bad. Because the history damns you and whispers in Black tongue, *You a lie.* Because there's been a whole #MeToo movement of women, whose originator was Black but whose public faces were largely white, protesting sexual violence, and I missed the part where white women called for the jailing of Carolyn Bryant Donham.

In 1955, she used a fourteen-year-old Emmett Till to work out some violent codependence with her old man—see the *Life* photos of her and her husband kissing after he was acquitted of murdering Till. Bryant, who accused Till of whistling at her, recanted late in life the most lurid parts of the story that got Till killed. In 2023, she died at age eighty-eight, having never been held to account, except perhaps by her Maker. Though there was plenty of time for white women to do so, at least rhetorically. Just as there was plenty of time during the height of the #MeToo movement for white women to acknowledge their deeply problematic history.

Their white innocence includes claiming the mantle of color blindness, swearing to it, tearfully sometimes, and denying that they have a single racist bone in their bodies (which is not a thing anatomically, BTW), while using performative ignorance to disregard the centrality of race in determining social, political, and economic outcomes throughout American history and contemporary life. Their privilege has made them soft, and not in a good way. Their innocence makes white women (as a cohort, not individuals) untrustworthy and unsafe to Blackness.

It is all so very tiresome, and all of this, all at once, is what Black women, particularly Black mothers, often see, just like our mothers and grandmothers did before us, when we see white women. When I worried aloud to my mother about sending my son down South to attend college and play football, she went straight to our collective shorthand about the dread fates of Black bodies.

"Don't worry," my mother told me. "He won't whistle at any white girls."

✼ ✼ ✼ ✼

When my son was about eight or nine, he was at baseball practice when a white coach's daughter jumped on him. Literally. And the two started to wrestle. The coach and the girl's mother, standing close by, ignored it.

I was aghast.

"Get up off him! Get up off him!" I sat in my car yelling, not trusting myself to get out. I very possibly would have physically lifted that little girl from atop my son and had words for the parents. The Black mothers I know would've charged the field if that were their daughters, I fumed. I felt like I had no play.

I had no ability to gauge how egregious the jump may have been, but the trigger was old, old. And it always carries the possibility of uneven sanction. Centuries of racialized judgments and sexual violence directed at Black people, combined with adultification of Black children, have simply made us less available for roughhousing. And for every time someone tells us we're overreacting, there's a "Cornerstore Caroline," who in 2018 called the police on a nine-year-old Black boy she said had sexually assaulted her after his backpack brushed her butt at a Brooklyn bodega, causing the little boy to burst into tears. Prior to cell phones, a Black child's vulnerability often went unrecorded.

Beyond the peril, at least in our Black momma minds, we don't think anything about girls jumping on our sons is cute. But of course, getting jumped on by a girl is just the kind of thing a preteen boy finds very compelling. As I yelled inside the car, a male friend I was on the phone with said, "Get used to it. In two years, that white girl will be asking him for his phone number, while all the Black girls will be standing at their lockers dogging them both out."

My frames of reference are middle-aged, my kids' and their friends' dating observations are middle-class, anecdotal, heteronormative, and perhaps offer nothing more than a snapshot of their custom experiences, but Black girls don't typically walk up and ask boys for their phone numbers or even social media information.

But either way, what is also true is that white girls have always had better PR.

In 2004, the dearly departed Gwen Ifill, the pioneering journalist who spoke such sisterly words to so many of us, coined the phrase "missing white woman syndrome" to describe media coverage of white women who have gotten nabbed, lost, or are otherwise gone. "If there's a missing white woman, you're going to cover that, every day," Ifill said.

When I was a girl, the world was Black, but from the time I began watching television, all I saw were white girls. And sometimes, they filled our waking minds.

As children, we used to be intrigued by the lone white woman left behind in the three- or four-year exodus from the time the first Black person moved into the neighborhood to the time it took for our South Side Chicago block to flip.

The white woman lived at about nine years old, using around-the-way math. It's a measurement of how old you are relative to how far down the block your momma would let you walk if you were by yourself, and she was paying attention. It was more art than science, a kind of knowing, triggered by heavy footfalls, unfamiliar doorsteps, and people who looked bigger than they looked closer to home. As kids, we used to imagine we saw the white woman in the shadows, peering out at us through her big picture window. Nobody ever seemed to get a real look at her though. We couldn't say how tall she was, what she wore, or whether she even really existed. She wasn't a white woman so much as a rumor of a white woman.

You could forget about seeing a white kid in my far South Side neighborhood, and we didn't think about them one way or the other, but we did like their antics on television. And also, their hair. We loved their hair. Or at least I assumed we loved it. Why else would our mommas sit us in the chairs of women who'd make us hold our ears while they put an iron comb, fresh off the flame, as close to our scalps as they could come without burning us? Though sometimes they did burn us. And sometimes they didn't, but we'd flinch. Then the woman whose chair we were in would threaten, "Move again and I'mma hit your knuckles with the hot comb." This continued for about an hour or so, depending on how much hair needed to be pressed. And it doesn't include hair-washing days. It doesn't include the tearful time it took to shampoo, pull apart, painfully detangle, and comb through each section of hair. *Washday's child is full of woe.* But while it was more painful than the everyday pain of getting your natural Black hair combed, at least that was also a pain at your momma's hand. It didn't involve burners, or stoves, or the sizzle as the hot comb met the grease in the "kitchen" that sat low on your neck.

The result—bone-straight hair, once or twice a year—was

transformative. For a brief moment, or up to two weeks if you didn't swim or sweat, our hair looked more like theirs, which always got encoded as neat. Presentable. Pretty.

The desire for this look doesn't happen in a vacuum. The white girls on television taught it to us growing up. They taught it to the known world, and every metric of attractiveness was set up to reinforce that lesson, so that even Black girls who spent their childhood utterly walled off from white people could credibly want to be Miss Clairol, or Samantha in *Bewitched*, or Jeannie in *I Dream of Jeannie.*

And don't even get me started on that bitch Truly Scrumptious.

Man, I loved Truly Scrumptious.

Black girls were, at least partially, indexed, and indexing themselves by the same kinds of white-girl standards that remain in the ether. They show up in every form of media we consume. They are meant to make us covet.

I don't know what the psychic mechanism was that allowed you to live in an all-Black world, where you watched television and saw nothing but white girls flipping their hair, and still managed to stay sane. But that's what we did, more or less. What we still do. Most of us, most of the time anyway.

As a Black mother (who still has a mildly tangled relationship with her natural Black hair), it can be a thankless task trying to counter that cinematic backlighting. That shimmery white-woman agitprop mau-mauing our children.

It can also make us look, ahem, startlingly intense, even though, as it turns out, the research and science backs us up all the way.

As a cohort, Black women's concerns are as nuanced as the history that gave rise to them. Black women's bodies represent the reproduction of slavery, Brittney Cooper wrote, so our bodies are "cast as the unique and singular site for unfreedom." White women can represent the opposite. Can represent freedom from that specific centuries-old sexual baggage and fallout. From the cultural strictures that warned us, in the most strident and judgmental terms, against being a fast-tailed girl while teaching us nothing about birth control, sex, or sexuality. That disallow roughhousing and discourage our daughters from asking a cute Black boy for his phone number. From all of our Momma Susies yelling "Keep your legs closed!"

In the broadest strokes, white women (as a cohort) can become a kind of romantic carve-out that gets shorthanded as racial progress. Shorthanded as moving on and seeing past race—without society having done anything close to the work of all of that, which requires a reckoning with history and legions of inequities.

Inequities that show up in the white girls we watched on television, and in all our instincts and visceral reactions to what we were seeing, and can be attributed to what researchers who study lookism and stratification call a "halo effect."

It relates to the greater social and bodily capital that accrues to those who most closely match European standards of beauty—lighter skin, blue eyes, blond hair, slimness, and certain types of facial features, according to the researcher and sociology professor Ellis Monk. And this finding is true worldwide. There's a system of beliefs about what all those European standards add up to, "and then there are all the consequences of that system of beliefs about people—and how aspects of our appearance are allegedly some kind of a cue or a signal to the quality and value of a person."

And about whether people find them attractive.

The biggest predictor of whether people perceive someone as attractive is skin color, irrespective of other traits, with the second being hair, Monk wrote. This means white women get spotted two points before the dating game even begins. We didn't have these studies when we were in college, but over the centuries we've learned to be observant.

Conversely, darker skin tone and more Afrocentric facial features are associated with appearing more masculine, according to researchers. Which often means Black women as a whole, and "especially darker-skinned Black women, may be penalized for being perceived as not feminine enough." But dark-skinned Black men "in particular, and Black men, in general, may not be as harshly penalized with respect to perceptions of perceived attractiveness."

It all just reminds me that when filmmakers want to make a white man look cool in a movie, they give him a Black friend. Before we know anything else about people, their color is already doing myriad forms of work.

"When it comes to white women, in order for them to achieve the apex of desirability, there has to be a foil to that, there has to be something else," said Jo Von McCalester, a professor of social and public policy and intersectionality. "And we're the something else. . . . Most folks don't know how far back this goes."

After the Civil War, when newly emancipated Black people were fashioning their post-enslavement identities, Black men often didn't want their women to work, because white men didn't have their wives working. Black men were trying to replicate white European gender roles. Though I saw my grandmothers, Pocahontas Bibb and Minnie Bibb, listed in census records as housekeepers, my Bibb and Blackwell grandmothers and aunties owned real estate, ran "tip boards," and in Momma Susie's case, loan sharked. Historian LaShawn D. Harris notes, these are all part of the ways Black women found to participate in the underground economies they historically relied on to provide runway for their families.

And sometimes that wasn't enough for some Black men, not because of who we were, but who we were not, in relation to who *they* were trying to be.

The cultural and economic stakes of all of this racial and sexual baggage can feel formidable, with generational impacts. Intermarriage can take people from the heart of the community, though it doesn't have to happen. A non-Black spouse can always decide to help carry the weight, but the worry is that our Blackness gets faded, our people become less connected, our resources get thinned. It may be the case with interracial marriage where the white spouse is brought in and becomes as comfortable and literate in Blackness as any Black cousin. Becomes versed in Black culture as a repository of creativity, joy, and activism. Becomes sanguine about the long lines of Black life—understanding that it simply takes eight hours to vote. But the worry is that our grown Black children become less tethered to Blackness (corny, perhaps, though that is not, by far, the worst that could happen). More significantly, that our Black sons could become less incubated in the kind of critical thinking that two partners with skin in the game, who understand the stakes, bring to the myriad judgments of Black parenting. Which is the same as all parenting.

Except Black.

The worry is that Black men, most especially, in interracial relationships will allow a white spouse to replicate white innocence and cluelessness about our collective peril. Will allow them to teach inanities, like "I don't see race," rendering our grandchildren utterly unable to make sense of the world except through white eyes, even the fairly enlightened of which (as a cohort) feel most comfortable being blinkered. They will teach children not to talk about race, as if that's a good thing—instead of just a white thing. As if that equips anybody to understand and contextualize the most urgent issues of our life and times. As if we are like them and talking about race leads to violence.

Love is personal, highly subjective, love is love, and we recognize that, but in the broadest strokes, we do not see the choice to partner with white women as unconnected with the larger history of race in this country. What we are more likely to see, fundamentally, are the women who have always made our work as Black people, and on behalf of Black futures, so very much harder.

I tell my children, especially my sons, when the elevator of life is carrying Black people, there are those who will not get on. Others will step inside but they will bail on the early floors. The elevator music will feature Sarah Vaughan, Jill Scott, Stevie Wonder, and others (Solange, Frank Ocean. Also Kendrick Lamar, J. Cole, and Megan Thee Stallion. There will actually be a fight on the elevator over the elevator music). And some of our dear white friends and family will ride with us happily for a good long while. With few exceptions, though (Teena

Marie springs to mind), nobody rides the elevator all the way up with Black people, come whatever may, but Black people, even though we have so often been found going the distance with everybody else. To be clear, we are not rooting against anyone else, we are just rooting for ourselves to win. And on balance, Black mothers, especially, think the best way to do that is with each other.

If it sounds too zero-sum, that is not our creation, or formulation. We don't shun children, let alone turn over buses. We embrace. We forgive. We love. And we try our best to shield our children from the shimmery backlight of whiteness, the sole purpose of which is to blind them.

CHAPTER 12

LAND AS FAR AS THE EYE CAN SEE

After learning about Momma Susie's people, and our ancestors in Bibbtown, my cousins and I talked about what it meant to be a descendant. We talked about land and inheritance. Traci, Ronald, and Amber were more familiar with this subject, having a set of grandparents who owned land in Centralia, as did the Bibbs and O'Neals—although I didn't know this at the time. And I later remembered my mother talking about her own family's land ownership in Centralia.

It all felt very abstract. My own modern Black life had only ever included a quarter acre and seven-eighths of an acre and 7,500-square-foot single-family lots. We were nearly two hundred years removed from Bibbtown and decades away from Centralia. While the Bibbtown history felt significant, I couldn't rightly say what, if anything, I cared about this distant farmland.

But that's the thing about a new, long-submerged history come to light. It occasions new conversations and connects you to novel ways of thinking about things you had only vaguely paid attention to. Things that provided a dignity and focus that was central to the lives of the people who came before you. It is a parcel of their identity and self-concept that they passed down and that you are able to build on. Whether you rightly know that is what has happened or not.

Land and inheritance was the thread between a Black past and a Black future. And of all the existential questions raised by enslavement, I have always understood those to be the most central, even as they have felt the most complicated, the most politically charged, the furthest from my grasp. A question of America that surpasses all understanding.

On the final day of that inaugural Bibb reunion, carloads of descendants walked the land of our forebears, who'd been manumitted pre–Civil War, when less than 4 percent of Black people were free in a state that for decades to come would still have white enslavers all around them. The small enclave of Bibbtown, about ten miles outside Russellville, was the last stop on that weekend speed-walk through family history. A chance to connect the ancestral work of Black people generations ago with the work before us now.

In many ways, I had found myself unable to keep up.

Bibbtown was split into two parcels. There was the twelve hundred acres of good, tillable land called Upper Bibbtown, which was inherited by three families emancipated by Major Richard Bibb. This includes the land Granny Kate and her aunt Rachel (my great-great-great-grandmother) donated for the Arnold's Chapel Church, an antecedent of which was founded in Bibbtown decades before John Bigger Bibb officially deeded them the land. (That entire weekend, Granny Kate, who also founded a school, had been staring out at me from her picture, looking like Momma Susie.)

Two other families inherited Lower Bibbtown, with three hundred acres roughly nine miles northeast of Russellville that was sufficient for personal use but not particularly arable or worth much on the resale market.

It had been almost two hundred years since all those calculations—who got what, based on who meant what to whom—had been made.

But long after the original Bibbtown residents had died and their families scattered, some of the Black Bibb descendants had reunited back in a physical and psychic space where what was left of the people was the land.

That is the thing about the kind of unresolved history America is built on. No sooner are you confronted with the emotion of finding out you had white people in your family than you are asked to consider the property values of everything that came with that realization.

Before Granny Kate died, she deeded her land to her children or grandchildren, in twenty-three-acre plots. As the heirs left the area, went north, or passed away, Ms. Mamie Gill, Granny Kate's granddaughter, who was the next to the last Bibb descendant, kept paying taxes on the land. When Mamie died, because she had paid taxes on some of the land and had farmed some of the land, she had a legal right to claim it. Her daughter, Marilyn Gill, inherited the land from her.

In 2016 Marilyn Gill, who was ninety years old, died in a trailer fire that burned hot enough to melt coins. She left seventy acres of land to a white man she had befriended, and his son, whom she babysat and helped raise. After she died, these men went to court to claim that the additional Bibb land she had been paying taxes on should go to them as well.

"But our contention is they shouldn't get the land. It's not theirs. And where we can find the heirs, I'm trying to get the heirs to come back and claim it," Michael Morrow said at the 2019 reunion. But "we're still in the process of trying to figure all that out. I've been working on it for about thirty years," he said. There was one hundred acres still in the name of one of the original formerly enslaved Bibbtown residents. He just had to find a descendant to substantiate a claim and keep at least some of the land in Black hands.

At the Bibb House, where I'd come face-to-face with the brick-and-mortar of slavery and felt the hollows behind the walls, I'd met the white lawyer Gran Clark. Clark had worked to keep the site as a true historic memorial, and in doing so acted, perhaps, as an intercessor in this life on behalf of those dear to him whose past lives might need squaring. He was soft-spoken and thoughtful, and I had heard how subtle realizations showed up in his voice. It is Clark, a true scion of old Kentucky, who had always felt to me like the seeking-est part of the SEEK Museums he helped found. His great-great-uncle and namesake was in the posse that tried to catch the Jesse James gang when a few members of the gang robbed Russellville's old Nimrod Long Bank in 1868. Gran Clark still owns an antique pistol from that bygone era. Clark heads a title company and practices what he calls

Michael Morrow stands for a portrait at Bibbtown Church in Logan County, Kentucky on September 18, 2022.

nonconfrontational law. He helped clarify where things stood with the Bibbtown land.

"Kentucky, like a lot of states, has laws that say that adverse possession for at least a fifteen-year period of time can create ownership rights. So, if somebody goes out and claims property as their own and does that openly and adversely and continuously for fifteen years, they've got a right to go to court"—and claim the land as theirs—said Clark.

He covered the finer points of Kentucky law, and—like the George Mortimer Bibb interpretation of his father's will, and the way John Bigger Bibb executed the will's directions—property law felt like more legal dress-up, one of the byproducts of which was to keep Black heirs from land that should by spirit and rule have gone to their children, and their children's children, and so on. And unlike Chancellor Bibb's interpretation of the law, which admittedly dealt with a cutting-edge legal issue of that time, this particular aspect of current Kentucky property law had enjoyed generations to grow thick, viny, and impenetrable. I understood, conceptually, the bitter harvest of Clark's words, but it wasn't until much later that I began to understand the corporeal sense of this legacy, and what it meant to my ancestors to walk on soil they called their own, in a way that called them home.

Dr. Blondean Y. Davis, a Chicago Public Schools educator who also served as a suburban superintendent, was born and raised in Chicago. But she spent every summer of her childhood on a Bibbtown farm with her grandmother Mamie Gill, much the same as my siblings, cousins, and I had spent ours in Centralia. Hers is a twentieth-century feel for the land, which isn't to say it doesn't stretch back even further in lore and lure and blood. By the time Davis was growing up, the area was called Lewisburg, after the nearest town. Davis hadn't known the Bibb history and had simply heard it was property that had been left to the formerly enslaved. But she had grown up with the stories, Davis told filmmaker and scholar Le Datta Grimes in an interview for the documentary *Invented Before We Were Born*, by white Bibb descendants Jonathan and Rachel Knight.

Gill used to keep a freezer full of rabbit, venison, and pig meat, Davis said. "It would be unbelievable these days, but do you know that she probably fed my immediate family and other families that had moved away" all year? Gill would send food "North," as she called it, to sustain people who were distant but dear.

Land anchored the family. It represented continuity and stability to the Black Bibbs, and as families and descendants grew older and moved away, those who remained on the Bibbtown land vowed to keep it in the family, which didn't include husbands and wives, just the brothers, sisters, and children. People who had that Bibbtown earth in their blood. Davis recalled a tree from her childhood adjacent to a burial ground that was more than a century old. Mamie Gill's house didn't have running water, because the lines would have to disturb the cemetery, and Davis said her grandmother considered that ground consecrated. And that to disturb it was a sin that could not be forgiven. Gill is buried there, as were the children she outlived. When Davis's mother fell ill with ovarian cancer, she left Chicago to be cared for "at home," where it was safe to die. She looked out over the trees and said, "Isn't that pretty," as she drew her last breath.

Going to Kentucky for the summers where Davis had to draw water from a pond every day was "probably one of the best things that ever happened to me because sitting with my grandmother, she told me about our legacy. Our legacy was the land, and she said, 'It's as far as you can see, sweetheart.'"

There weren't enough people, or money, for a full-time minister, but whenever there were services at Arnold's Chapel, the extended family would walk from all parts of their land. About a mile or so out, a distance they knew by the cuts and clearings and mile markers of meadows, they'd begin to sing "Rough Side of the Mountain," until they all became one chorus. After service, they had "basket dinner," where everyone would open their trunks to reveal *God only knows* how much food.

James "Peg" Gill, Davis's uncle, accidently drowned while fishing on the banks of the lake behind Bibbtown, and there was no one to keep the farm going. Mamie Gill rented some of the land outside of family, "because the only people who had money were white people.

Looking back, I knew it was never rented at the price that it should have been," said Davis. Lumber companies would come knocking, but Gill wouldn't sell a single tree.

As a young woman, Davis became concerned that her grand-mother was paying taxes on land she didn't have a clear title to. Land the family had known by informal markers. Land they had force-of-willed to one another, but not legally willed to one another as people passed away. "I have clear title if I say I do," Gill had told Davis.

But what she had were letters from brothers and sisters saying what family member they wanted their land to go to. Mamie Gill was land rich, people said, but there was never a point where some-one went through the legal hoops to clear the titles and centralize her ownership. When Mamie died in 1990 at age eighty-eight, her daughter Marilyn Gill inherited seventy acres. Marilyn Gill had been stationed overseas, in Paris and London, among other places, during her career in the Women's Army Corps. She later worked for Reuters news service as their communications liaison and lived with Davis and her mother in Chicago for a time. After she'd retired, and divorced, she told Davis she needed to go home. Davis had been profoundly shaken by her aunt Marilyn Gill's death in that 2016 trailer fire. It was some-thing she couldn't think about for long.

She wished her aunt had shared her plans to leave the land to a white man. "I do feel that my aunt was confused. Had she addressed this with me, because I was at a different point in time, different point in my life, I might not necessarily have moved down there, but I would have stabilized the land situation and made sure it stayed in the family."

Mamie Gill would have hated the land leaving the family, but "maybe some things are not meant to last forever," said Davis. And the Bibbtown legacy that lasted more than a century provided the family enough time—time to fortify, to stabilize, to build the kind of social capital that allowed descendants to make their way in the wider world, she thinks.

It was also enough time for the world to change. For research tools to get better. For the kinds of details you know about people in small towns, and those people's people, to do some of its own work. And for the nation to develop something of an appetite, or at least an awareness, around reuniting Black people with the land under their feet. If not the dirt, then at least the pride. The surety. And the ability to leverage it for money.

Major Richard Bibb left hundreds of acres to his trusted carriage driver, Ben Winn Bibb. Ben Winn often drove Major Bibb out to the country, where the two would only have each other for company, and any matter of vengeance or violence could have happened with nary an eye to witness. Ben Winn died before John Bigger Bibb got around to deeding him the land—a parcel somewhere in size between the 400-acre tract Clark found in the records and the 750 acres that Michael Morrow had discovered he'd paid taxes on. Ben Winn's land went to his children, one of which was Matilda Bibb, who got about 100 acres.

After Marilyn Gill's death, in addition to her seventy acres, it was that one hundred acres that the two local white litigants claimed they were entitled to, since Marilyn Gill had paid taxes on it. For years, nothing happened with the lawsuit, but then the white litigants began paying taxes on those smaller twenty-acre tracts that Granny Kate had left her descendants, so that was yet another thing Clark and Morrow had to keep their eyes on.

Over more than thirty years, Michael Morrow had made it his mission to find out what happened to everybody who was deeded land in Major Bibb's will. He understood the intricacies of how Black land was transferred. How sometimes families just keep living on the land, but nobody ever comes after them. With the Bibb heirs, people moved north, or just away, and sold their land. They left it to kids, who lived on it for years and then sold it or left it to their kids and grandkids. There was always a way to follow the dispensation. Morrow knew that Major Richard Bibb's former carriage driver had been paying taxes on 750 acres, and he knew there was at least 100 acres that belonged to his daughter, Matilda, that had never been sold or deeded.

Morrow and Clark knew that if Historic Russellville could find a descendant of Matilda, they could make a claim. So Morrow began digging.

He reached out to a likely heir and got hung up on a couple of times. "Somebody pops up and tells you you're heir to one hundred acres of land, people think, oh hell, he's trying to beat me," Morrow said. He traced six generations through marriage records, census records, school records. Not only did he have to prove that Matilda had a living descendant, he had to prove Matilda was married to the father of her children, since an old Kentucky property law contended "that illegitimate children did not inherit from their father's estate," said Clark. It was overturned by the Supreme Court in 1979, but states were allowed to decide how to apply the property law prior to the court's ruling. Kentucky decided not to make the ruling retroactive. Matilda's heir would have had to prove that all of his ancestors after her death had been born as legitimate children in order to claim any inheritance rights.

Throw the rock, hide your hand, pass a law that made the arrangements of Black life illegal in concert with a system of plunder to ease your way. Before the Civil War, an enslaved person couldn't get married.

Matilda had gotten married during enslavement. But she was free. That meant the marriage was recorded legally, in the white marriage records in Logan County.

Once Morrow had a last name, he traced it three generations to a guy he grew up with. A guy whose granddaddy had the same last name. He used death certificates to help Gran Clark make the legal case.

In 2024, Historic Russellville Inc. reached a settlement with Marilyn Gill's white legatees that gave Matilda's descendant a cash settlement that would equate to the value of about five acres of Matilda's farm. The white legatees received 160 acres near Matilda's house. In exchange for his cash settlement, Matilda's descendant would not claim ownership rights for Matilda's farm, located south of Granny Kate's old farm. That land, totaling forty-three acres around Arnold's Chapel AME Zion Church, is now held in trust for the benefit of the Bibb descendants, including me and mine. The land has rearranged me. Partially.

Arnold's Chapel, which stood for something, and stands for something still, has been renovated, I fantasize that my children, or some other Bibb descendant, will get married there one day. That we will gather in celebration, awe, and our own anthems of love and community (like "Before I Let Go" by Frankie Beverly and Maze). I believe Granny Kate, and my great-great-great-grandmother Rachel, would be proud of the work Morrow and Clark, both sons of Logan County, did so that the Black Bibb inheritance will see life, use, and, God willing, joy again. Before we return to our own homes, our own lives and legacies, all around the country.

Lonnae in front of Arnold's Chapel in Bibbtown with young cousins.

CHAPTER 13

POST RACIST

The night my family and I moved into our new house, one of our new neighbors called the police on us.

It was 2019, but I'd been looking for this house most of my adult life, or so it seemed. I'd stopped to gather myself at way stations in Washington, DC, and suburban Maryland, but I couldn't shake my longing for somewhere else. The right arrangement, perhaps found only in my imagination, of migration and arrival.

My urban suburb, with its mix of architectural styles and neighborhood vibes, along an arts corridor minutes from the DC line, fit the bill. It was bungalows, Cape Cods, and Craftsman Revival homes. Wine crawls, porch fests, and historic house tours featuring colorful Victorians called the Painted Ladies. Every step outside my door was canopied by old trees and took me past backyards that still filled with lightning bugs at sunset. I'd discovered the neighborhood decades earlier and become enchanted with the old-as-new notion of mixed-use housing and neighborhoods you can walk.

Really, my writing eyes had grown weary of subdivisions, and I longed for the sidewalks and corner stores that reminded me of childhood. Of bungalows and block clubs on the South Side of Chicago where gloriously free-range kids lived by the simple, everyday rule that when the streetlights come on, it's time to get gone.

My new neighborhood had reminded me of home. And I am always trying to go home.

But this time, on far better terms.

My town of about twenty thousand people, incorporated in the late-nineteenth century, was roughly a third Black, a third Hispanic, and a third white when I moved in, with a smattering of two-or-mores, and people-of-color others. It sits in Prince George's County, which, for decades, had been the wealthiest majority Black county in the country, before slipping to second in 2020.

For more than a century, Prince George's (which was founded on tobacco cultivation and enslaved more than twelve thousand people, the most in Maryland, prior to the Civil War) had been largely rural and white, with a long history of segregation and police brutality. The county became more educated and more affluent as it became more Black, which was, to some, surprising. But it was of a piece with my family history, where the Black Bibbs owned land they farmed over generations for sustenance, for stability, and in the furtherance of Black futures. It followed John and Pocahontas Bibb's move from Bibbtown to Centralia, where Black people built community with small businesses and industrial jobs mixed with side hustles. And their grandchildren sent their children to college. It was of a piece with my childhood on the far South Side of Chicago, where my Washington Heights neighborhood had gone from nearly all white to, *oh dear God*, nearly all Black almost overnight after the 1968 passage of the Fair Housing Act.

That neighborhood was a haven for educators and civil servants with great expectations for their children. It remained solidly middle-class for decades before the long, slow decline of disinvestment and plundering, punitive or indifferent public policies that hound Black steps whenever we get a foothold, began to catch up. The South Side of my childhood was set to music from open windows and the smell of freshly cut grass that you *better not* step on. (I once interviewed a lieutenant from the Disciples street gang back when they had more defined hierarchies, and even gang violence had rules. He said they couldn't step on anybody's grass either.) The South Side shaped my head, the way old Black women used to shape the heads of newborn babies.

Prince George's County represented my approximation of the South Side of Chicago. The latest iteration and my specific leg of more than two centuries of Bibb (Blackwell, O'Neal, and Black) migration. It represented my search for that New Jerusalem, which to my mind meant a place where Black folks could build, grow, and hold cultural sway, along with everybody else who was cool with that. My former husband and I bought our first house in our mid-twenties. It was a far-suburban, car-dependent, cookie-cutter new construction that felt next level and impressed our parents, who didn't know to tell us which houses made the best investments. Because it wasn't just wealth, in the form of a down payment, that Black people missed generationally.

It was the kinds of insights that were accumulated in places our parents were prohibited from entering.

Later, we bought a big house, in a neighborhood full of big houses, where nearly every family looked like mine. I exposed my children to white people through extracurriculars like piano (which I'd taken as a child and which actually codes as very middle-class and Black, and also just part of Americana). I put them in ballet classes, which I also took as a young girl, and dragged them with me across the DMV to parks, plays, panels, and recitals. If you live Black, I told other young mothers, you have to be intentional about exposing your children to some fraction of white people, so they learn to navigate the wider world. If you live in white spaces, you must create significant opportunities sustained over years to be with Black people, because Blackness refracted back at them through white eyes could make them unlovable or, far worse, unknowable to themselves. It is an evolution of the issues faced by my parents, grandparents, and Black Bibb ancestors living side by side, or at least white adjacent, in America.

Momma Susie served white customers, made small talk with white suppliers and teachers, and kept Daddy's white high school teammate fed—while remaining attentive to all the ways whiteness could bad-touch her family. This as the more opaque threats from other Black folks whose margins of everything were far too thin and who were in too close continued to creep up on her. She controlled all she could as she stood at the fence line of mid-twentieth-century segregation in a small southern Illinois town with an integrated high school that helped with surface civility, while across the nation and in hamlets minutes away, the fight against racism was becoming a Civil Rights Movement. She remained planted in her community for good and for ill as she reached across that fence line as often as she could to secure the resources from white spaces that could make the lives of her family, and perhaps her people, better.

To my mind, staging from a place of Blackness anchored us in community and creativity but helped me teach my children powers of discernment. What of Black culture could you throw yourselves into and what might get you killed. For more than two decades, as a writer for the *Washington Post*, I took them with me on assignments to all the places they could go. I wanted for them what I had for myself, an ability to run up one side of the culture and slide down the other, or so I imagined.

These are the calculations, probabilities, ratios that make for a kind of Black math that you don't have to be my uncle David Blackwell—that luminary Centralia native son—to figure. It is simply an everyday requirement of the descendants of slavery. It's a constant figuring I've had to do in my life and the lives of my children, like Momma Keziah, Momma Rachel, Momma Pokey, Momma Minnie, Momma Susie, my dearest momma, and my Black ancestors before me. I've added to that tradition and customized my formulations. I've taught my children what scholar Sheryll Cashin calls "cultural dexterity," as I gerrymandered their childhoods like a voting district in Texas.

My first husband and I divorced, we both remarried, and after a brief stint in a northern Virginia exurb with my new husband, I was ready to move back to Prince George's County—by then the kids said the *PG* stood for "Pretty Girl"—and resume my quest for that New Jerusalem. I chose a charming neighborhood full of millwork and memory, a place I'd written about twenty years before and thought I knew. My new house looked like me, my ex-husband told me. The night I moved into my renovated American Foursquare house, in my walkable neighborhood, in my diverse little town, in my majority Black county, with my all-Black movers, and had to explain myself to the local police, I realized something.

I hadn't done enough reporting.

We are the only Black family on our immediate block, which was a more granular demographic consideration than I'd usually undertaken. If you count our neighbor across the street, on the next block, we are one of two Black households out of two dozen on our section of the street. There's also a Black-white interracial couple. In this neighborhood, I've seen more yard signs affirming Black people than I've seen actual Black people, and I feel strongly that these two things are related. As was the armed welcome wagon my new neighbors rolled out for us.

I had to help my children understand why someone would call the police on us as we moved in, beyond the regrettable fact that our moving truck necessitated a detour around our one-way block. I don't argue that my neighbors weren't inconvenienced. Only that they could have introduced themselves, asked us to move the truck so that they could ease by, or given grace since moving is universally understood to be challenging. In calling the police on their new Black neighbors, knowing that when it comes to police and Black people the margins of error are thin, they were cartoonish.

The expectation that white people will never encounter an inconvenience or annoyance that they simply have to manage with self-regulation and creativity, that the police are always available as a bulwark or a racial concierge to alleviate their discomfort at the public nature of the world, was built into my neighborhood. And, I suspected, codified.

I visited our local community development nonprofit, part of a collaborative Mapping Racism project, to test my hunch. My search went back to the beginning, when the town was young, and white land-owners sold the American dream subject to restrictions. Here's the 1924 covenant that governed my new house:

"First, that therein described piece or parcel of land or any part thereof, or any improvements thereon shall never be sold or conveyed to, or used, or in any manner occupied by any Negro or by any person of the Negro race or having Negro blood."

Along with no nuisance, "noisy trade," or extra building permitted within twenty feet of the street line, "These covenants are to be taken as running with the land and bind all parties hereto, their heirs and assigns forever. . . ."

What had I done? I wondered. This place, where I had moved my family, how did it deserve us?

It is a question I'd asked of other places in other times. And learned to answer for myself. Because in the centuries-old-and-counting argument over America, we cannot simply wait on white people to see around corners. Some are simply starting from too far back.

In 2015, I wrote a column about being stopped by the police for a broken headlight less than a minute from my house, with my seventeen-year-old daughter, who was driving, and my thirteen-year-old son, who was tall for his age, in the back seat. My daughter had forgotten her learner's permit at home, so the officer ran her name but couldn't find her in his system. The situation was starting to tick up, and he went back to his car to do more checking. I had an idea about how to resolve things, and I got out of the car, carrying nothing, wearing tight, pocketless leggings and a fitted, pocketless short-sleeved T-shirt, to tell him. I'd been stopped for speeding the year before by a Black officer who'd merely waved me away before issuing a ticket, but this time the officer began screaming. He exited the car and began a slow, menacing count to five, as I stood paralyzed, at a fifteen-foot distance, near the rear wheel well of my car.

I wrote:

> I should have moved quicker. But sometimes, I freeze. Freeze, fight, flee. It's a matter of basic wiring. It's a fact people seem to understand intuitively when passengers on a Metro train fail to come to the aid of a man being stabbed to death in front of them, but often lose sight of when police encounters go left.
>
> "FOUR..." the officer yelled.
>
> "I'm a reporter for the *Washington Post!*" I blurted. Then I finally found my legs and dashed to my car.
>
> The officer was calm when he approached me again. He allowed my son to run home and grab his sister's permit. I asked his name, but I was shaking too badly to write it down. My daughter rubbed my hand. I asked why he had screamed at me so.
>
> He asked, "I'm not going to read about this,

am I?" He leaned a little into my passenger's side window. I found the question coercive. I told him no, but I wrote about it anyway (without using his name, or the name of his police department).

I know it can be a dangerous job, but it's a danger officers sign up—and presumably train—for. One that requires discernment. Every time someone is left humiliated or frightened by one of these stops (let alone bloody or dead), some of what binds us is lost. By a thousand cuts, you are losing your nation's respect.

The day my column ran, I was told I shouldn't have gotten out of the car or called out that I was a reporter for the *Post*. I shouldn't have written the column in the first place, was the gist of it. And perhaps all of that was true. But there was something wrong with the policing part of that encounter. And I needed to be able to think and write about it using a standard other than getting shot or killed to make it worthy of contemplation. I needed a wider lens and a Blacker understanding. Every pressurized system needs a release.

It was 2015, and something was coming to a head in America. I could feel it. Like I could feel my daddy was going to die. And my newsroom, where I spent nearly my entire adult life, was unprepared. As was I. The difference was I knew it. Like I knew my daddy was going to die. The following year, when I was offered another job in a well-resourced, Black-led newsroom focused on race, sports, and culture, I wept. Then I left. Being in a Black-centered newsroom didn't mean I agreed with every line of inquiry or perspective. It simply meant there were layers of translation I did not have to do, which put time back on my clock. It made me less encumbered to "compose with purposeful fury," as scholar and author Jabari Asim said of Black writers. It helped me bust out of L Seven square, in the visionary words of Rick James. *We done braided our hair / We don't mind if you stare.*

In 2017, the *Post* adopted the slogan "Democracy Dies in Darkness," and I was reminded that threats don't become real until they are real to the white people in charge, and by then, for some of us, it's already far, far too late. It is why we can't wait on the logic of "the white moderate, who is more devoted to 'order' than to justice," in the words of Martin Luther King Jr. Just like Granny Kate and Rachel Bibb couldn't wait on John Bigger Bibb to finally decide to deed them their Bibbtown land. So, they donated parts of parcels, which they did not even have title to, and raised a school to lift their children, and built a church to praise the Lord, with a spirit and a faith that turned into legacy that lives still, in the descendants of the enslaved.

In 2019, when I moved into my new house, and certainly by 2024, with the American experiment and Black lives and women's lives again (always) in the balance, I continued to believe the transaction costs of moderation and the go-along-to-get-along of America had shifted. The wages of whiteness had to be paid.

And not simply by the descendants of enslavement.

It's a thought that came to me when I decided to attend that inaugural Russellville reunion and I stood for the first time inside the Bibb

House plantation. I'm here to give you back all your bags to carry. And all your crosses to bear.

I've been having an imaginary exchange with one of my white neighbors for some time. It's a replay of a couple of real conversations I'd had with him after we moved in. I was in the front yard and said hi or waved to him and his family. He stopped to talk one of these times. More specifically to ask me, without preamble, *Do you live here?*

I found the question curious. I'm sure I told him I'd just moved in or some such before saying goodbye. I didn't think much of it until I saw him again and waved.

He asked me if I lived there. Again. I don't remember what I said. I probably just answered him and may have even reminded him that we'd already met. But now I made a different judgment about our exchange. As a neighbor, he'd probably seen the house being renovated in ways that made it among the newest on the block. He could see that I was Black, or at the least a woman of color, and had the luxury of working from home during the covid pandemic, or perhaps he assumed I didn't work. He might have noticed all the Black teens and young adults in and out of the house. He might have heard an old-school R&B, or Chicago Hot Mix 5 compilation, playing in my backyard.

He privileged his curiosity, his desire to have me explain myself, presumably because he was working some version of all of that wonderin' out in his head. Or just because he felt entitled enough to ask a rude-ass question, *twice.*

I wish I had said something clever at the time, but in my experience, that's not usually how these encounters go. Since we take for granted a general comity and right to take up space while Black, that specific white urgency about needing us to answer to them is always disconcerting. Still, I'm hoping one day he'll ask me again, because I've had a good time thinking about how that might go.

White neighbor: "Do you live here?"

Me: "I'm sorry. I don't recognize your standing to ask me that question."

Then I go on about my own Black business.

Or:

White neighbor: "Do you live here?"

Me: "Interestingly, despite slavery, Jim Crow segregation, and continued structural inequality, my husband and I were able to save enough from our Black jobs to secure this modest dwelling right here, in your same neighborhood. Crazy, huh?"

But this is my favorite:

White neighbor: "Do you live here?"

I stare at him, and also past him. I am an enigma, but I allow a slight smile to play across my lips.

"You know, who's to say?" I ask. "Who's to say?"

Then I laugh, a light, tinkling thing, the trill of which follows him home.

I made no attempts to find out who called the police on us that night, though the reporter in me was tempted. I reached for grace instead. I arrived at my own terms, which disallowed anyone to steal my hard-earned joy. Or my hope for that New Jerusalem. The next morning, my son remarked, "This neighborhood is not as Black as I thought it would be. And not as friendly." It's not the South Side of my youth, I told him, but nothing ever will be again, and besides, that was not my final stop.

I never did return to my backyard garden, all those years ago.

When I got back from Home Depot, I forgot to separate my seed packets, and by the time I realized that, it was too late. My daughter had already planted two rows of Bibb lettuce. In an instant, my back-yard garden felt despoiled. Despoiled. I have never even been able to love the idea of it again.

My enthusiasm for the nearby tomatoes withered, and I watched what I thought was the Bibb lettuce grow from a safe distance. One day, randomly, outside of any proper cultivation cycle, I broke off a leaf and tasted it. The bitterness surprised me. It shouldn't have. That is what happens when you don't account for your harvest.

But after a few years, I started another tentative garden, this time in my front yard. Right next to my front porch. A white neighbor, who I would see walking with her husband or dog, noticed my digging. She filled a wheelbarrow full of dirt and sunflowers that she gifted to me and which promptly died. If my neighbor realized my gardening was performative—gloves, hat, and tools notwithstanding—she wisely said nothing. I think my gardening is more haunted than anything. But these days me and my ghosts are more simpatico. I think we've come to a truce. We are at least on more solid ground.

The next season, I got into a conversation with that same neighbor about tomatoes, the plants I love most in the world, and she brought me a few, already thinned out and rooted in their own container. This time I devoted myself to watering them, pulling away weeds, and tend-ing to my garden in ways that so reminded me of my childhood and planting with my mother. It may even have reminded me of a Black truck farmer named John W. Bibb.

After a couple of months, I was able to pick my cherry tomatoes. I shared the news with my neighbor the next time I saw her, and tears sprang to my eyes. It was the first time in years, in decades, I had eaten from my own garden, I explained self-consciously. I thanked her, genuinely, for that, and she blew me a kiss. It wasn't a fancy lettuce that bore my family's name, I'm still coming to terms with that, but it was something real and grounded. Something to grow on.

We've staked our lives on a vision of America with ancestors and children who both require truth, and tending. I've looked back over seven generations of my family history set against the sweep of American history, so I understand all the things that can be true at once. Especially in Bibb Country, where my ancestors gifted me with all they had, even when it wasn't nearly enough, and my children authorize me to continue negotiating with the nation on their behalf. All kinds of seeds have been allowed to take root in America. Some grow in ways that see them wither and die on the vine. Others have yet to flower.

On this leg of my family's long migration, I've gotten myself to the point where I'm beyond the reach of the worst of America. Or so I've told myself. Beyond the need to explain myself to people who can't hear me. Beyond even the desire to turn and meet them halfway, since, come what may, we are not going back, so I am hoping they'll catch up. Because it would be (potentially, with caveats) lovely to walk together. I proclaim myself, with more than a little self-importance, decolonized.

Every day, I think about Momma Keziah, not as an old Black woman who fell out of the history and records of her former enslavers, but as the brave young girl who walked from Virginia to Kentucky with a will to be free.

I'm past the reach of white folks, I call out to the Momma Keziah I hold in my mind's eye. My fourth great-grandmother turns to me and smiles. She is a child, but she speaks of generations. *You would not be the first of my daughters to think so,* she tells me. She waves at me as she turns to continue walking. She's beckoning me forward. Always forward.

She is telling me to keep up.

ACKNOWLEDGMENTS

I may need to write another book just to thank all the people who made this one possible.

Finding out your family is descended from enslavers, and learning those same enslavers, or others, are also your ancestors rearranges you. I am deeply grateful to my longtime editor and friend, Steve Reiss, who saw all the story possibilities in that. In 2019, when I sat in his office, in tears and anger, I knew Steve was already seeing the book to come. Thank you for walking with me. You are a gift to writers.

Michael Morrow brought this history to light and made this book possible. Thank you for telling Bibb stories for more than three decades—just long enough for them to find the Centralia Bibbs. I wish your grandmother, Ms. Henrietta Beal, and her best friend, Ms. Mattie Bell-Morman, could see how keeping your promise transformed the Black Bottom. Thank you for picking up the phone every time I called, and thank you for answering every call since. Joe Gran Clark, thank you for having the tenacity, heart, and vision to have the Bibb house and history tell a deeper story of America. You give me more hope.

Love and gratitude to my agent, Joy Harris. Thank you for being with me through many, many seasons. Your belief, nurturing, and fierce advocacy sustain me and give me courage to face the hard parts.

Thank you to the Andscape imprint family. To my superbly talented editor, Aliya S. King Neil, your patience, collaboration, and thought work helped me turn a corner, and find my Bibb voice. Thank you for calls and cautions about writing and life that lingered on my mind after we hung up. Jennifer Levesque, thank you for being excited from our first call. I'm grateful for your insights, steady leadership, and for helping convince me to lean into the lettuce. Olivia Zavitson, yours is a rare, wonderful combination of gifts that carried me over the finish line. I am grateful for your discernment as both a talented writer and editor and as an enormously capable process whiz. I am glad I met you young because I already see your future. I am also thankful to the photo researchers, copy editors, and production teams that made this book better.

To my ESPN/Andscape (and former Undefeated) family, I could not have done this without you. Thank you Kevin Merida and Raina Kelley for your newsroom leadership. Thank you for believing in this story, granting me space to write it, and being in my corner. I love you both for that. Kevin thank you (and Gary, Indiana's own Donna Britt) for being part of every inflection point in my career.

A hearty thank you to Jason Aidoo and Dwayne Bray, who made this book possible. Thank you for being a home for big ideas and giving me runway. Thank you to my colleagues, former colleagues, and friends whose support and kindness has meant the world to me. Marc Spears, Marcus Matthews, Bill Rhoden, Jesse Washington, Domonique Foxworth, Martenzie Johnson, Jason Reid, Jerry Bembry, Kelley Carter, Brittany Grant, Kelley Evans, Karin Berry, Justin Tinsley, Aaron Dodson, Beth Stojkov, David Dennis, Mia Berry, Channing Hargrove, Britni Danielle, Sheila Matthews, and Mary Almonte. Sabrina Clarke, thank you for years of smarts and newsroom talks. Everything runs better with you!

To my friends who are like sisters, I love you deep! Thank you for your love, light, and wisdom when writing and times got hard.

My dear line sisters, Tracy D. Holliway, Kim Rutherford, Tatia Jones, Angela Campbell, and Pamela Hemphill, we have been fellow travelers for decades and you lift me daily. Tracy, thank you for always calling on the spirit, and the work, that takes us where we need to go. Captains are alive!

My dear Lafayetta Bowling, thank you for being my first writer's retreat (open ended!) and for always being there for me, and for Momma. We love you and I couldn't have done this without you. Terina Winfrey and Shonda Sims, *my girls,* we go back like rocking chairs! Bless and love you my dear sisters for being on deadline with me, counting the words, the milestones and all these days of our lives, together. Thank you, Dana Brunson and Stephanie Crockett, for breakfasts, lunches, walks, talks, concerts, tears, and especially, your capacious wisdom and love. I'm so grateful for you, and that the band is back together! My dear Michele Booth Cole, your friendship, faith, keen insights, and intellect are a gift to my life. Thank you for lunches and tools that sustain me. We're always on for lunch! To Gretchen Holloman who has the words, spirit, and deep understanding about our world, inside and out. We are thrilled that you are near and dear! Liana Asim, I call you Liana Love. Everybody who knows you understands that. Your wisdom and faith change the world, as well as honor Ms. Susie Ward.

Thank you to those sisters whose hours-long Zoom writing sessions turned into every kind of space I needed. Dear Sydney Trent, thank you for knowing routine saves the day, and for your deep well of empathy, love, and kindness. What a gift you are! Jenée Desmond-Harris, thank you for your brilliant reading eyes and writer insights.

I love you and yours and I'm thrilled to have you back close! Dr. Carla Cheatham, it was a joy to reconnect and write together. Thank you for years of friendship and prayers.

Blaise Allysen Kearsley, your writing space, empathy, and brilliance = how my soul got over. I loved doing this work with you, which was the only way I could have gotten it done. Much gratitude to Camille Wanliss and those Saturdays with Galleyway. My dear Deesha Philyaw, thank you for your sagacity, brilliance, deep well of sisterhood, and the pop-up space that saved me!

Carole Sargent, your Georgetown writing groups and expert research advice gave me the community and insight essential to getting started, and I am deeply grateful. Thank you Kate, for a home away from home, to lay our heads. Thank you Irene, for all your love and care.

I am a club woman, like my mothers before me. Thank you to my Sojourner sisters for your support, love, and fire. You tuned in, so I didn't have to. I love you all dearly! Thank you to my Butterflies, especially Kimberley Alfonso, for building a strong, enduring sisterhood, wholly in the tradition.

To Carole Feldman and the Georgetown School of Continuing Studies, thank you for your deep belief in the power of journalism and calling me to teach! I am grateful to work with you. Love and thank you to my coteacher, Jonathan Franklin for your agile mind, fierce multiplatform journalism, and of course, tech help. Along with talented video producer, Jonelle Scafe La Foucade, you both kept me in the game! Thank you to *the* Jon Cherry for your sensitivity, and for artfully capturing Russellville in photos.

Thank you to all the subject matter experts I interviewed for this

book, especially the brilliant genealogist, Nicka Sewell-Smith, scholars LaShawn Harris, Jo Von McCalester, Ellis Monk, Andrew Agha,
Kurt Metzmeier, Yuki Kato, and Angelyn Mitchell. Your voices were
essential in shaping my thinking. Thank you to the Filson Historical
Society and Frankfort historian Russ Hatter and the Capital City
Museum for bringing Kentucky history to life. Much gratitude to
Kentucky State University's Marcus Bernard, Shawn Lucas, and the
young scholar Jordan Bennett for helping me understand the lettuce,
the soil, and the dirt. And a big thanks to the University of Kentucky,
Franklin County Extension. A hearty thank-you to Alison Flowers and
Sam Stecklow at the Invisible Institute for navigating and talking me
through all of those CPD records. Your help was invaluable.

Lynn Medford and Jeff Leen. Thank you for your honesty, assess-
ment, and friendship. Tom Shroder, thank you for the advice that
helped me turn the corner.

Thank you Magda Jean-Louis for research that made the centuries
more legible. And for finding my Hattie Mae Bibb for me. Blessings!
Javier Sampedro, thank you for turning my analog soul digital. For
your technical expertise, literary bent, and for saving lost documents.
I am blessed to have found you. Clarence Williams, my friend, bless
you for the countless times your smarts saved the day. Thank you to
documentarians Jonathan and Rachel Knight (the white cousins!) and
Le Datta Grimes for all your work and insights in bringing the Bibb
story and legacy to light. I am grateful to you! Joshua Niedwick, thank
you for your fierce intellect and your artistry in telling the 1908 story
of Logan County.

Peg Ivanyo, your Illinois land reports made the land of my ancestors so much more clear. I am grateful for your painstaking, tenacious

work. Denise Shoulders, thank you for your genealogical research that showed me all the ways that tells its own story. A hearty thank you to Michael Middleton, and Peggy Jones at Centralia Historical Society for detailing the nuances of Centralia backstories and timelines. Fascinating!

To Evangeline Tierney, I hear your wisdom and guidance in my head. The space we built together endures. Claudia Cauterucci, thank you for all the tools, gifts, and healing you share with the world. Dr. Stanley Riddley, thank you for your many tools and Riddleyisms that helped carry me through this project.

Finally, to my dearest family, friends, and fellow travelers, thank you. I love you, I hold your stories close, and I am grateful beyond measure.

To the Bibb men who drove me, sheltered, and fed me and put stories in my head: Kyle Patrick Westbrook, Tyrone Hill, David Braswell, Marvin Vaughn, and Ronald D. O'Neal, Jr. All of Centralia is proud of you. Charles A. O'Neal. Keep choo-chooing, my brother, you are loved. Morris Douglas Bibb rest in peace. Rolland Lawson, thank you and rest well.

Thank you, my dearest cousins Sharon Bibb Vaughn, Traci Ellis, Amber O'Neal, Nina Franklin, Malynda Bibb, Lisa Blackwell, Keppen Fitzhugh (your brilliance and light have been missed!), Lana O'Neal, Cathy O'Neal-Windom, Cynthia Hill, Herb Williams, Harold David Bibb Jr., and my niece Brittany Anderson. Cris Cawthon, your research was clutch! Thank you, Aunt Carolyn, Aunt Charlotte Washington, Joel Berkley, Gail Pang, Lemuel Flagg, Otis Downey, Paul Adams, Aunt Dorothy Williams, and Mrs. Eleanor Tate. To my dear Godmother Joan Eaton (née Webber), rest well.

Ralph Parker, thank you for the photos, the Matt's, and the support. You are much appreciated! Toya Evans, thank you for inspiring all our young women!

To my dear friends, Robert Pierre, Darryl Fears, Sofia Lenzin, Rhome Anderson, Krissah Thompson (love live Kris-Lon, sis!), Aaron McGruder, and The Jabari Asim. Your talent is blazing. Your friendship lifts me and I love you all.

To my darling Sydney, Savannah and Satchel, Marshall, Gabby and Brooke, you mean everything to me! Savannah, bless you for your research help and your literary eyes and ears.

And to Thomas, for reading, editing, listening, making coffee, and thinking through all the things. For driving me to see Momma during late nights, hard roads, and for that day in June, when I despaired, thank you. This book and this family doesn't happen without you. I have undoubtedly forgotten someone whose support has been very meaningful. Please forgive me, and know that you are also appreciated.

AUTHOR'S NOTE

Thank you very much for reading *Bibb Country*! Some of you may have read the beginnings of this exploration in my 2019 article on The Undefeated website (now Andscape.com). I'm humbled, years later, to be at the end of this book, having covered so much more ground.

Perhaps a heightened sense of time and distance is to be expected when you're reaching back centuries for data points, and tracing a family migration over thousands of miles. Of course, I wasn't just researching the past. I was experiencing these historic connections breathing all over the here and now.

I was directed by the belief that to understand Black ancestors, you have to get subterranean. You have to follow the coins and spare change below the cushions to where the coils and springs are unupholstered—that's if you want to understand how and where we all sit.

As it turns out, getting subterranean was also a good way to think about white Bibb history—particularly the development of Bibb lettuce. For that, I used a kind of farm-to-table approach. How is this lettuce grown? What's its cultural significance? What's the dirt on it? How does it taste? It was my field (greens) reporting that helped me research this chapter of Bibb history, and piece together its disparate layers of meaning.

Chapter by chapter, I was reminded how America's racial history can be most intuitively understood as it played out in families. You have to accrete context and meaning even when the fact patterns and expertise to do so are constantly subject to sanction, revision, and slant. I heard numerous cautions against "presentism," making judgements about historical events using current knowledge and norms. I found that argument to be a sleight of mind. Black people have been "present" at every point in American history. They had thoughts, feelings, calculations, and takeaways about everything happening around them, but no one was asking them. Further, there was no common standard of safety, citizenship, or welcome for them to answer deeply anyway. Often, that remains the case.

Early on, the writing felt like a sprawling ragtime opera. There were dissimilar lines of inquiry, often philosophically and rhythmically opposed, that I needed to put my fingers on simultaneously. What is and what was the history and significance of the Kentucky Derby, for example, and how are we to understand it as both *this* and *that,* in Black and white? (BTW, there's an old hip-hop song, which, like ragtime, was invented by Black people, that asks *this* or *that*? *this* or *that*? repeatedly addressing our multinodal existentialism. W.E.B. Du Bois wrote that Black people experience double consciousness, but whatever you call it, this dual, triple, quadruple apprehension of ourselves is a central underpinning of Black creativity.)

If you can imagine a ragtime version of the American songbook, you start to feel historic riffs, parallels, and jumps like your grandmother felt them, which is what drove her to cuss. (Try as I might, though, I never did understand why she pronounced Wisconsin, where my cousin, Lana Sue, went to college, as "Wesconscious.") In the Henry Bibb narrative, I heard the tools of American expansion and seizure in the chords that bound both personal and national histories together. It was a crime against antebellum custom and law to speculate about the white father of an enslaved child, wrote Bibb, who was a child of such a union. More than a century later, Charles Bibb, a white Bibb family historian, considered it a mystery and a shame that the most storied branch of the white Bibbs wasn't more complete and forthcoming about detailing all their children and heirs.

For centuries, the Bibbs in Black and white have kept separate time signatures in the same American movement, and it was with that understanding that I researched and wrote Bibb Country.

SOURCES

WEBSITES (BY CHAPTER)

Chapter 1: Harvest and Bond.

Hughbanks, Katie. "Seeking History." Kentucky Monthly, October 29, 2020. http://www.kentuckymonthly.com/culture/history/seeking-history.

O'Neal, Lonnae. "The bitter harvest of Richard Bibb: A descendant of slavery confronts her inheritance." Andscape, October 14, 2019. https://andscape.com/features/the-bitter-harvest-of-richard-bibb-a-descendant-of-slavery-confronts-her-inheritance

PBS Learning Media. "Bibb House / Kentucky Studies." https://ca.pbslearningmedia.org/resource/bibb-house-video/kentucky-studies.

Chapter 2: The Bibb Begotten

Brain, Jessica. "The Huguenots – England's First Refugees." Historic UK, September 10, 2021. https://www.historic-uk.com/HistoryUK/HistoryofEngland/The-Huguenots.

Harper, Adelle Bartlett. "What's Your Family Line?" *Georgia Magazine*, June-July 1969. https://static1.squarespace.com/static/5802c4d9414fb5e45ce4dc44/t/5998b486e45a7ccab71bf254/1503179913747/Bibb.pdf

Reynolds PA to VA. "Benjamin Bibb." Last modified May 27, 2020.https://reynoldspatova.org/getperson.php?personID=I6688&tree=reynolds1.

Chapter 3: Bibb Lettuce

Bundy, Molly. "Glenn was a 'Louisville, national treasure'." The Courier-Journal, February 10, 2010. https://www.newspapers.com/article/the-courier-journal-camille-glenn-obitua/35328887.

Chilton, Charlotte and Meg Donohue. "The Fascinating History of The Kentucky Derby." Town & Country, February 6, 2024. https://www.townandcountrymag.com/leisure/sporting/a27255219/kentucky-derby-history.

Dana, Robert W. "Little Club Attracts Stars of Theater." Tips on Tables, November 6, 1957. https://www.tipsontables.com/littleclub.html.

Downs, Jere. "Churchill Downs to spotlight local foods." Courier Journal, last updated April 28, 2015. https://www.courier-journal.com/story/entertainment/events/kentucky-derby/2015/04/28/churchill-downs-boast-local-foods/26515507.

Eisenberg, John. "Off to the Races." Smithsonian Magazine, August 2004. https://www.smithsonianmag.com/history/off-to-the-races-2266179.

Fanto Deetz, Kelley. "How Enslaved Chefs Helped Shape American Cuisine." Smithsonian Magazine, July 20, 2018. https://www.smithsonianmag.com/history/how-enslaved-chefs-helped-shape-american-cuisine-180969697.

Farmers' Almanac. "Kentucky Derby Traditions: The History Behind The Run For The Roses." Last updated May 2, 2024. https://www.farmersalmanac.com/the-kentucky-derby-12144.

Fischer, Nan. "The History of Lettuce." Mother Earth Gardener, February 21, 2018. https://www.motherearthgardener.com/plant-profiles/the-history-of-lettuce-zm0z18szphe.

Food Network Kitchen. "What Is Bibb Lettuce?" February 4, 2022. https://www.foodnetwork.com/how-to/packages/food-network-essentials/bibb-lettuce.

Hecker, Donna. "A Lettuce by Any Other Name." Holly Hill, 2023. https://www.hollyhillandco.com/stories-recipes/a-lettuce-by-any-other-name.

"John Bigger Bibb Obituary." The Courier Journal, Louisville, Kentucky, April 15, 1884.

Kunik, Kelsey. "Butter Lettuce Nutrition: Benefits, Risks, Recipes, and Storage Tips." Livestrong.com, last updated October 1, 2021. https://www.livestrong.com/article/38948-nutritional-value-butter-lettuce.

Loosemore, Bailey. "'We Can't Forget': Kentucky is (slowly) recognizing the role of slaves in bourbon's legacy." Courier Journal, last updated June 10, 2021. https://www.courier-journal.com/story/life/food/spirits/bourbon/2019/06/27/kentucky-bourbon-slaves-contributions-industry-being-recognized/1418931001.

Lumen Learning. "25.1:The Agricultural Revolution." *History of Western Civilization II*. https://courses.lumenlearning.com/ suny-hccc-worldhistory2/chapter/the-agricultural-revolution.

MacGuill, Dan. "Did Colonel Sanders Steal the KFC Original Recipe From a Black Woman Named 'Miss Childress'?" Snopes. com, September 13, 2019. https://www.snopes.com/fact-check/ colonel-sanders-kfc-miss-childress.

Newsham, Gavin. "Inside the overlooked history of black horse race jockeys." The New York Post, last updated May 6, 2023. https://nypost.com/2023/05/06/ inside-the-overlooked-history-of-black-horse-race-jockeys.

Produce Blue book. "Romain Lettuce Market Summary." https:// www.producebluebook.com/know-your-produce-commodity/ romaine-lettuce.

Rozsa, Lori. "Saving the manatees-rescue by rescue, rehab by rehab." The Washington Post, January 23, 2022. https://www. washingtonpost.com/climate-environment/2022/01/23/ saving-manatees-rescue-by-rescue-rehab-by-rehab.

Scherer, Lauri. "How and Why Black Riders Were Driven from American Racetracks." National Bureau of Economic Research, December 28, 2020. https://www.nber.org/digest/202101/ how-and-why-black-riders-were-riven-american-racetracks.

Schrieberg, Felipe. "Bourbon's black fans are changing the whiskey world for the better." Whisky Mag, Iss. 175, April 30, 2021. https://whiskymag.com/articles/ bourbons-black-fans-are-changing-the-whiskey-world-for-the-better.

Science in the News. "The Fight Over Inoculation During the 1721 Boston Smallpox Epidemic." December 31, 2014. https://sitn.hms.harvard. edu/flash/special-edition-on-infectious-disease/2014/the-fight-over- inoculation-during-the-1721-boston-smallpox-epidemic.

Slack, Paul. "England's Improvement." *The Invention of Improvement: Information and Material Progress in Seventeenth-Century England*. Oxford Academic, October 23, 2014. https://doi.org/10.1093/acprof: oso/9780199645916.003.0007.

Smith, K. Annabelle. "When Lettuce Was a Sacred Sex Symbol." Smithsonian Magazine, July 16, 2013. https://www.smithsonianmag. com/arts-culture/when-lettuce-was-a-sacred-sex-symbol-12271795.

Syme, Rachel. "Laurie Colwin's Recipe for Being Yourself in the Kitchen." The New Yorker, October 11, 2021. https://www.newyorker.com/magazine/2021/10/18/laurie-colwins-recipe-for-being-yourself-in-the-kitchen.

Vecsey, Laura. "Doris Day and Caesar Salad Made a Big Splash in 1947 at NYC's Little Club." StreetEasy, May 13, 2019. https://streeteasy.com/blog/doris-day-and-caesar-salad-made-a-big-splash-in-1947-at-nycs-little-club.

Walker, DeArbea. "Black jockeys once dominated the Kentucky Derby. Why is it so rare to see them today?" Insider, last updated May 6, 2022. https://sports.yahoo.com/black-jockeys-once-dominated-kentucky-225836502.html.

Zelitch, Israel. "Why Lettuce Bolts, and What You Can Do About It." KitchenGardener Magazine, Iss. 27, June 2000. https://www.finegardening.com/article/why-lettuce-bolts-and-what-you-can-do-about-it.

Chapter 4: Chancellor Bibb and the White Man's Burden

"A chronological list of senators since the First Congress in 1789." https://www.senate.gov/artandhistory/history/resources/pdf/chronlist.pdf.

Biographical Directory of the United States Congress. "Bibb, George Mortimer." https://bioguideretro.congress.gov/Home/MemberDetails?memIndex=B000433.

Goff, John S. "THE LAST LEAF: GEORGE MORTIMER BIBB." *The Register of the Kentucky Historical Society* 59, no. 4 (1961): 331–42. http://www.jstor.org/stable/23374698.

Hardy, Michael. "America's Other Great Depression." *Brandeis Magazine,* Spring 2013.

https://www.brandeis.edu/magazine/2013/spring/inquiry/depression.html.

https://csrd.asu.edu/sites/default/files/2024-06/January%2010%2C%202022%20More%20than%201%2C800%20congressmen%20once%20enslaved%20Black%20people.%20This%20is%20who%20they%20were%2C%20and%20how%2-0they%20shaped%20the%20nation.pdfMetzmeier, Kurt X. "The Jurist." Kentucky Scholarship Online, November 2016. https://doi.org/10.5810/kentucky/9780813168609.003.0005.

National Agricultural Library. "Heirs' Property." https://www.nal.usda.gov/farms-and-agricultural-production-systems/heirs-property.

Post, Edward M. "KENTUCKY LAW CONCERNING EMANCIPATION OR FREEDOM OF SLAVES." *The Filson Club History Quarterly* 59, no. 3 (July 1985). https://filsonhistorical.org/wp-content/uploads/publicationpdfs/59-3-4_Kentucky-Law-Concerning-Emancipation-or-Freedom-of-Slaves_Post-Edward-M..pdf.

Robinson, Morgan. "The American Colonization Society." The White House Historical Association, June 22, 2020. https://www.whitehousehistory.org/the-american-colonization-society.

Weil, Julie Zauzmer, Adrian Blanco, and Leo Dominguez. "More than 1,800 congressmen once enslaved Black people. This is who they were, and how they shaped the nation." The Washington Post, January 10, 2022.

Wills, Eric. "The Forgotten: The Contraband of America and the Road to Freedom." National Trust for Historic Preservation, *Preservation*, May/June 2011. https://savingplaces.org/stories/the-forgotten-the-contraband-of-america-and-the-road-to-freedom.

Chapter 5: My Old Kentucky Home

Bingham, Emily. "Emily Bingham on the Material Culture of White America's Song to Itself: "My Old Kentucky Home." Lit Hub, May 16, 2022. https://lithub.com/emily-bingham-on-the-material-culture-of-white-americas-song-to-itself-my-old-kentucky-home.

Bingham, Emily. "History of 'My Old Kentucky Home' examines how Black performers had to act out caricatures of plantation life." Andscape, May 3, 2022. https://andscape.com/features/history-of-my-old-kentucky-home-examines-how-black-performers-had-to-act-out-caricatures-of-plantation-life.

Brockell, Gillian. "'My Old Kentucky Home,' Kentucky Derby anthem, has racist past." The Washington Post, May 7, 2022. https://www.washingtonpost.com/history/2022/05/07/old-kentucky-home-racist.

Burbridge, Sue H. Sue H. Burbridge to Abraham Lincoln, January 20, 1861. Library of Congress. https://tile.loc.gov/storage-services/service/mss/mal/064/0645300/0645300.pdf.

Carmi, Ziv. "Kentucky: Historical Context." State of the Confederacy, n.d. https://stateoftheconfederacy.sites.gettysburg.edu/confederatemonumentmaps/kentucky.

Clark, Lewis Garrard. "Narrative of the Sufferings of Lewis Clarke, During a Captivity of More Than Twenty-Five Years, Among the Algerines of Kentucky, One of the So Called Christian States of North America." 1845. https://docsouth.unc.edu/neh/clarke/clarke.html.

Cullen, Jim. "Father of the self-made man." American History Now, December 1, 2012. http://amhistnow.blogspot.com/2012/12/father-of-self-made-man.html.

Doolin, Garner, "Dr Beverly Anthony Allen, 1757-1816." Internet Archive, January 1990. https://archive.org/details/beverly-allen-garner-doolin-notes.

Egerton, John. "Heritage of a Heavyweight." The New York Times, September 28, 1980. https://archive.nytimes.com/www.nytimes.com/books/98/10/25/specials/ali-heritage.html.

Eslinger, Ellen. "The Shape of Slavery on the Kentucky Frontier, 1775-1800." *The Register of the Kentucky Historical Society* 92, no. 1 (1994): 1-23. https://www.jstor.org/stable/23383130.

Gibson, Campbell and Kay Jung. "HISTORICAL CENSUS STATISTICS ON POPULATION TOTALS BY RACE, 1790 TO 1990, AND BY HISPANIC ORIGIN, 1970 TO 1990, FOR THE UNITED STATES, REGIONS, DIVISIONS, AND STATES." U.S. Census Bureau, September 2002. https://www.census.gov/content/dam/Census/library/working-papers/2002/demo/POP-twps0056.pdf.

Goodwin, Bruce, II. "A Brief History Of Fried Chicken, And It's Complicated." Cassius, April 18, 2017. https://cassiuslife.com/187/history-of-fried-chicken.

"Henry Clay and Slavery." *The Henry Clay Estate*. https://henryclay.org/henry-clay/henry-clay-and-slavery.

King, Gilbert. "The Day Henry Clay Refused to Compromise." Smithsonian Magazine, December 6, 2012. https://www.smithsonianmag.com/history/the-day-henry-clay-refused-to-compromise-153589853.

Lander, Art, Jr. "Art Lander's Outdoors: Early Kentucky's era of exploitation awakened conservation movement." Northern Kentucky Tribune, June 21, 2017. https://nkytribune.com/2017/06/art-landers-outdoors-early-kentuckys-era-of-exploitation-awakened-conservation-movement.

Lee, Jason H. "Minstrelsy and the Construction of Race in America." Brown University Library Center for Digital Scholarship, Spring 2004. https://library.brown.edu/cds/sheetmusic/afam/minstrelsy.html.

Lewis, Patrick A. "The Democratic partisan militia and The Black Peril: the Kentucky militia, racial violence, and the fifteenth amendment, 1870-1873." *Civil War History* 56, no. 2, June 2010. https://go.gale.com/ps/i.do?id=GALE%7CA228432758&sid=googleScholar&v=2.1&it=r&linkaccess=abs&issn=00098078&p=AONE&sw=w&userGroupName=anon%7E34649779&aty=open-web-entry.

Lincoln, Abraham. *Abraham Lincoln papers: Series 1. General Correspondence. 1833-1916: Sue H. Burbridge to Abraham Lincoln, Sunday, January 20, 1861 (Slavery)*. January 20, 1861. Manuscript/Mixed Material. https://www.loc.gov/item/mal0645300.

"Logan County (KY) Enslaved, Free Blacks, and Free Mulattoes, 1850-1870," *Notable Kentucky African Americans Database*, Last updated June 20, 2024. https://nkaa.uky.edu/nkaa/items/show/2439.

"Longhunter, Southern Kentucky Genealogical Society Newsletter." *Southern Kentucky Genealogical Society* 27, no. 3 (Summer 2004). https://digitalcommons.wku.edu/cgi/viewcontent.cgi?article=1102&context=longhunter_sokygsn.

Manuscripts & Folklife Archives. "Lewisburg United Methodist Church - Lewisburg, Kentucky (MSS 94)." March 29, 2008. *Manuscript Collection Finding Aids*. Paper 404. https://digitalcommons.wku.edu/cgi/viewcontent.cgi?article=1406&context=dlsc_mss_fin_aid.

Miller, Adrian. "Gospel Bird: The Sacred Roots of Fried Chicken." Allrecipes.com, February 14, 2024. https://www.allrecipes.com/article/gospel-bird-how-fried-chicken-went-to-church.

National Archives and Records Administration, "Bounty-Land Warrants for Military Service, 1775-1855." Last updated December 2010. https://www.archives.gov/files/research/military/bounty-land-1775-1855.pdf.

National Archives. "Black Soldiers in the U.S. Military During the Civil War," last reviewed October 4, 2023. https://www.archives.gov/education/lessons/blacks-civil-war.

National Park Service. "Civil War Timeline," Last updated October 6, 2022. https://www.nps.gov/gett/learn/historyculture/civil-war-timeline.htm.

Reid, Darren. "Walking the line of fire: violence, society, and the war for the Kentucky and Trans-Appalachian Frontier, 1774-1795." PhD Thesis, University of Dundee, 2011. https://discovery.dundee.ac.uk/en/studentTheses/walking-the-line-of-fire-violence-society-and-the-war-for-the-ken.

Risen, Clay. "When Jack Daniel's Failed to Honor a Slave, an Author Rewrote History." The New York Times, August 15, 2017. https://www.nytimes.com/2017/08/15/dining/jack-daniels-whiskey-slave-nearest-green.html.

Sexton, Don. "Wallens Creek Revenge: The Isaac Crabtree Story." The Notorious Meddler, February 20, 2009. http://www.randyspecktacular.com/2009/02/wallens-creek-revenge-isaac-crabtree.html.

"Slave Population of the United States." *United States Census*, n.d. https://www2.census.gov/library/publications/decennial/1850/1850c/1850c-04.pdf.

"Slavery in Kentucky." *The Journal of Negro History* 3, no. 3 (July 1918). https://penelope.uchicago.edu/Thayer/E/Journals/JNH/3/3/Slavery_in_Kentucky/Development*.html.

Smithsonian American Art Museum, "The Age of the Common Man." https://americanexperience.si.edu/historical-eras/colonization-revolution-and-new-nation/pair-daniel-lamotte-independence-squire-jack-porter.

Tapp, Hambleton, and James C. Klotter. *Kentucky: Decades of Discord, 1865-1900*. University Press of Kentucky, 1977. https://core.ac.uk/download/pdf/232564314.pdf.

The Underground Railroad in the Kentucky, Ohio, and Indiana Borderland. "Slavery in Kentucky, Indiana, & Ohio," Fall 2012. https://urrrborderland.omeka.net/exhibits/show/ugrr/slavery/slaveryky#_ftnref3.

This Far by Faith. "1776-1865: from Bondage to Holy War: Abolition and the Splintering of the Church." PBS. https://www.pbs.org/thisfarbyfaith/journey_2/p_5.html.

Tuttle, Ellen E. "Miners, Moonshiners, and Men of the Mountains: The Effect of Violence in Central Appalachia Through the Reconstruction Era." Senior Thesis, Salve Regina University, December 2017. https://digitalcommons.salve.edu/cgi/viewcontent.cgi?article=1114&context=pell_theses&httpsredir=1&referer=.

U.S. Department of the Interior, "Origin of Names of US States." January 4, 1974. https://www.bia.gov/as-ia/opa/online-press-release/origin-names-us-states.

West Ficklin, Marilou. "Colonial Kentucky Frontier: Speculators and Explorers Push further into Shawnee and Cherokee Territory." *Westerly Journeys*, 2006. https://www.westerly-journeys.com/colonial/colokent.html.

Wigger, John. "Introduction." *American Saint Francis Asbury and the Methodists*. New York: Oxford University Press, September 1, 2009. https://doi.org/10.1093/acprof:oso/9780195387803.003.0001.

WikiTree. "Brig Ajax's Company, arrived at Monrovia July 11, 1833," n.d. https://www.wikitree.com/wiki/Space:Brig_Ajax's_Company%2C_arrived_at_Monrovia_July_11%2C_1833#Slave_Owners.

Wolf, Stephanie. "'My Old Kentucky Home' will be performed at the Derby this weekend by a marching band and choir." Louisville Public Media, May 2, 2022. https://www.lpm.org/news/2022-05-02/my-old-kentucky-home-will-be-performed-at-the-derby-this-weekend-by-a-marching-band-and-choir.

Chapter 6: Centralia

African American Heritage Trail. "African Americans and the Illinois Central Railroad," n.d. https://ccafricanamericanheritage.org/trail-stop/railroad.

Bartlett, H.O. H.O Bartlett to Anna May Price, February 28, 1934. In *The Illinois State Archives*. https://www.ilsos.gov/departments/archives/teaching_packages/hard_times/doc27.html.

Beduya, Jose. "Exhibit sheds light on railways' discriminatory history." Cornell Chronicle, February 12, 2020. https://news.cornell.edu/stories/2020/02/exhibit-sheds-light-railways-discriminatory-history.

Bunch, Charles F., Sr. "Charles F. Bunch, Sr. Interview Tape 2 of 4." Oral History Collection of the University of Illinois at Springfield, 1974. https://www.idaillinois.org/digital/collection/uis/id/1171/rec/1.

Bunch, Charles F., Sr. "Charles F. Bunch, Sr. Memoir – Part 2." Oral History Collection of the University of Illinois at Springfield, 1974. https://www.idaillinois.org/digital/collection/uis/id/5325/rec/1.

Contributors to Mwal Wiki. "List of Negro League Baseball Teams." Mwal Wiki, n.d. https://mwal.fandom.com/wiki/List_of_Negro_League_baseball_teams.

DeWitt, Larry. "The Decision to Exclude Agricultural and Domestic Workers from the 1935 Social Security Act." *Social Security Bulletin* 70 no. 4 (2010). https://www.ssa.gov/policy/docs/ssb/v70n4/v70n4p49.html.

Ely, James W., Jr. "Abraham Lincoln as a Railroad Attorney," Indiana Historical Society, n.d. https://indianahistory.org/wp-content/uploads/51a319bce67b7f5614886cd3a4504ef7.pdf.

Hankey, John P. "Illinois Central Railroad." Encyclopedia of Chicago, n.d. https://encyclopedia.chicagohistory.org/pages/627.html.

Iowa PBS. "The Great Depression Hits Farms and Cities in the 1930s," n.d. https://www.iowapbs.org/iowapathways/mypath/2591/great-depression-hits-farms-and-cities-1930s.

Jones, Julius L. "The Red Summer of 1919." Chicago History Museum, July 26, 2019. https://www.chicagohistory.org/chi1919.

Lueckenhoff, Sandra K. "A. Lincoln, a Corporate Attorney and the Illinois Central Railroad." Missouri Law Review 61, no. 2 (1996). https://scholarship.law.missouri.edu/mlr/vol61/iss2/3.

"Negro League Games by Location," n.d. Retrosheet, last updated January 8, 2025. https://www.retrosheet.org/NegroLeagues/ballparks.html.

Office of the Illinois Secretary of State. "Charter for the Illinois Central Railroad (1851)." https://www.ilsos.gov/departments/archives/online_exhibits/100_documents/1851-il-central-railroad.html.

Raines, Edgar F., Jr. "The Ku Klux Klan in Illinois, 1867-1875." *Illinois Historical Journal* 78, no. 1 (1985): 17–44. http://www.jstor.org/stable/40191819.

Ryans, Kevin. "Centralia, IL rallies around its historic high school basketball program." Fox 2 Now, January 18, 2024. https://fox2now.com/sports/prep-zone/centralia-il-rallies-around-its-historic-high-school-basketball-program.

See Centralia. "Centralia Boys Basketball-Winningest Team in the Nation," n.d. https://seecentralia.com/centralia-boys-basketball-winningest-team-in-the-nation.

Southeastern Illinois College. "Legends and Lore". June 21, 2022. https://sic.edu/about/facts-and-history/legends-and-lore.

The Library of Congress. "Race Relations in the 1930s and 1940s," n.d. https://www.loc.gov/classroom-materials/united-states-history-primary-source-timeline/great-depression-and-world-war-ii-1929-1945/race-relations-in-1930s-and-1940s.

Chapter 8: Chicago, A Blues Song for Lonnie Gerald

Chicago Police Department. "About / History," n.d. https://home.chicagopolice.org/about/history.

"Chicago Population History | 1840 - 2023," n.d. https://www.biggestuscities.com/city/chicago-illinois.

Great Cities Institute. "Fact Sheet: Black Population Loss in Chicago." July 2019. https://greatcities.uic.edu/wp-content/uploads/2019/08/Black-Population-Loss-in-Chicago.pdf.

Hagedorn, John et al. "Crime, Corruption and Cover-ups in the Chicago Police Department." University of Illinois at Chicago Department of Political Science, January 17, 2013. https://pols.uic.edu/wp-content/uploads/sites/273/2018/10/ac_policecorruptionb6e6.pdf.

Hassett-Walker, Connie. "The racist roots of American policing: From slave patrols to traffic stops." The Conversation, last updated June 2, 2020. https://theconversation.com/the-racist-roots-of-american-policing-from-slave-patrols-to-traffic-stops-112816.

Illinois State Museum. "Congressman Oscar de Priest." https://story.illinoisstatemuseum.org/content/congressman-oscar-de-priest.

Illinois State Police. "Director Joseph Bibb," n.d. https://isp.illinois.gov/DiversityEquityInclusion/DirectorJosephBibb.

Lawrence, Daniel S., Jessica Dockstader, Karen Solomon, Lewis Z. Schlosser, and Joe Willis. "Law Enforcement Deaths by Suicide." *CNA*, March 20, 2024. https://www.cna.org/reports/2024/03/law-enforcement-deaths-by-suicide.

Lewis, Patrick A. "The Democratic partisan militia and The Black Peril: the Kentucky militia, racial violence, and the fifteenth amendment, 1870-1873." Civil War History 56 no. 2 (2010). https://go.gale.com/ps/i.do?id=GALE%7CA228432758&sid=googleScholar&v=2.1&it=r&linkaccess=abs&issn=00098078&p=AONE&sw=w&userGroupName=anon%7E34649779&aty=open-web-entry.

Library of Congress. "Consumer Advertising During the Great Depression: A Resource Guide." https://guides. loc.gov/consumer-advertising-great-depression/ black-businesses-and-advertising-industry.

Lyman, Brian. "UA's decision to add first Black student's name to Bibb Graves building sparks retelling of Graves' history with KKK." Montgomery Advertiser, last updated February 7, 2022. https://www. montgomeryadvertiser.com/story/news/2022/02/04/bibb-graves-alabama-governor-kkk-ku-klux-klan-member-university-building-autherine-lucy-foster/6661814001.

Maynard, Alicia. "The Assassination of Fred Hampton." Digital Chicago / Lake Forest College, n.d. https://digitalchicagohistory.org/exhibits/ show/fred-hampton-50th/the-assassination.

McDonald, Soraya Nadia. "A triumphant 'Judas and the Black Messiah' unfurls the life and death of Fred Hampton." Andscape, February 12, 2021. https://andscape.com/features/a-triumphant-judas-and-the-black-messiah-unfurls-the-life-and-death-of-fred-hampton.

Moore, Natalie. "Burge Torture Survivors Seek Support For Counseling, Public Memorial." WBEZ Chicago, January 27, 2020. https://www. wbez.org/race-class-communities/2020/01/27/burge-torture-survivors-seek-support-for-counseling-public-memorial.

NBC 5 Chicago. "White Flight, By The Numbers." May 6, 2013. https://www.nbcchicago.com/news/local/chicago-politics/ white-flight-by-the-numbers/1951412/.

National Archives. "Fred Hampton (August 30, 1948 - December 4, 1969)." August 25, 2020. https://www.archives.gov/research/ african-americans/individuals/fred-hampton.

National Endowment for the Humanities / Chronicling America. "About the Chicago whip." https://chroniclingamerica.loc.gov/lccn/ sn86056950.

PBS. "The Chicago Defender," n.d https://www.pbs.org/blackpress/ news_bios/defender.html.

Serrato, Jacqueline, Pat Sier, and Charmaine Runes. "Mapping Chicago's Racial Segregation." WTTW Chicago, n.d. https://interactive.wttw. com/firsthand/segregation/mapping-chicago-racial-segregation.

The Library of Congress. "The African-American Mosaic. Chicago: Destination for the Great Migration," n.d. https://www.loc.gov/ exhibits/african/afam011.html.

Chapter 9: The Lynching Tree

Carmi, Ziv. "Kentucky Historical Context." State of The Confederacy, n.d. https://stateoftheconfederacy.sites.gettysburg.edu/confederatemonumentmaps/kentucky.

Lartey, Jamiles and Sam Morris. "How white Americans used lynchings to terrorize and control black people." The Guardian, April 26, 2018. https://www.theguardian.com/us-news/2018/apr/26/lynchings-memorial-us-south-montgomery-alabama.

Swietek, Wes. "Hidden history: Effort aims to memorialize Logan lynchings." Associated Press, last updated August 26, 2018. https://apnews.com/general-news-a16e6acf543b43ee86c29d87c979a585.

Chapter 10: Colorism

Ali, Wajahat. "How to Teach a Little Girl to Love Her Brown Skin." The New York Times, November 13, 2021. https://www.nytimes.com/2021/11/13/opinion/culture/racism-colorism-parenting.html.

Bradt, Steve. "'One-drop rule' persists." The Harvard Gazette, December 9, 2010. https://news.harvard.edu/gazette/story/2010/12/one-drop-rule-persists.

Davis, Michaela Angela. "My Light Skin and Loose Curls Give Me Even More Responsibility to Advocate for Other Black Women." Allure, May 14, 2022. https://www.allure.com/story/light-skinned-black-women-liberation-movement.

Dennis, Angela. "Colorism: Raising A Dark Skinned Daughter As A Light Skinned Woman In An Anti-Black Society." Medium, June 5, 2019. https://medium.com/@AngelaDennisWrites/colorism-raising-a-dark-skinned-daughter-as-a-light-skinned-woman-in-an-anti-black-society-18d9cf3471bd.

Monk, Ellis P., Jr. "The Unceasing Significance of Colorism: Skin Tone Stratification in the United States." *Daedalus* 150, no. 2 (Spring, 2021). https://www.ellismonk.com/home/unceasingcolorism.

Williams, Vanessa. "Dark and Lovely, Michelle." The Root, January 13, 2009. https://www.theroot.com/dark-and-lovely-michelle-1790868592.

Chapter 11: Beware of Becky

Brown, Alana C. "What is the connection between domestic violence, sexual assault, and reproductive justice and how does it impact Black women?" National Resource Center on Domestic Violence, January 20, 2021. https://vawnet.org/news/what-connection-between-domestic-violence-sexual-assault-and-reproductive-justice-and-how-does.

Buckhead Heritage Society, "Mary Elizabeth Tyler House," n.d. https://buckheadheritage.com/mary-elizabeth-tyler-house.

Clark Hine, Darlene. "Rape and the Inner Lives of Black Women in the Middle West." *Signs* 14, no. 4 (1989). https://blackwomenintheblackfreedomstruggle.voices.wooster.edu/wp-content/uploads/sites/210/2019/01/Darlene-Clark-Hine_Rape-and-the-Inner-Lives-of-Black-Women.pdf.

DuRocher, Kristina."'Is this the man?': White Girls' Participation in Southern Lynchings," in Raising Racists: The Socialization of White Children in the Jim Crow South (University Press of Kentucky, 2011). https://doi.org/10.5810/kentucky/9780813130019.003.0007.

Greenidge, Kaitlyn. "Here's How 40,000 Black Women Mobilized on Zoom for Kamala Harris." Harper's Bazaar, July 23, 2024. https://www.harpersbazaar.com/culture/politics/a61679211/win-with-black-women.

Grigsby-Bates, Karen. "What's In A Name? The History of Karens, Beckys And Miss Anns." NPR Morning Edition, August 5, 2020. https://www.npr.org/2020/08/05/899230724/whats-in-a-name-the-history-of-karens-beckys-and-miss-anns.

Hernandez, Nestor and Paul Hemez. "Some Demographic and Economic Characteristics of Male and Female Same-Sex Couples Differed." United States Census, November 8, 2023. https://www.census.gov/library/stories/2023/11/same-sex-couple-diversity.html.

Lartey, Jamiles and Sam Morris. "How white Americans used lynchings to terrorize and control black people." The Guardian, April 26, 2018. https://www.theguardian.com/us-news/2018/apr/26/lynchings-memorial-us-south-montgomery-alabama.

Mays, Jeffery C. and Sean Piccoli. "A White Woman, Teresa Klein, Called the Police on a Black Child She Falsely Said Groped Her." The New York Times, October 12, 2018. https://www.nytimes.com/2018/10/12/nyregion/woman-calls-police-black-boy-brooklyn.html.

McDonald, Soraya Nadia. "In 'They Were Her Property,' a historian shows that white women were deeply involved in the slave economy." Andscape, March 15, 2019. https://andscape.com/features/in-they-were-her-property-a-historian-shows-that-white-women-were-deeply-involved-in-the-slave-economy.

Monk, Ellis P. Jr., Michael H. Esposito and Hedwig Lee. "Beholding Inequality: Race, Gender, and Returns to Physical Attractiveness in the United States." *American Journal of Sociology* 127, no. 1 (July 2021). https://scholar.harvard.edu/files/monk/files/monk_-_beholding_inequality_-_ajs.pdf.

National Sexual Violence Resource Center. "Part 1 - Sexual Violence Against African American Slaves And Its Legacy Today - Interview with Dr. Crystal Feimster," November 10, 2023. https://www.nsvrc.org/blogs/resource-online-magazine/part-1-sexual-violence-against-african-american-slaves-and-its.

Pérez-Peña, Richard. "Woman Linked to 1955 Emmett Till Murder Tells Historian Her Claims Were False." The New York Times, January 27, 2017. https://www.nytimes.com/2017/01/27/us/emmett-till-lynching-carolyn-bryant-donham.html.

Salem, Sara. "White Innocence as a Feminist Discourse: Race, empire and gender in performances of 'shock' in contemporary politics." *London School of Economics*, n.d. https://www.academia.edu/37735749/White_Innocence_as_a_Feminist_Discourse_Race_empire_and_gender_in_performances_of_shock_in_contemporary_politics?email_work_card=titles.

Sartore, Melissa. "Meet The Evil, Racist Mastermind Who Saved The KKK From Going Extinct." Ranker, last updated April 22, 2024. https://www.ranker.com/list/how-mary-elizabeth-tyler-saved-the-kkk/melissa-sartore.

Slatton, Brittany C. "A Body That Does Not Compare: How White Men Define Black Female Beauty in the Era of Colorblindness." Genders, 2012. https://www.colorado.edu/gendersarchive1998-2013/2012/10/01/body-does-not-compare-how-white-men-define-black-female-beauty-era-colorblindness.

Wells-Barnett, Ida B. "Southern Horrors: Lynch Law in All Its Phases." New York, New York, United States of America, October 5, 1892. https://awpc.cattcenter.iastate.edu/2020/09/21/southern-horrors-lynch-law-in-all-its-phases-oct-5-1892.

West, Carolyn M. and Kalimah Johnson. "Sexual Violence in the Lives of African American Women." National Online Resource Center on Violence Against Women, March 2013. https://vawnet.org/sites/default/files/materials/files/2016-09/AR_SVAAWomenRevised.pdf.

West, Ella-Marie. "Before 'Loving'." Washington University Arts & Sciences, 2017. https://artsci.wustl.edu/before-loving.

Williams, Heather Andrea. "Compartmentalizing Slavery." Slate, June 17, 2015. https://slate.com/human-interest/2015/06/how-white-people-justified-and-struggled-with-separating-slave-families.html.

Wilson, Dominique R. "Sexual Exploitation of Black Women From The Years 1619–2020." Journal of Race, Gender, and Ethnicity 10 (Spring 2021). https://digitalcommons.tourolaw.edu/cgi/viewcontent.cgi?article=1079&context=jrge.

Chapter 13: Post Racist

Farhi, Paul. "The Washington Post's new slogan turns out to be an old saying." The Washington Post, February 24, 2017. https://www.washingtonpost.com/lifestyle/style/the-washington-posts-new-slogan-turns-out-to-be-an-old-saying/2017/02/23/cb199cda-fa02-11e6-be05-1a3817ac21a5_story.html.

Institute for Health Metrics and Evaluation, "The Lancet: More than half of police killings in USA are unreported and Black Americans are most likely to experience fatal police violence." September 30, 2021. https://www.healthdata.org/news-release/lancet-more-half-police-killings-usa-are-unreported-and-black-americans-are-most-likely.

The Maryland-National Capital Park and Planning Commission, "Geographic and Historical Overview," March 2010. https://www.pgplanning.org/wp-content/uploads/2024/03/Chapter-02-Geographic-and-Historical-Overview.pdf.

FILMS

Brown, Margaret. *Descendant*. Participant, Night Tide Production, Two One Five Entertainment, 2022. https://participant.com/campaign/descendant.

Hoffman, John and Christine Turner. *The Barber of Little Rock*. Story Syndicate, 59th & Prairie Entertainment, 2023. https://www.youtube.com/watch?v=1amOPUn49aM.

Knight, Jonathan and Le Datta Grimes. *Invented Before You Were Born.* TruJuLo Media, 2022. https://www.bibbfilm.com.

Moore, Michael. *The Big One.* BBC Productions, Dog Eat Dog Films, 1997. https://www.youtube.com/watch?v=sDKUL1YRZZs.

Niedwick, Josh. *By Parties Unknown.* WKU PBS, 2022. https://www.pbs.org/show/parties-unknown.

PLACES TO VISIT

Carter G. Woodson Library, Chicago, Illinois. https://www.chipublib.org/locations/81.

Centralia Area Historical Museum, Centralia, Illinois. https://seecentralia.com/historical-society-museum.

SEEK Museum, Russellville, Kentucky. https://seekmuseum.org.

PODCASTS

Stuff You Missed in History Class, "Lettuce, Slavery, and the Bibb Legacy," iHeartRadio, July 6, 2022. https://www.iheart.com/podcast/105-stuff-you-missed-in-histor-21124503/episode/lettuce-slavery-and-the-bibb-legacy-99102223.

BOOKS

Anderson, Carol. *White Rage: The Unspoken Truth of Our Racial Divide.* New York: Bloomsbury Publishing USA, 2016.

Asim, Jabari. *We Can't Breathe: On Black Lives, White Lies, and the Art of Survival.* New York: Picador, 2018.

Ball, Edward. *Slaves in the Family.* New York: Farrar, Straus and Giroux, 2017.

Berry, Daina Ramey, and Kali Nicole Gross. *A Black Women's History of the United States.* Boston: Beacon Press, 2020.

Bibb, Charles William (1941). *The Bibb Family in America, 1640-1940.* Baltimore, Maryland, 1941.

Bingham, Emily. *My Old Kentucky Home: The Astonishing Life and Reckoning of an Iconic American Song.* New York: Knopf, 2022.

Cashin, Sheryll. *White Space, Black Hood: Opportunity Hoarding and Segregation in the Age of Inequality.* Boston: Beacon Press, 2021.

Coleman, J. Winston, Jr. *Slavery Times in Kentucky.* Chapel Hill: University of North Carolina Press, Johnson Reprint, 1940.

Collins, Patricia Hill. *Black Sexual Politics: African Americans, Gender, and the New Racism.* New York: Routledge, 2004.

Cooper, Brittney. *Eloquent Rage: A Black Feminist Discovers Her Superpower.* St. New York: Martin's Press, 2018.

Dexter, Darrel, and John A. Beadles. *Pulling Off the Sheets: The Second Ku Klux Klan in Deep Southern Illinois.* Carbondale: Saluki Publishing, 2024.

Finley, Alexander C. *The History of Russellville and Logan County, Ky: Which is to Some Extent a History of Western Kentucky.* CreateSpace Independent Publishing Platform, 2013.

Fischer, David Hackett, and James C. Kelly. *Bound Away: Virginia and the Westward Movement,* Charlottesville and London: University of Virginia Press, 2000.

France, Kimberly. *Black Settlements in Southern Illinois.* Charleston: History Press, 2024.

Glaude, Eddie S., Jr. *Begin Again: James Baldwin's America and Its Urgent Lessons for Our Own.* New York: Random House, 2021.

Glazier, Jack. *Been Coming through Some Hard Times: Race, History, and Memory in Western Kentucky.* Knoxville: Univ. of Tennessee Press, 2013.

Jacobs, Harriet. *Incidents in the Life of a Slave Girl. Written by Herself.. Edited by L. Maria Child.* Boston, 1861.

Johnston, Amber O'Neal. *A Place to Belong: Celebrating Diversity and Kinship in the Home and Beyond.* New York: Penguin, 2022.

Jones-Rogers, Stephanie E. *They Were Her Property: White Women as Slave Owners in the American South.* New Haven & London: Yale University Press, 2019.

Loewen, James W. *Sundown Towns: A hidden dimension of American Racism.* New York: New Press, 2005.

Lucas, Marion Brunson, and George C. Wright. *A History of Blacks in Kentucky: From Slavery to Segregation, 1760-1891.* Frankfort: Kentucky Historical Society, 1992.

Masur, Kate. *Until Justice Be Done: America's First Civil Rights Movement, from the Revolution to Reconstruction.* New York: W.W. Norton and Company, 2021.

Norwood, William R. *Cleared for Takeoff: A Pilot's Story of Challenges and Triumphs*. Carmel: Dog Ear Publishing, 2014.

O'Neal Parker, Lonnae. *I'm Every Woman: Remixed Stories of Marriage, Motherhood, and Work*. New York: Amistad, 2005.

O'Neal, Traci D. *The Exceptional Negro: Racism, White Privilege and the Lie of Respectability Politics*, Atlanta: Icart Media LLC, 2018.

Perry, Imani. *South to America: A Journey Below the Mason-Dixon to Understand the Soul of a Nation*. New York: Ecco, 2023.

Salafia, Matthew. *Slavery's Borderland: Freedom and Bondage Along the Ohio River*. Philadelphia: University of Pennsylvania Press, 2013.

Swarns, Rachel L. *The 272*. New York: Random House Publishing Group, 2023.

Twitty, Michael W. *The Cooking Gene: A Journey Through African-American Culinary History in the Old South*. New York: HarperAudio, 2023.

Van Der Kolk, Bessel A. *The Body Keeps the Score: Brain, Mind, and Body in the Healing of Trauma*. New York: Penguin Books, 2015.

Wiencek, Henry. *The Hairstons: An American Family in Black and White*. Grand Haven: BrillianceAudio, 2020.

Wright, George C. *Racial Violence in Kentucky, 1865-1940: Lynchings, Mob Rule, and "Legal Lynchings."* Baton Rouge: Louisiana State University Press,1990.